SEP – 9 2009

3.21.2010 (10)
6-12 (13)
8.7.15 (17)

Classic Lebanese Cuisine

Classic
Lebanese Cuisine

170 Fresh and Healthy Mediterranean Favorites

Chef Kamal Al-Faqih

ThreeForks®

GUILFORD, CONNECTICUT
HELENA, MONTANA

AN IMPRINT OF THE GLOBE PEQUOT PRESS

To my mother Hind and my aunt Effat
Thank you for your patience and guidance

ThreeForks is an imprint of The Globe Pequot Press.
ThreeForks is a registered trademark of Morris Book Publishing, LLC.

Text designed by Sheryl P. Kober
Layout by Nancy Freeborn
Photo credits: pp. vi, x, xii, xvii, xviii, 216, 223, 226 © Shutterstock. All others courtesy of Kamal Al-Faqih and Andreas Frank.

Library of Congress Cataloging-in-Publication Data

Al-Faqih, Kamal.
Classic Lebanese cuisine : 170 fresh and healthy Mediterranean favorites / Kamal Al-Faqih.
p. cm.
ISBN 978-0-7627-5278-2
1. Cookery, Lebanese. I. Title.
TX725.L4A42 2009
641.595692—dc22

2009013815

Printed in China
10 9 8 7 6 5 4 3 2 1

Contents

Foreword by Nora Boustany   vii

Acknowledgments   ix

Introduction   xi

How to Use This Book   xiii

Helpful Techniques   xiv

Before the Guests Arrive   xvi

Appetizers (Mezza)   1

Salads (Salata)   49

Main Dishes (Chicken/Lamb/Beef/Fish/Vegetarian)   65

Side Dishes (Vegetarian/Chicken/Lamb/Beef)   131

Desserts (Hillou)   171

Suggested Menus   217

The Pantry   219

Metric Conversion Tables   224

Index   227

About the Author   238

Foreword

BY NORA BOUSTANY

Climbing up my grandmother's pine trees shading a carpet of rust needles was only half the fun. The cones we coaxed to drop to the ground did not stay there for long, at least not in the village where I spent my summer holidays, Dibbiyeh in the Chouf Mountains of Lebanon. The cones were burned to extricate the hard, brown shells encasing the nut and were then crushed with the nearest pebble or stone. Washed and dried, the peculiar buttery treats were then tossed into a hissing frying pan to adorn the typical meat and onion fillings of a whole array of Lebanese dishes.

Golden and glistening, these pine nuts topped my mother's upside-down cake mold filled with chicken and rice, like jewels on a crown. The lemon sauce on the side added flavor to the mouthfuls of moist chicken and crunchy treats.

Sunday lunches around my Grandmother Rose's dining room table, with everyone fussing over the latest details, were a special family bonding ritual. My uncles and father cracked jokes, their wives laughed or hummed disapproval, and we squealed with joy. The showstoppers were the Sunday menus, with mloukhiyeh, a leafy green stew over rice, toasted Arabic bread, and chicken topped with a vinegar-and-onion salsa; sayadiyeh, an exquisite mix of fish over rice with caramelized onions and cumin topped with roasted almonds; and of course the legendary kibbi bi sayniyeh, a pie of cracked wheat and lamb, stuffed with a rich lamb filling.

Therese, our nanny, housekeeper, and friendly kitchen mole, would wrap her head in a white cotton scarf and start pounding the slab of lean lamb with her large and heavy wooden pestle, striking it into a large stone urn, the jurn, early that morning.

Unrelenting thuds to beat the meat into creamy submission alternated with church bells and the muzzin's call to prayer from a neighboring town. We woke up to that telltale rhapsody promising a scrumptious oven dish in its early stages, a process now easily replaced with the efficient buzz of a meat grinder. Soaked cracked wheat would get folded into the jurn with white onions, spices, a sprig of wild thyme or basil, a dash of salt and cinnamon, and a couple of cubes of ice to keep the meat fresh.

While my mother sautéed the minced lamb with onions, pine nuts, and pomegranate paste for the filling, my twin sister and I would hide behind the drying laundry clutching wet sheets for cover to get our stolen mouthful of fresh raw kibbi before it was all kneaded and flattened into a great, round pan and etched with a sharp knife into a mosaic of diamond shapes.

Shameless little beggars that we were, we would tiptoe around to enter the main kitchen door on the lookout for leftover morsels, this time brazenly and in broad daylight, before they too were balled and stuffed for frying or freezing. The aromas wafting out of the kitchen those blessed Sundays were meant for the gods. The accompanying salad of finely shaven, hair-thin cabbage and boiled beets slathered in a garlicky vinaigrette and sprinkled with dried and crushed mint leaves from the garden was another step up to heaven. The homemade yogurt, fermented in a clay pot and wrapped in an old towel overnight, was a must.

As war ravaged Lebanon and parts of the Middle East, I would hark back to those tastes and smells savored in acres of carefree time with a hole in my heart for those shared pleasures and that sublime way of life.

A Lebanese family table is a spiritual exercise of togetherness and cultural, culinary communion. The piles of rolled-up leaves picked from our own vine trees in Dibbiyeh were another woman-made miracle. As a graduate student later in Columbia, Missouri, I sought to replicate my mother's delicacies for a graduation dinner I had organized for classmates. I called Beirut, panic-stricken, when the vine leaves started opening up: "What shall I do, what shall I do? The guests are coming in 45 minutes!" I yelled over the phone. My mother laughed, reminding me of the age-old trick of weighting the contents of the pot with a heavy plate plunged into the water to keep the little green cigars from unraveling.

I became bolder and more daring as I finally set up house alone as a foreign correspondent. Traveling through Syria, Iraq, Iran, Morocco, Algeria, and Libya, I was constantly reminded while strolling through their souks of the riches of scents, flavors, spices, and condiments the region had to offer. I grew to appreciate the strong element of organic, tasty vegetables that shaped the Leba-

nese, Mediterranean, and Middle Eastern diet. The dark purple basil grown in Iran enhanced the blissful marriage of fresh feta and warm, Persian bread with its earthy perfume.

Once I settled in Washington, D. C., no dinner party I gave was complete without Kamal's personal and professional contributions as a friend and caterer. He shared some tricks and helped me heal the deprivations of exile, as I treated my guests to nostalgic flights into the magical evenings at home I wished had never been interrupted. Kamal's perfected and time-tested techniques steeped in the authenticity and ethos of the dishes he grew up with make that unique culinary voyage possible anywhere.

Our ingredients of fresh olive oil, dried thyme, sesame paste (tahini), and sumak are now gourmet staples and can be found on shelves of delicatessen stores and mainstream supermarkets all over America. Hummus is part of the South Beach Diet! My beloved worlds have come together.

The refreshing tart sweetness of pomegranates, both raw and processed, which has laced dishes from Morocco to Beirut and from Baghdad to Kabul, is the hottest new antioxidant. It is as though my grandmother's backyard of heavy, golden yellow lemons, ruby pomegranate fruit, pearl-blossomed almond trees, and emerald patches of basil, mint, and parsley has gone global.

Let me invite you to that garden and to Kamal's chest of Mediterranean treasures of the palate, lovingly and artfully presented in this gem of a book.

Acknowledgments

A mosaic of people, events, and circumstances have conspired over the years to end up in the compilation of this book. It all began with experiences and memories from my childhood, when our family would spend summers in Lebanon.

I would stand in the kitchen, watching my grandmother, aunts, and a ton of cousins preparing what always seemed to be a feast. The aroma of fresh parsley as someone's hands flew over a chopping board to make tabbouli, the sizzle of a kibbi ball splashing into hot oil—these were my early connections to a cuisine and culture I came of age with. The diversity and healthy, earthy ingredients of the Lebanese table always fascinated me. It has endured over the ages and traveled across borders to all kinds of palates.

To me, a day at home in the kitchen with my mother was a special event all by itself. I would happily turn the handle of our manual meat grinder screwed to the side of the countertop as meat, onions, and cracked wheat would pass through to produce that softened texture for kibbi. As she mixed and molded, then stuffed the hollowed cavities with minced meat and pine nuts, I would be crushing freshly roasted coffee beans with a handheld mill into a fine powder, giving off the scent that I forever associate with steaming Turkish coffee.

When I started a catering company with my family in Washington, D.C., my skills grew and I perfected our recipes and Lebanese-style tapas or mezza, pastries, and dishes to suit all kinds of occasions. Embassy receptions, holiday parties, weddings, bar and bat mitzvahs, graduation celebrations, museum openings, and official government events commanded our specialties in a myriad of variations. I was inspired by and adapted to certain occasions, alternating the range of ingredients, thus amassing a body of techniques and innovations of old traditions that are the foundation of this book of recipes.

My mother Hind and aunt Effat deserve my deepest thanks for their culinary prowess and authenticity. Their generosity, devotion, and time helped make this book possible. My father Wajih always supported my efforts and my dream. I would like to thank cousins Mimo, Nada, and Diana Takieddine, who were catalysts at the very beginning, and dear Betty Takieddine, who separated parsley for tabbouli in the early days.

Thanks to all of those individuals who worked in our company over the years; they too helped make this book possible. My brothers Faisal and Fadey worked day in and day out at Med Catering, enabling me to grow as I traveled along this unique journey. Thanks to my friend Ed Statland, who always encouraged me and wisely reminded me to keep my eye on the ball. To my friend Michael Giacopelli—thank you for all those early-morning phone conversations we had. You helped me focus on the task at hand.

I would like to thank my agent, Andrea Hurst, for her support and the good advice she offered me along the way. A big thank you to Heather

Carreiro, Jenn Taber, Jane Crosen, Sheryl Kober, Nancy Freeborn, Melissa Evarts, Lori Enik, and the entire team at The Globe Pequot Press for believing in this book.

A special thanks to all those who spent their time and gave constructive comments in testing the recipes: Sonia Hamra, Diane Buchta, Sami and Emily Takieddine, Sara Takieddine, Hank Hury, Jim Cross, Bob and Freya Loftus, Leila Assaf, Ghassan Al-Faqih, Peter Chenoweth, Rick Tedesco, Tim Wheat, Therese Pratt, May Hassan, Ann Tanous, Lara Hines, Kara Lilian, Deeb Keamy, John Bonkoske, Barbara Hekimian, Kirk Snyder, Pat Christ, Lori Hoolihan, Helen McNeal, Tom Falise, Lynne Wertheimer, Laura Cassagnol, Alan Miller, Stan Drake, Sharon Brown, Craig Mahfood, Joy and Pablo Weiser, David Mathews, Gail Rich, and Mitch Plave, all foodies and soul mates; I am immensely indebted to them.

Special thanks to my friend Nora Boustany and her positive energy. We share the same vision.

My deepest appreciation goes to my dear friend Andreas Frank. You devoted weekends and evenings working with me on the recipes and the book. Thanks for your faith in me, and in a project you knew was close to my heart. I hope you will enjoy preparing these recipes with your families and friends.

Introduction

Often, on Saturday nights when I was growing up in Washington, D.C., a steady flow of guests would arrive at the home of my parents. Hors d'oeuvres (mezza) would be passed and drinks offered, all under the watchful eye of my mother. My brothers and I were the waiters, bartenders, and kitchen help. Being the youngest, I was always in the kitchen with my mother. (Little did I know that I was a work in progress.) Everything ran according to plan, the table had been set the night before, silver polished days in advance, and all food preparations completed before the first guests arrived. Following dinner and dessert, Turkish coffee (qahwa) would be offered to most, while white coffee (qahwa bida) was offered to others. Some guests would begin to leave, while others stayed late into the night playing backgammon and telling jokes. Others would play cards and listen to the latest Farouz tape.

My parents entertained often, and at the end of each meal their guests would comment on the food. While Lebanese cuisine was new to some, to others it was familiar and part of their daily meals. Everyone always agreed that it was among the best food they had ever had—a phenomenon that occurs in many Middle Eastern homes. The truth of the matter is that the food my parents served really was quite good. My mother came to the United States in the early 1950s just after marrying my father. She brought with her a multitude of perfected techniques, distilled flavors, and time-tested recipes. Generations of knowledge of our Lebanese culinary traditions were passed on to her by my grandmother, which my mother has passed on to me.

Years later we began to give serious thought to opening a catering company. Where would we begin? We agreed the first step was organizing the recipes, which were all in my mother's head. There really were no recipes in writing. It was a coffee cup of this, a big spoon of that, a large onion—you know. The size of a ball? Yikes! So the process began—turning a pinch of this and a spoon of that into cups, teaspoons, and pounds.

After two years of measuring, weighing, dicing, slicing, baking, and frying, we opened our catering company. Over the years our company evolved into the premier Mediterranean catering company in Washington, D.C. Eventually we had the good fortune to have catered thousands of events. Events that ranged from a welcoming luncheon for her Majesty, Queen Noor of the Heshemite Kingdom of Jordan, a reception to welcome Crown Prince Abdullah of Saudi Arabia, receptions at the home of Selwa "Lucky" Roosevelt (President Ronald Reagan's chief of protocol), and a multitude of events held at the Smithsonian, art galleries, private homes, and even the White House—occasions that ranged from weddings to birthdays, bar and bat mitzvahs, graduations, engagements, and a host of holiday parties. Over the years I had the pleasure of being part of these occasions in a very special way—the food.

For two decades I had the opportunity to prepare recipes in different ways. Feedback from clients, friends, and family over the years allowed me to focus on each dish individually and adjust the ingredients and flavors, developing my signature recipes. Our foods incorporate a large variety of earthy ingredients, fresh vegetables, heart-healthy grains, yogurt, olive oils, and spices. Preparing various recipes multiple times allowed me to accurately balance these ingredients and offer a large variety of Lebanese classics ranging from entrees to hors d'oeuvres, salads, desserts, and side dishes. I have spent the past two years preparing these recipes at home for this book.

I have always enjoyed preparing our foods and sharing them with friends and family. My love for our cuisine continues to grow. I will always consider myself very fortunate to have been trained by one of the best natural chefs I have known, my mother. From my family to yours, Sahtain (double health).

How to Use This Book

Each recipe begins with an English title. These titles are descriptions of the recipe and are not literal translations. The traditional name is under the English title. To the right of that is the traditional name spelled phonetically. There are 170 recipes and variations. The format of each recipe informs you if special kitchen equipment or special ingredients are required and whether the recipe can be prepared in advance. Vivid color photography helps simplify preparation techniques and presentation. The book is linked to the website, www.cookingwithkamal.com, offering additional information.

Lebanese cuisine consists of a variety of heart healthy, fresh, vegetarian recipes, salads, earthy grains, poultry, meats, seafood, and stews that are considered to offer a well-balanced diet. Included are variations of the recipes giving you the option of preparing several of them vegetarian style or adding chicken, lamb, or beef. Most often the foods are baked, grilled, or sautéed in olive oil, which is high on the heart smart list.

While preparing the recipes, keep in mind that some ingredients such as lemons may vary in their intensity and flavor. Onions and garlic can also vary in their intensity and flavor, as well as herbs and spices. Freshly ground spices have a more intense flavor, so you may want to consider adding a bit less when using them. I encourage you to taste the recipes while preparing them. You may adjust the lemon, salt, or spice to suit your personal taste. My recommendation is to use the suggested ingredient list and follow the procedure the first time you prepare a recipe. Make notes directly in the book for future adjustments.

All recommended baking temperatures are based on standard gas or electric ovens and do not include using the convection setting of your oven. If you use the convection setting, you will need to decrease the baking time accordingly. Temperatures vary between ovens, so baking times may vary as well. Make certain your oven temperature is properly calibrated. The thickness of a skillet, pot, or pan may determine the level of heat you should use while preparing recipes. Thinner ones will heat rapidly while the opposite will occur when using thicker ones.

There is a section that describes techniques such as rinsing and storing produce, handling fillo dough, the recommended procedure for measuring flour, and others. The pantry describes and defines ingredients, sauces, flavorings, oils, and spices. There is a section on suggested menus, which recommends combinations of recipes that you may want to consider when planning a cocktail party, brunch, afternoon luncheon, or dinner. Also included is information discussing how to prepare before the guests arrive.

Helpful Techniques

Handling Fillo Dough: Bring fillo dough to room temperature before handling it. Never remove frozen fillo dough directly from the freezer to the counter; thaw it gradually in the refrigerator overnight, then let it come to room temperature the following day (several hours on the counter should do it). Follow the instructions on the package for handling fillo dough. Always prepare all the ingredients you need before opening the package. Once opened, cover the dough with plastic wrap to retain the moisture.

Measuring Flour: My recommendation for consistency is to use dry cups (dry of any moisture), scooping the flour into the measuring cup, then leveling excess flour off the top with a straight edge. Never plunge the measuring cup into the flour or pack flour into the cup, or you will end up with a different amount of flour each time.

Recycle Oil: Every type of oil has a specific smoke point. Every time you fry with a batch of oil, the smoke point is slightly reduced. After frying, I recycle the oil when there is about a cup or more left over. Once the oil has cooled, pass it through a fine-mesh sieve lined with a cotton ball to catch small particles. Store the oil in a jar and label it. You can fry a couple of more times using this oil, adding some fresh oil if needed. When frying items with strong flavors such as falafel or fish, that recycled oil should be used again only for falafel or fish.

Rinsing and Storing Produce: It may not always be possible to rinse and air-dry produce a day or two in advance, but if you can, great. Placing them in the refrigerator makes lettuce crispier, herbs firmer, and in my opinion it yields crunchier salads. Various vegetables are rinsed differently.

Place a large, clean towel on the counter before you begin. Bunches of vegetables such as parsley, mint, oregano, cilantro, or dill should be plunged into a bowl of cold water to rinse out deeply embedded debris and sand. Change the water several times until it runs clear. Shake out as much of the excess moisture as possible from the bunches. You can use a salad spinner, if you have one, to remove excess moisture.

Transfer rinsed vegetables to the towel to allow them to air-dry (not wilt) for several hours, turning them from time to time. Roll the individual items in dry paper towels or dry kitchen towels, then place them in individual plastic bags and refrigerate overnight.

When rinsing romaine lettuce, remove several of the larger outer leaves until you reach the tender leaves that make up the heart, and keep those intact. Rinse all the leaves as well as the heart. Drain them to allow the excess water to run off. After an hour or two, wrap the leaves in paper towels or a dry kitchen towel and place them in a plastic bag in the refrigerator overnight. As for other vegetables, after they are rinsed and air-dried, place each in its own plastic bag in the refrigerator until needed. Leave the bags slightly open overnight to keep condensation from forming within the bag, and seal the following day.

Segmenting Whole Chicken: Place the chicken on a cutting board, back down. Remove the wings by cutting right at the joint. Remove the leg and thigh together as one piece. To cut the leg and thigh into two pieces, bend them at the joint with your fingers on the joint. Carefully cut exactly at the joint where you feel a slight indentation. Sit the chicken up on the board and cut it in half; remove the back and discard it. Cut the breast in half lengthwise into two full half breasts. Then cut each half breast in half widthwise. Your yield will be ten pieces (four pieces of breast, two legs, two thighs, and two wings).

Tying a Roast: Shape the roast into a cylinder (fatty side facing upwards) while tucking any loose pieces in and under the roast. Try to keep the roast uniform in size from one end to the other so it will bake evenly. Use individual pieces of twine to tie around the roast at 2-inch intervals. Tighten the twine just enough so it presses firmly against the meat but is not cutting into it.

Alternatively, you can cut a piece of kitchen twine about ten times the length of the roast. Loop the string around one end of the roast (so it presses firmly against the meat without cutting into it), about 2 inches in from the end. Run the string down 2 inches along the top of the roast and then wrap it around the roast, making a loop. Pass the string under the loop and gently pull, tightening the loop around the roast. Move down the roast, making three additional loops at about 2-inch intervals, and tighten each one so that the string is pressing firmly against the meat. Flip the roast and pass the string in and out through the loops along the bottom until you are back at the top where you made the first loop. Tie these off together.

Before the Guests Arrive...

Whether you are entertaining four or forty guests, nothing will serve you better than a little planning and preparation. Complete all shopping in advance, and complete most of the food preparation before your guests arrive. Try not to put anything off that can be prepared in advance. Take a few minutes to walk through the party in your mind. As you think of things, write them down. This list will serve as your "reminder" list later.

While waiting for your guests to arrive, remove the glasses from the cabinet and place them close by so they are easy to access. Light any votive candles around the room in advance. If you have a non-smoking home, place an ashtray outside to accommodate smokers. If you are hosting a seated dinner party, set the table in advance or even the day before. One time I set the table two days before our big Thanksgiving Day dinner.

Prepare lemons, limes, or other garnishes for drinks before your guests arrive. For larger gatherings, plan in advance which platter you are going to use for each dish. Label the platters and have them close by in one convenient area. Add to your list the foods that you want to place on the table. Use it to confirm that everything is on the table; it will help you avoid leaving a dish out.

Buy and arrange flowers a day or two in advance. Empty the dishwasher early in the day. Remove all dishes, cutting boards, and utensils from the sink before guests arrive. Put in a new roll of paper towels and place a couple of clean, dry kitchen towels on the counter for later use. Empty the kitchen trash can before the first guests arrive so it doesn't bubble over with trash within the first hour.

When hosting outdoor events, have everything set up and ready to go beforehand. Set up drink and food areas in advance. Make sure they are well equipped with all the necessary cups, napkins, cutlery, ice, beverages, and utensils. Place large trash receptacles close by so your guests will know where to put trash.

For larger numbers of guests, you will find it useful to have someone in the kitchen who can give you a hand—not just a friend or family member, but someone that you have hired. While that is not always a necessity and may not always be in the budget, when you are having a lot of guests it pays to have that extra set of hands.

In my opinion, the kind of occasions at which you can call on friends and family for help are casual family dinners and gatherings like Thanksgiving or holiday and birthday parties. Friends and family are more than happy to pitch in and give a hand.

Appetizers

(MEZZA)

I have fond memories of the meals we enjoyed in the town of Zahle in Lebanon. Zahle sits in a prime location in the Beqaa Valley and is the site of many well-known outdoor restaurants, where gentle breezes blow over the canopies and peaceful meandering streams flow between the walkways. Throughout the day and night, tabletops brim with an enticing selection of *mezza* in what always seems to be a grand feast.

Mezza are sumptuous, small finger foods that set the tone for what is to follow. What I've always enjoyed about mezza is the diversity of textures and flavors. These Lebanese-style tapas are a great choice for cocktail buffets, tray-passed hors d'oeuvres, or when you simply want something delectable to snack on. Spinach Triangles, Hummus with pita dippers, Thyme Pizzettas, Pumpkin Kibbi Balls, Olives, Pickles, Cheese, and Crudités, Vegetable- or Lamb-Stuffed Grape Leaves, Fried Cauliflower with Tahini Sauce . . . the combinations are endless. All of them are easy to pick up and delicious to eat. Add Parsley and Bulgur Wheat Salad (tabbouli), a selection of Lebanese Mixed Grill, Basmati Rice with Cumin, Lentils, and Onions, fresh fruit, and baklava, and the meal becomes a lavish event.

Crispy Bean & Herb Patties 2
Feta Cheese Crescents 4
Pomegranate-Beef Crescents. 6
Fried Cauliflower with Tahini Sauce 7
Hummus 8
Hummus with Minced Lamb and Pine Nuts   11
Lamb Turbans 11
Mini Dill Omelets 14
Olives, Cheese, Pickles, and Crudités. 15
Pickled Turnips 17
Pomegranate Beef and Cheese Pies 18
Basic Dough 20
Pumpkin Kibbi Balls 21
Potato Kibbi Balls 23
Lamb Kibbi Balls. 24

Robust Garlic Puree 26
Smoked Eggplant Dip 28
Spicy Red Pepper and Walnut Spread 30
Spinach Triangles 31
Garbanzo Bean Triangles with Beef Confit . . 33
Tabbouli Bites 34
Tangy Beef Fillo Rolls 35
Thyme Pizzettas 37
Red Pepper Pizzettas. 39
Toasted Pita Dippers. 40
Vegetable-Stuffed Grape Leaves 42
Lamb-Stuffed Grape Leaves 45
Yogurt Cheese Canapés. 46
Yogurt Cheese 47

Crispy Bean & Herb Patties

ABOUT 15 PATTIES

Falafel (fa-le-fill)

The aroma that fills the air while these crispy patties are being prepared will make you eager to bite into one. Offer them as an appetizer with tahini dip or in a pita wrap sandwich with chopped lettuce, tomato, radish, pickled turnips, and tahini sauce. Traditionally, skinless fava beans are combined with the garbanzos, but they vary so much from market to market that I have decided to leave them out.

Specialty ingredients: Tahini, found in specialty markets or online.

Special equipment: A food processor and a candy/fry thermometer.

Prepare ahead: The raw patties can be frozen for several weeks. Freeze uncovered on a plastic-lined baking sheet, then transfer to an airtight container. Fry as directed without thawing. **Note:** The beans must soak overnight.

FOR THE FALAFEL

1 cup dry garbanzo beans (soak overnight)

½ teaspoon and ¼ teaspoon baking soda, divided

2 tablespoons coarsely chopped garlic

¼ cup coarsely chopped yellow onion

¼ cup coarsely chopped green onion

¼ cup coarsely chopped flat-leaf parsley; use green leafy parts and tender stems

¼ cup coarsely chopped cilantro; use green leafy parts and tender stems

1¼ teaspoons salt

¼ teaspoon coarsely ground black pepper

¼ teaspoon ground allspice

¹⁄₁₆ teaspoon cayenne pepper

¾ teaspoon ground coriander

2 tablespoons all-purpose flour

2 teaspoons raw sesame seeds (for topping)

2 cups canola oil (for frying)

FOR THE TAHINI SAUCE

1 recipe Tahini Sauce (see page 7)

To soak the beans for the falafel

*Soak the beans in 4 cups water (so they are submerged) with ½ teaspoon baking soda overnight at room temperature, uncovered. (**Note:** The baking soda will soften the beans.)*

To prepare the falafel (the following day)

Drain the beans. Place them on a kitchen towel and dry them well. Pat the vegetables dry to remove excess water (too much moisture in the mixture makes it difficult for the patties to hold together).

Place the beans in a food processor fitted with a metal blade. Add the garlic, both types of onion, the parsley, and the cilantro. (I use a 12-cup food processor; smaller ones may require processing one half at a time.) Pulse several times until the beans are coarsely chopped. Scrape down the sides, then slowly pulse and process until the beans are finely chopped (not pureed) and the mixture begins to hold together. (Test a small amount by squeezing it in the palm of your hand.)

Transfer the mixture to a bowl. Add the salt, spices, flour, and ¼ teaspoon baking soda, and mix well. Measuring the falafel mixture into 2-tablespoon por-

tions, place each portion in your palm and press it into a 2-inch round dome-shaped patty (like a crab cake) using your other palm (or use a falafel mold; see below). Place the patty on a plastic-lined baking sheet, dome-side up. Repeat with the remaining portions. Sprinkle a few raw sesame seeds on top of each and gently press them into the patties with your finger. (Do not use toasted sesame seeds; they will not stick.)

To make the tahini sauce

Follow the recipe and the procedure to prepare the tahini sauce as described on page 7.

To fry the falafel

Heat the oil to 375°F in a small saucepan over medium-high heat (the oil should be about 1 inch deep). Use a candy/fry thermometer to measure the temperature of the oil for accuracy. Fry 5 patties at a time. Once they are golden brown, remove them with a slotted spoon to a paper towel–lined plate. Fry the remaining falafel. Make sure the temperature of the oil remains at 375°F so the patties fry evenly.

Recycle the oil: *See page xiv.*

To serve

Serve with warm pita bread and tahini sauce on the side. Offer with Pickled Turnips (page 17) to kick up the flavors.

Falafel molds

Handheld molds can be found in specialty markets or online. They consist of two pieces: a small circular mold attached to a spring-loaded handle, and a flat paddle. Hold the lever down on the handle as you fill the mold with the falafel mixture. Pack it down into the mold using the paddle as you press the mixture into a dome-shaped patty. Gently release the lever and transfer the patty to a plastic-lined tray. If you plan on making falafel often, it is worth purchasing one of these. The final number of patties may vary based on the size of the mold you use. Try to find one that is about 2 inches in diameter.

Feta Cheese Crescents

ABOUT 2 DOZEN

Sambousik bi Jibni (sam-boo-sick bee jib-nee)

This pastry is simple to prepare and easy to handle. The crispy outer layers taste as though you are biting into a pillow filled with warm cheese. They are perfect for tray-passed hors d'oeuvres, on a cocktail buffet, or as a mid-afternoon snack. You can also use this filling when preparing the Greek layered pastry called tyropita.

Specialty ingredients: Bulgarian feta cheese (other brands will do).

Special equipment: A pastry blender, a 2½-inch round cookie cutter, and a candy/fry thermometer.

Prepare ahead: The uncooked crescents can be frozen for several weeks. Freeze uncovered on a plastic-lined baking sheet, then transfer to an airtight container. Fry as directed without thawing.

FOR THE SAMBOUSIK PASTRY

1½ cups unbleached flour

6 tablespoons chilled butter, diced

¼ teaspoon salt

¼ cup and 1 tablespoon cold water

2 cups canola oil (for frying)

Measuring flour: See page xiv.

4

FOR THE FILLING

¼ pound Bulgarian feta cheese, crumbled

¼ cup minced yellow onion

¼ cup finely chopped flat leaf parsley; use green leafy parts and tender stems

¼ teaspoon salt

¼ teaspoon coarsely ground black pepper

To prepare the sambousik pastry

Combine the flour, butter, and salt in a bowl. Using a pastry blender in a rocking motion, cut the butter into the flour by pressing it up against the sides and the bottom of the bowl until all the pieces of butter have been cut in and the mixture resembles cornmeal. (If you do not have a pastry blender, use the tines of a fork to press the butter into the flour; it takes a bit longer, but it will work.)

Add the cold water, mixing quickly with your hand to form the dough. Shape the dough into a disc about 1 inch thick. Wrap the disc in plastic wrap and refrigerate; this allows the dough to rest. After 1 hour, remove the dough from the refrigerator and let it stand for 10 minutes at room temperature prior to rolling.

To prepare the filling

Separately press the feta cheese and onion between paper towels until they are dry. Combine the feta cheese, onion, parsley, salt, and pepper in a bowl. Use the tines of a fork to mix the ingredients until they are well combined. Portion the cheese into 1 teaspoon, egg-shaped balls and place them on a plate double-lined with paper towels to absorb excess liquid. Loosely cover with plastic wrap and refrigerate until needed. Remove the filling from the refrigerator 10 minutes prior to preparing the crescents.

To prepare the crescents

On a lightly floured surface, roll the dough out to ⅛-inch thickness. Gently hold the rolled-out dough by the edges and lift it about 2 inches off the counter (this will allow any contraction in the dough to occur before cutting). Cut the dough into 2½-inch rounds using a cookie cutter; make one cut directly next to the other to maximize the number of rounds. Cover the rounds with plastic wrap to avoid drying. Pick up 1 round at a time and flip it over so that you are placing the filling on the underside of the dough (or whichever side seems stickier). Place a portion of cheese in the center. Fold the dough over the cheese so it forms a half-moon crescent. Firmly pinch the edges together with your fingers, securing the cheese inside while forming an outer rim ¼ inch wide. (Avoid getting cheese trapped in between the edges; this may cause the crescents to open later.) Fill the remaining rounds.

Place the crescents flat on your work surface. Using the tines of a fork, press firmly along the outer rim of each crescent to crimp the edges, locking the cheese inside. Be careful not to pierce the dough. Alternatively, you can crimp the edges as you would a piecrust.

Heat the oil to 375°F in a small saucepan over medium-high heat, using a candy/fry thermometer for accuracy. The oil should be about 1 inch deep. Fry 6 crescents at a time until golden brown, then transfer to a plate double-lined with paper towels. Fry the remaining crescents. Make sure the temper- *ature of the oil remains at 375°F so that the crescents fry evenly. Let them cool for several minutes prior to serving.*

Recycle the oil: *See page xiv.*

Pomegranate-Beef Crescents

ABOUT 2 DOZEN

Sambousik bi Lahmi (sam-boo-sick bee lah-me)

Specialty ingredients: Sumak and dibs ruman, (pomegranate molasses), found at specialty markets or online.

FOR THE DOUGH
1 recipe sambousik pastry (see the previous recipe)

FOR THE FILLING
1 teaspoon extra-virgin olive oil
¼ pound ground beef (80% lean)
¾ cup diced yellow onion (⅛ inch)
½ teaspoon salt
⅛ teaspoon coarse ground black pepper
¼ teaspoon ground allspice
⅛ teaspoon ground cinnamon
1½ tablespoons freshly squeezed lemon juice
1½ teaspoons sumak
2½ teaspoons dibs ruman
1 tablespoon toasted pine nuts
(**You can substitute** ground lamb or ground chicken for the beef.)

To prepare the dough
Follow the procedure for the sambousik pastry as described in the previous recipe.

To prepare the filling
Preheat the olive oil in a small skillet over medium-high heat. Add the ground meat and cook while breaking it into small, minced pieces. Once the meat is no longer pink, add the onions, salt, pepper, allspice, and cinnamon, reduce the heat to medium-low, and cook until the onions are tender. Add the lemon juice and simmer until the moisture is absorbed. Remove from the heat and mix in the sumak and dibs ruman. Spread the filling over a flat dish and cool uncovered in the refrigerator for 30 minutes prior to using.

Preheat the oven to 350°F. Spread the pine nuts over a foil-lined baking sheet and toast in the center of the oven, shaking the tray occasionally, for 5 to 7 minutes, or until they are golden. Cool the pine nuts before using.

To prepare the crescents
Follow the same procedure described for the Feta Cheese Crescents in the previous recipe, placing 1 teaspoon meat filling and 2 pine nuts in the center of each round.

Fried Cauliflower with Tahini Sauce

SERVES 4

Arnabeet Mickli ma Taratoor (ar-na-beet mick-lee ma tara-tour)

This is a different way to offer cauliflower as an appetizer or with the main meal. The combination of the lightly fried florets with the tangy tahini sauce is delicious. As you cut through the tender pieces of cauliflower, it's like slicing through creamy butter.

Specialty ingredients: Tahini, found at specialty markets or online.

Special equipment: A pestle (a garlic press will do) and a candy/fry thermometer.

Prepare ahead: The cauliflower can be fried early in the day. Refrigerate loosely covered until needed. Reheat at 400°F for 5 to 7 minutes. Serve as directed. The tahini sauce can be prepared up to 3 days in advance.

FOR THE CAULIFLOWER
2 teaspoons salt
1 head cauliflower (about 2½ pounds)
3 cups canola oil (for frying)

FOR THE TAHINI SAUCE
1 large clove garlic
1 teaspoon salt
½ cup tahini (mix well before using)
⅓ cup freshly squeezed lemon juice
¼ cup water
¼ cup finely chopped flat-leaf parsley; use green leafy parts and tender stems

To prepare the cauliflower
Place a large pot with 8 cups water and the salt over high heat. Cover and bring to a rolling boil. Meanwhile remove all the leaves from around the stem of the cauliflower. Cut the florets off the central stem into 2- to 3-inch pieces, keeping them consistent in size.

Place the florets in the boiling water. Return the water to a rolling boil and cook uncovered, stirring a couple of times, for 5 minutes. Drain, then evenly spread the florets over a flat tray and cool for 30 minutes uncovered. The steamed florets must cool prior to frying, or they will fall apart.

Heat the oil in a medium saucepan over medium-high heat to 375°F, using a candy/fry thermometer for accuracy. The oil should be about 1½ inches deep. Fry 4 to 5 florets at a time until golden brown and the edges are crispy. Remove them with a slotted spoon to a paper towel–lined dish. Make sure the temperature of the oil remains at 375°F so that the florets fry evenly. Fry the remaining pieces of cauliflower. (If you prefer, you can serve the cauliflower steamed.)

Recycle the oil: *See page xiv.*

To prepare the tahini sauce

In a small bowl, mash the garlic and salt to a pulp using a pestle. Add the tahini, lemon juice, and water. Whisk until smooth and creamy; the consistency will be like pancake batter.

Use a spoon to mix in the parsley. Cover and refrigerate until needed. Tahini sauce may thicken once refrigerated. Thin it with lemon juice or water.

To serve

Place the tahini sauce in a small bowl in the center of the platter. Arrange the warm or room-temperature cauliflower around the tahini.

Selecting Cauliflower

Choose creamy white compact heads with bright green leaves. Avoid heads that have brown spots. Cauliflower is a member of the cabbage family.

Hummus

SERVES 4 TO 6 (ABOUT 1 PINT)

Hoummos bi Tahini (hum-moose bee ta-hee-nee)

Between the nutty-tasting tahini and the buttery texture of the garbanzo beans, this dish is not only flavorful, but a good source of protein. Prepared hummus is available in many markets, but the flavor is not like that of homemade hummus, which is so easy to prepare—especially using canned garbanzos—you may never buy it again. Another option is to soak dry garbanzo beans overnight and cook them the following day. Serve hummus with toasted pita dippers, crackers, fresh vegetables, or your favorite rustic bread.

Specialty ingredients: Tahini, found at specialty markets or online.
Special equipment: A food processor.
Prepare ahead: You can prepare hummus several days in advance and refrigerate it in an airtight container. Serve as directed.

FOR THE BEANS
½ cup water
1 (15- or 16-ounce) can garbanzo beans (drained), about 1¾ cups

alternatively: 1¼ cups dried garbanzo beans
  4 cups and 6 cups water, divided
  ½ teaspoon and ¼ teaspoon baking soda, divided
  ½ teaspoon salt

FOR THE HUMMUS
2 large cloves garlic
1 teaspoon salt
⅓ cup freshly squeezed lemon juice
⅓ cup tahini (mix well before using)

Opposite page: Hummus

8

To prepare the beans

In a small saucepan, place ½ cup water and the drained canned garbanzo beans (reserving 3 beans for the garnish) over high heat. Bring to a rolling boil and cook uncovered for about 1 minute, allowing half of the water to evaporate. For thicker hummus, let most of the water boil off.

Alternatively, *to prepare dry beans, soak the beans in 4 cups water (so they are submerged) and ½ teaspoon baking soda overnight at room temperature, uncovered. (**Note**: The baking soda will soften the beans.) The following day, drain the beans and place them with the ½ teaspoon of salt in a medium-sized saucepan with 6 cups fresh water. Bring to a boil over high heat. Skim any foam off the top, then reduce the heat to medium-low and add ¼ teaspoon baking soda. Cover and let the beans simmer for 20 to 30 minutes or until tender. Place 1¾ cups of the drained beans plus ½ cup of the cooking liquid in a small sauce pan and boil off half the water to prepare the hummus. Freeze the remaining 1¾ cups beans (see below).*

To prepare the hummus

Pour the boiled garbanzo beans and the remaining cooking liquid into a food processor fitted with a metal blade. Add the garlic and salt and process for 2 minutes. Use a spatula to scrape down the sides. Add the lemon juice and tahini and process for 1 minute more.

Transfer the hummus to a container and cover with a paper towel and refrigerate. Cover with the lid once cooled. Serve at room temperature.

To serve

Place room-temperature hummus in the center of a flat serving dish. Use the back of a spoon to spread the hummus over the dish so there is an outer raised lip around the perimeter, with a central "canal" around a raised mound in the center. Place a radish star on the raised mound surrounded by 3 garbanzo beans. Garnish with a few sprigs of parsley and sprinkle the center and around the perimeter with paprika. Pour extra-virgin olive oil in the central canal formed with the back of the spoon. Offer with warm pitas or pita dippers (page 40).

To Freeze Cooked Garbanzos

Place the beans in a container and cover them with their cooking liquid. Freeze up to 4 months.

{VARIATIONS}

Hummus can be varied by adding one of the following ingredients.

Roasted Red Bell Pepper: Mix ¾ cup drained and coarsely chopped roasted red bell pepper into the room-temperature hummus. (See "Roasting Fresh Red Bell Peppers," page 30.)

Cumin: Mix in 1 teaspoon ground cumin.

Horseradish: Mix in 2 tablespoons of prepared horseradish.

Sun-dried Tomato: Mix in ¾ cup drained and coarsely chopped sun-dried tomatoes.

Hummus with Minced Lamb and Pine Nuts

SERVES 4

Hoummos bi Tahini ma Lahm Mafroom (hum-moose bee ta-hee-nee ma lah-him ma-froom)

For a quick, delicious meal or hearty appetizer, top hummus with warm minced lamb, toasted pine nuts, and a drizzle of olive oil and offer with warm pita bread and a salad on the side.

Prepare ahead: You can prepare the hummus and the topping 2 to 3 days in advance (refrigerate separately). Serve as described.

FOR THE HUMMUS WITH MINCED LAMB AND PINE NUTS

1 recipe Hummus (see previous recipe)

1 recipe Kibbi Filling (pages 24–25)

(**You can substitute** ground beef or ground chicken for the lamb in the Kibbi filling.)

To prepare the hummus

Prepare the hummus, following the recipe and procedure described in the previous recipe.

To prepare the filling

Prepare the Kibbi filling, following the recipes and procedures on page 25.

To serve

Spread room-temperature hummus over a flat platter. Top with the warm meat filling and sprinkle with pine nuts. Drizzle olive oil over the top. Serve with warm pita bread.

Lamb Turbans

ABOUT 2 DOZEN

Lahm bi Ajeen (lah-him bee a-jeen)

Not only are these unique lamb turbans beautiful to look at, they are delicious too. A tasty combination of lamb, onions, tomato, and pomegranate with toasted pine nuts is wrapped up and baked to perfection in these stylish appetizers shaped like turbans.

Special ingredients: Dibs ruman (pomegranate molasses), can be found at specialty markets or online.

Special equipment: A 1¼-inch round cookie cutter, cheese grater, fine-mesh strainer.

Prepare ahead: The turbans can be refrigerated for several days or frozen for several weeks. Freeze uncovered on a plastic-lined baking sheet, then store in an airtight container. Reheat thawed turbans at 350°F for 5 to 7 minutes.

FOR THE DOUGH

½ cup plus 1 tablespoon lukewarm water
¼ teaspoon dry active yeast
⅛ teaspoon sugar
1½ cups unbleached flour
½ teaspoon salt
2 tablespoons olive oil (for dipping)

Measuring flour: See page xiv.

FOR THE FILLING

¾ cup grated onion
¼ pound (coarsely ground) lean lamb
¾ cup peeled and seeded tomato, chopped in
 ¼-inch pieces
¾ teaspoon salt
¼ teaspoon black pepper
¼ teaspoon allspice
¼ teaspoon cinnamon
⅛ teaspoon ground ginger
1 tablespoon dibs ruman
1 teaspoon freshly squeezed lemon juice
1½ tablespoons toasted pine nuts
(**You can substitute** ground beef or ground
 chicken for the lamb.)

To prepare the dough

In a small bowl, dissolve the yeast and sugar in the water. Mix well. Cover with a dish and set aside for several minutes to proof the yeast (until it foams). Meanwhile combine the flour and salt in a separate bowl. Pour all of the yeast mixture over the flour. Using one hand, quickly mix and knead the ingredients into a dough. Use both hands to shape the dough into a ball. (If the dough seems sticky, dip your hands in a bit of flour.)

On a lightly floured surface, roll the ball of dough out to ¼ inch thickness. Gently hold the rolled-out dough by the edges and lift it about 2 inches off the counter (this will allow any contraction in the dough to occur before cutting).

Cut the dough into 1¼-inch rounds using a cookie cutter; make one cut directly next to the other to maximize the number of rounds. Dip the pastry rounds into the olive oil and place them side-by-side on a dinner plate. Cover them with plastic wrap and set the plate aside, allowing the pastry to rest for 1 hour. In the meantime, prepare the filling. Reserve the leftover olive oil.

To prepare the filling

Grate the onion using the large holes of a cheese grater. Place the grated onion in a fine-mesh strainer and, using the back of a spoon, press the onion against the mesh to remove as much of the liquid as possible. Combine the onions with the next 9 ingredients, all but the pine nuts. Mix well, cover, and refrigerate the filling until needed. Keep the fine-mesh strainer aside for later use.

Preheat the oven to 350°F. Spread the pine nuts over a foil-lined baking sheet and toast in the center of the oven, shaking the tray occasionally, for 5 to 7 minutes, or until they are golden. Cool the pine nuts before using.

To prepare the turbans

After the dough has rested 1 hour, transfer the plate of rounds to your work area. Put the filling into the fine-mesh strainer. Place the strainer over the bowl used for the filling, allowing excess liquid to drain (you will later discard this liquid).

Line a baking sheet with foil and generously grease it with some of the reserved olive oil. Set this next to your work area. Preheat the oven to 425°F.

With a dessert plate on the counter in front of you, transfer 1 round of dough to the center of the plate. Use your fingers to flatten it into a round 3½ inches in diameter, dipping your fingers in some of the olive oil as you open the round. Place 2 teaspoons of filling in the center of the dough. Use your fingers to lift one side of the dough over the filling, as you form a hood over half of the filling. Press the edges down on either side with your fingertip, securing the filling under the hood. Start from one side by lifting and wrapping the dough up, over, and around the filling. Repeat this 3 more times. As you lift and wrap the dough around for the third time, make sure to tuck the final stretch of dough under the turban to prevent the dough from unraveling while it bakes.

The turban should look like a rosebud at this point. Transfer it to the greased tray. Repeat with the remaining rounds of dough, placing them 1 inch apart on the tray. Insert 3 pine nuts into the meat filling at the top of each turban.

Place the tray on the middle shelf of the oven and bake at 425°F for 18 to 20 minutes, or until the pastry edges of the turbans are golden brown. Allow them to cool for several minutes before serving.

Mini Dill Omelets

ABOUT 15

Ijjie Shimra (ij-jee shim-ra)

The wonderful thing about these pillow-like omelets is that they are prepared using an egg ring so they are the perfect serving size. The basic recipe is with onion and dill, but they can also be prepared using zucchini, potato, or beef confit. The omelets are served slightly warm or at room temperature and are delicious with Pickled Turnips (see recipe on page 17) and warm pita bread.

Special equipment: Two (3–3½-inch-diameter) egg rings and a candy/fry thermometer.

Prepare ahead: The omelets can be prepared up to 3 days in advance, and refrigerated. They can be frozen for several weeks. Freeze them uncovered on a plastic-lined baking sheet, then transfer to an airtight container. Reheat thawed omelets at 375°F for 8 to 10 minutes, then serve as directed.

FOR THE OMELETS

6 large eggs, beaten
3½ cups diced yellow onion (¼ inch)
1 cup finely chopped dill; use threadlike leaves
   and tender stems
¾ teaspoon salt
¼ teaspoon coarsely ground black pepper
3 tablespoons flour
¾ teaspoon baking soda
1 cup olive oil (for frying)

To prepare the omelets

Combine all the ingredients in a bowl (except the oil) and mix thoroughly with a fork. Preheat the oven to 350°F. Double-line a baking sheet with paper towels and set aside.

Pour ½ inch oil into a medium-sized skillet and heat to 375°F over medium-high heat. Use a candy/fry thermometer to ensure proper temperature.

Place the 2 egg rings in the pan, and portion 2 heaping tablespoons of egg mixture into the center of each ring, making certain to distribute the mixture up to the edges of the rings. Using a large spoon, scoop and baste hot oil from the sides of the pan over the tops of each mini omelet. Continue basting the omelets with hot oil until the tops puff up and are golden brown, resembling the top of a muffin.

Using tongs, remove the rings (leaving the omelets in the pan) and set the rings aside. Carefully flip each mini omelet as you would a pancake and brown the underside. Once browned, transfer the omelets to the paper towel–lined tray. Return the rings to the skillet and repeat until the egg mixture is finished. Stir the egg mixture periodically to prevent it from separating. Make sure the temperature of the oil remains at 375°F so that the omelets fry evenly.

Place the tray of omelets on the middle rack in the oven and bake for 15 minutes, then set them aside to cool for 10 minutes. Garnish with sprigs of fresh dill. Serve slightly warm or at room temperature with warm pita bread.

{VARIATIONS}

Mini Zucchini Omelets (Ijjie Cousa): Substitute 1 cup grated zucchini (squeeze out the moisture before combining it with the eggs) for the dill.

Mini Potato Omelets (Ijjie Batata): Substitute 1 cup peeled and grated russet potato for the dill.

Mini Beef Confit Omelets (Ijjie Qawarma): Substitute 1 cup beef confit (see page 136) without the rendered fat for the dill. Break the beef confit into small pieces.

Olives, Cheese, Pickles, and Crudités   SERVES 8 TO 10
Zeytoon, Jibni, Kabeese ma Khudra (zey-toon, jib-nee, ka-beese, ma khud-dra)

An assortment of olives, cheeses, pickles, and raw vegetables is a colorful and interesting addition at mealtime or with drinks. It makes a beautiful centerpiece, and your friends and family will enjoy the different and delicious flavors and textures.

Specialty ingredients: Pickled turnips (page 17), micti pickles, kalamata and green Greek olives, Kashkaval cheese, Halloumi or Ackawi cheese, or braided string cheese, all found at specialty markets or online.

Prepare ahead: You can prepare the individual items one day in advance. Refrigerate them separately. Serve as directed.

FOR THE OLIVES, CHEESE, PICKLES, AND CRUDITÉS

15 slices cucumber, striped and cut ¼ inch thick

10 sticks green bell pepper, cut ¼ inch wide lengthwise

2 green onions, cut in 2-inch lengths

16 pickled turnips (prepared fresh as on page 17, otherwise store-bought)

4 micti pickles, halved and cut in 2-inch lengths

1 lemon, cut in 8 wedges

8 radishes (greens attached when available), cut into flowers

24 black kalamata or Moroccan olives

24 Greek green olives

½ pound Kashkaval cheese, cut into bite-sized wedges

½ pound Halloumi or Ackawi cheese, cut in bite-sized cubes

or: ½ pound braided string cheese, cut in 1-inch lengths (separate the braids)

15

To prepare the olives, cheese, pickles, and crudités

Prepare the cucumber, bell pepper, green onion, pickled turnips, micti pickles, and lemon and set them aside. (If micti pickles are not available, use your favorite pickles and cut them in half, then into 2-inch lengths). To prepare the radish flowers cut the root tip off. Make 4 surface cuts (about ⅛ inch deep) in each side of the radish to resemble petals. Soak in an ice water bath for 1 hour, and the petals will open. Drain radish flowers. Prepare the remaining items. Cover and store the prepared ingredients individually in the refrigerator until ready to serve.

To serve

Platter up to 5 hours in advance. Arrange chilled items on a flat serving dish over leaf lettuce and parsley sprigs. Refrigerate covered until ready to serve.

{VARIATION}

Include other pickled items (such as peppers or cauliflower), olives (such as olives stuffed with jalapeño or sun-dried tomato), or different cheeses (such as Bulgarian feta) or vegetables (such as red, yellow, and orange bell peppers).

Choosing Cheeses

My favorite traditional cheeses are Bulgarian Kashkaval, Halloumi from Cypress, and Karoun brands of Ackawi and braided string cheese. The flavors of the cheeses vary between brands. Find a brand of each cheese that suits your palate, and stick with it.

Pickled Turnips

1 QUART

Lift (lift)

These pickled white turnips have it all. They are crispy and crunchy with a zesty bite. They get their brilliant pinkish-purple color from beets, and have a distinctively deep, rich tangy flavor, making them an interesting and unusual condiment. Offer these pickled turnips with falafel (page 2) or moujaddara (page 145), or even with olives and drinks.

Special equipment: A 1-quart storage container with a tight-fitting lid.

Prepare ahead: Pickled turnips must be prepared 6 days prior to using. Once pickled, they should last in the refrigerator for several weeks.

FOR THE TURNIPS

1 pound small white turnips, peeled

¼ pound fresh beets, peeled

¾ cup distilled white vinegar

¾ cup cold water

4 teaspoons salt

To prepare the turnips

Cut the tip and tail off each turnip, then peel. Cut each turnip into 4 equal wedges. Cut each wedge widthwise into pieces that are ½ inch thick. Prepare the beets the same way. Wear gloves if you have them, as beets stain easily.

Combine the pieces of turnips and beets in a quart container. Mix the vinegar, water, and salt together until the salt has dissolved. Pour this solution over the turnips and beets and mix well. Cover and refrigerate for 3 days; then stir the vegetables, exchanging the pieces at the top with the ones at the bottom. Return to the refrigerator for 3 more days before serving.

Selecting White Turnips

Choose smaller, smooth-skinned turnips that seem heavy for their size. Avoid soft ones with brown spots; they are porous and will not be crisp.

{VARIATION}

Add a couple of your favorite hot peppers in the vinegar mix for a spicy kick.

Pomegranate Beef and Cheese Pies

ABOUT 3 DOZEN

Sfiha Lahm (sfee-ha lah-him)

These pies are great as an afternoon snack, tray-passed hors d'oeuvres, or on a buffet. When you bite into one, the crisp texture of the edges complemented by the savory flavors in the filling will entice you back for another. The blending of the yogurt cheese with the dibs ruman keeps the meat moist with a slightly sweet yet tart flavor.

Specialty ingredients: Labni (yogurt cheese), dibs ruman (pomegranate molasses), and tahini, found at specialty markets or online. Yogurt cheese can also be prepared fresh (see page 47).

Special equipment: A 2-inch round cookie cutter.

Prepare ahead: The baked beef pies can be frozen for several weeks. Freeze uncovered on a plastic-lined baking sheet then store in an airtight container. Reheat thawed pies at 350°F for 5 to 7 minutes.

FOR THE DOUGH

1 recipe Basic Dough (see page 20)

$^1\!/_3$ cup extra-virgin olive oil (for dipping)

FOR THE TOPPING

⅓ cup toasted pine nuts

½ tablespoon melted butter

1 pound ground beef (80% lean)

3 cups diced yellow onion (¼ inch)

2½ teaspoons salt

½ teaspoon table-grind black pepper

1 teaspoon ground allspice

½ teaspoon ground cinnamon

¼ cup freshly squeezed lemon juice

½ cup labni (cream cheese will do)

2 tablespoons dibs ruman

1 tablespoon tahini (mix well before using)

½ cup pomegranate seeds (when in season
   October through January)

(**You can substitute** ground lamb for the beef.)

To prepare the dough

Prepare the dough as described on page 20, and set it aside to rise.

To prepare the topping

Preheat the oven to 350°F. Spread the pine nuts over a foil-lined baking sheet and toast in the center of the oven, shaking the pan occasionally, for 5 to 7 minutes or until the nuts are golden. Mix ½ tablespoon melted butter with the nuts. Transfer them to a paper towel–lined dish and set aside.

Preheat a large skillet over medium-high heat. Add the ground meat and cook while breaking it into small, minced pieces. Once the meat is no longer pink, add the onions, salt, pepper, allspice, and cinnamon. Reduce the heat to medium-low and sauté, stirring periodically, until the onions are tender. Add the lemon juice and simmer until the moisture is absorbed.

Remove the skillet from the heat. Add the cheese, dibs ruman, and tahini. Mix well and set aside until needed. Gently fold in the fresh pomegranate seeds, if in season.

To prepare the pies

Just before rolling the dough, preheat the oven to 450°F. Line a baking sheet with foil and set it within reach. Roll out half of the dough on a lightly floured surface to ¼ inch thickness. Gently hold the rolled-out dough by the edges and lift it about 2 inches off the counter (this will allow any contraction in the dough to occur before cutting). Cut the dough into 2-inch rounds using a cookie cutter; make one cut directly next to the other to maximize the amount of rounds.

Dip each round of dough in the olive oil and coat both sides. Place the rounds 1 inch apart on the foil-lined baking sheet. Roll out the remaining dough. Use your index and middle finger (close together) to open each piece of dough to 2½ inches in diameter. Press down on the center of each pastry round with your fingertips; this will prevent them from puffing up like pillows while they bake. Slowly rotate your hand in a circular motion (bobbing your fingertips up and down) as you work your way toward the edge of the pastry, leaving a ¼-inch lip around the edge.

Scoop 1 full tablespoon of topping into the center of each piece of dough. Use the tines of a fork to press and distribute the topping up to, but not over, the lip. Place 5 pine nuts on the meat topping of each pie and use the tines of the fork to gently press them into the topping.

Place the tray on the middle rack in the oven. Bake the pies for 10 to 12 minutes, or until the edges are a golden color. Cool slightly before serving.

{VARIATION}

Pomegranate Chicken and Cheese Pies (Sfi-ha Djeaj): Substitute ground chicken for the beef. The recipe and the procedure are the same as described above.

Basic Dough
(Ajeen)

ABOUT 1½ POUNDS

1 cup plus 1 tablespoon lukewarm water
1½ teaspoons dry active yeast
¼ teaspoon sugar
3 cups unbleached all-purpose flour
¾ teaspoon salt
3 tablespoons extra-virgin olive oil

Measuring flour: See page xiv.

To prepare the dough
In a small bowl, dissolve the yeast and sugar in the water. Mix well. Cover the bowl with a dish and set it aside for several minutes, allowing the yeast to proof (until it foams). Combine the flour and salt in a separate bowl.

Make a well in the center of the flour. Pour the yeast mixture into the well, followed by the olive oil. Using one hand, quickly mix and knead the ingredients to form the dough. (If the dough seems sticky, dip your hand in some flour to remove the dough that is sticking to you.)

Use both hands to lift the dough out of the bowl and tuck and shape it into a ball. Sprinkle flour around the sides and bottom of the bowl and place the ball in the center of the bowl. Sprinkle the top of the ball with some flour. Cover the bowl with a dish and set it aside in a warm place to rise. After 1 hour and 15 minutes, the dough is ready to roll.

As an alternative to making the dough from scratch, freshly prepared dough may be purchased; it varies in quality depending on the brand, so when you find one you like, stick with it.

Pumpkin Kibbi Balls

Kibbi Kebab Luctine (kib-bee kib-bab luck-teen)

ABOUT 2 DOZEN

People rave over the unique flavor of this vegetarian kibbi. The subtle taste of the pumpkin and bulgur wheat complements the filling of sautéed onions and walnuts, and the flavor of the pomegranate makes them tart yet sweet. Offer Pumpkin Kibbi Balls as part of a mezza buffet, tray-passed hors d'oeuvres, or an afternoon snack.

Specialty ingredients: Bulgur #1 (fine) and dibs ruman (pomegranate molasses), both found at specialty markets or online.

Special equipment: A food processor, meat grinder, and a candy/fry thermometer.

Prepare ahead: The Pumpkin Kibbi Balls can be frozen raw for several weeks. Freeze uncovered on a plastic-lined baking sheet, then store in an airtight container. Fry as directed without thawing.

Note: The kibbi must soak overnight.

FOR THE KIBBI

1¼ cups diced yellow onion (½ inch)
1 (15-ounce) can 100% pure pumpkin puree
1½ cups bulgur #1 (fine)
⅓ cup all-purpose flour
1¼ teaspoons salt
½ teaspoon coarsely ground black pepper
½ teaspoon ground allspice
¼ teaspoon ground cinnamon
3 cups canola oil (for frying)

FOR THE FILLING

2 tablespoons extra-virgin olive oil
3 cups (packed) sliced yellow onion (¼ inch)
½ cup coarsely chopped walnuts
¾ teaspoon salt
¼ teaspoon coarsely ground black pepper
1 tablespoon freshly squeezed lemon juice

2 tablespoons dibs ruman
¼ cup pomegranate seeds (optional, when in season)

To soak the kibbi (overnight)

Place the onion in a food processor fitted with a metal blade and process to a pulp. Combine the onion pulp in a bowl with the remaining ingredients for the kibbi (except the oil for frying). Mix well. Pat the mixture down, then cover the bowl with plastic wrap, sealing it around the edges. Refrigerate overnight, allowing the bulgur to expand. This will make it easier to work with once it is ground.

To prepare the filling

Preheat the olive oil in a large skillet over medium-high heat. Add the onions, walnuts, salt, pepper, and lemon juice. Stir well. Reduce the heat to medium-low, and sauté until the onions are limp and tender.

Remove from the heat. Add the dibs ruman and the optional ¼ cup pomegranate seeds when in season (October through January). Mix well and set aside to cool uncovered.

To prepare the kibbi (the following day)

Remove the kibbi mixture from the refrigerator and pass it through a meat grinder fitted with a fine-cutting plate. Measure the ground mixture into ¼-cup portions. On a flat surface, use your hands to roll and shape each portion into a 3-inch cylinder. (Do not skip this step; rolling them into cylinders makes opening them easier.) Cut each cylinder in half widthwise; each half will be a portion. Drape plastic wrap over the portions to prevent drying.

To open the kibbi balls

Set a small bowl of cold water within reach. Place one portion of kibbi in the palm of one hand. With your other hand, dip your index finger in the water

and rub some on the palm of the hand that is holding the portion. Insert your index finger into the circular top of the portion (not the side), making an opening toward the center while not poking a hole through the bottom or sides. Expand the opening to form a cavity by gently pressing against the sides of the portion with your finger and shaping it in your palm. Dip your finger in water once again to dampen your palm and finger so the kibbi ball will not stick to your palm or finger. The opened kibbi ball should have the shape of a football 2½ to 3 inches long and about 1½ inches around, with walls about ¼ inch thick. Repeat with the remaining portions.

To fill and close the kibbi balls

Use a demitasse spoon to fill the kibbi balls. They should be full but not stuffed; avoid getting filling on and around the lip. To close the kibbi ball, hold it in one hand, and with your other hand dip your index finger in the water and dampen the ridge between your index finger and thumb. Using the ridge between your index finger and thumb, apply pressure to the top of the kibbi and press the edges together until they are sealed. Repeat with the remaining kibbi balls.

To fry the kibbi balls

Heat the oil to 375°F in a medium saucepan over medium-high heat, using a candy/fry thermometer to measure the temperature of the oil for accuracy.

The oil should be about 1½ inches deep. Fry 6 kibbi balls at a time. Once they are golden, transfer them to a paper towel–lined dish. Make sure the temperature of the oil remains at 375°F so that the kibbi balls fry evenly. Repeat with the remaining kibbi balls. Cool for 10 minutes prior to serving.

Recycle the oil: *See page xiv.*

To serve
For best results, serve this kibbi slightly warm or at room temperature.

Potato Kibbi Balls

ABOUT 2 DOZEN

Kibbi Kebab Batata (kib-bee kib-bab ba-ta-ta)

Specialty ingredients: Bulgur #1 (fine), dibs ruman, and sumak, found at specialty markets or online.

Special equipment: A food processor, meat grinder, and a candy/fry thermometer.

Prepare ahead: The Potato Kibbi Balls can be frozen raw for several weeks. Freeze uncovered on a plastic-lined baking sheet, then store in an airtight container. Fry as directed without thawing.

Note: The kibbi must soak overnight.

FOR THE KIBBI
1 pound peeled russet potato (dice into 1-inch cubes)
1¼ cups diced yellow onion (½ inch)
1½ cup bulgur #1 (fine)
⅓ cup all-purpose flour
1¼ teaspoons salt
½ teaspoon coarsely ground black pepper
½ teaspoon ground allspice
¼ teaspoon ground cinnamon
1 teaspoon ground cumin
3 cups canola oil (for frying)

FOR THE FILLING
2 tablespoons extra-virgin olive oil
3 cups lightly packed sliced yellow onion (¼ inch)
½ cup coarsely chopped walnuts
¾ teaspoon salt
¼ teaspoon coarsely ground black pepper
¾ teaspoon ground cumin
4 teaspoons sumak
1 tablespoon dibs ruman

To soak the kibbi (overnight)
Begin with room-temperature potatoes. Weigh the potatoes after they are peeled to ensure you have 1

pound, then dice into 1-inch cubes. Place 4 cups of water and the cubed potatoes in a medium saucepan over high heat, uncovered. Once it comes to a boil, reduce the heat to medium-low and simmer covered for 15 minutes. In the meantime, place the diced onion in a food processor fitted with a metal blade and process to a pulp, then set aside.

Drain the cooked potatoes in a colander and set aside to cool, about 10 minutes; then transfer the cooled potatoes to a bowl and mash them using the tines of a fork. Add the onion pulp, bulgur, flour, salt, and spices. Mix well using one hand until evenly combined. Pat the mixture down, then cover the bowl with plastic wrap and seal it around the edges. Refrigerate overnight to allow the bulgur to expand.

To prepare the filling

Preheat the olive oil in a large skillet over medium-high heat. Add the onions, walnuts, salt, pepper, cumin, and sumak. Stir well. Reduce the heat to medium-low and cook until the onions are limp and tender. Remove from the heat. Add the dibs ruman, mix well, and set the filling aside to cool.

To prepare the kibbi (the following day)

Follow the procedure in the previous recipe for Pumpkin Kibbi Balls. Follow the procedure to prepare the kibbi, to open the kibbi balls, and how to fill, close, and fry them.

Lamb Kibbi Balls

ABOUT 20

Kibbi Kebab Lahm (kib-bee kib-bab lah-him)

My mother could not make enough of these when we were growing up. They are so easy to pick up and munch on. Even though the ingredients are identical to the tray form, (kibbi trays page 99), the crisp outer shell with the moist filling of meat, onions and pine nuts is irresistible. Choose either filling below for your kibbi balls. Filling #2 is excellent for kibbi balls in cilantro yogurt (kibbi labaniyeh).

Specialty ingredients: Bulgur #1 (fine), found at specialty markets or online.

Special equipment: A food processor, meat grinder, and a candy/fry thermometer.

Prepare ahead: The meat Kibbi Balls can be frozen raw for several weeks. Freeze uncovered on a plastic-lined baking sheet, then store in an airtight container. Fry as directed without thawing. **Note:** the bulgar must soak overnight.

FOR THE KIBBI

1¼ cups bulgur #1 fine (soak overnight)

1½ teaspoon salt

¼ teaspoon coarsely ground black pepper

½ teaspoon ground allspice

¼ teaspoon ground cinnamon

½ pound lean lamb (from the leg) cut into 1-inch cubes

¾ cup diced yellow onion (½ inch)

3 cups canola oil (for frying)

(You can substitute ½ pound beef—top round London broil—for the lamb.)

FOR FILLING #1

1½ tablespoons toasted pine nuts
½ tablespoon melted butter
1 tablespoon extra-virgin olive oil
½ pound ground lamb
1½ cups diced yellow onion (¼ inch)
¾ teaspoon salt
¼ teaspoon coarsely ground black pepper
½ teaspoon ground allspice
¼ teaspoon ground cinnamon

FOR FILLING #2

1 tablespoon extra-virgin olive oil
½ pound ground lamb
1 cup diced yellow onion (¼ inch)
1 cup diced red bell pepper (¼ inch)
¼ cup coarsely chopped walnuts
¾ teaspoon salt
¼ teaspoon coarsely ground black pepper
½ teaspoon ground allspice
¼ teaspoon ground cinnamon
1 tablespoon sumak
(You can substitute ground beef or ground chicken for the lamb in filling #1 or #2. The recipe and procedure remain the same.)

To soak the bulgur (overnight)

Combine the bulgur with ¾ cup water in a bowl. Stir well. Cover the bowl with plastic wrap sealing it around the edges. Refrigerate overnight to allow it to expand.

To prepare filling #1

Preheat the oven to 350°F. Spread the pine nuts over a foil-lined baking sheet and toast in the center of the oven, shaking the pan occasionally, for 5 to 7 minutes or until golden brown. Mix ½ tablespoon melted butter with the nuts. Transfer them to a paper towel–lined dish. Set aside to cool.

Preheat the olive oil in a medium skillet over medium-high heat. Add the ground meat and cook while breaking it into small, minced pieces. Once the meat is no longer pink, reduce the heat to medium-low. Stir in the onions, salt, and spices, and sauté until the onions are tender. Set aside to cool.

To prepare filling #2

Preheat the olive oil in a medium skillet over medium-high heat. Add the ground meat and cook while breaking it into small, minced pieces. Once the meat is no longer pink, reduce the heat to medium-low. Stir in the onions, red bell pepper, walnuts, salt, and spices, and sauté until the onions and bell pepper are tender. Set aside to cool.

To prepare the kibbi (the following day)

Remove the soaked bulgur from the refrigerator. Combine the salt, pepper, allspice, and cinnamon in a bowl. Pass the meat and onion (mixed together) through a meat grinder fitted with a fine-cutting plate into the bowl with the seasonings and mix well. Add the soaked bulgur. Using massage-like strokes, knead the bulgur into the meat until evenly combined. Pass the mixture once again through the grinder, then use massage-like strokes to combine the ground mixture.

Measure the ground mixture into ¼-cup portions. On a flat surface, use your hands to roll and shape each portion into a 3-inch cylinder. (Rolling them into cylinders makes opening them easier.) Cut each cylinder in half widthwise. Each half will be a kibbi ball. Cover with plastic wrap to prevent drying. (See Pumpkin Kibbi Balls pages 22–23 for diagram.)

To open, fill, close, and fry the kibbi balls
Follow the procedure on pages 22–23 for Pumpkin Kibbi Balls. Follow the procedure to prepare the kibbi, to open the kibbi balls, and how to fill, close, and fry them. The only difference is in the filling. Use a demitasse spoon to fill each ball. Fill it halfway, then add 3 pine nuts and then more filling. The kibbi balls should be full but not overstuffed; avoid getting filling on and around the lip.

To serve
For best results, serve these kibbi balls warm.

{VARIATION}
Chicken Kibbi Balls (Kibbi Kebab Djeaj):
Substitute ½ pound boneless/skinless chicken

breast for the lamb. The recipe and procedure remain the same.

Preparing Kibbi

It is important to get the moisture-to-bulgur ratio correct. Sometimes you may have to toss in a little extra bulgur if the kibbi mixture seems too damp, and at other times you may need to dip your hands in water to introduce additional moisture.

(**Note:** Several recipes recommend using a food processor to grind the kibbi mixture. I have not had good results using that method. I find it does not grind the bulgur wheat the same way as a meat grinder does.)

Robust Garlic Puree
Toom (toom)

ABOUT 6 CUPS

"Garlic mayonnaise" or "garlic spread" does not come close to describing the depth of flavor of this garlic puree. It will make your taste buds stand at attention! Traditionally offered with Grilled Chicken Kebabs (page 86), the spread can be enjoyed in many ways. If you are a garlic lover, then prepare yourself for complete satisfaction. It's great for making garlic bread, as well.

Special equipment: A food processor with a sharp metal blade.
Prepare ahead: You can prepare this several days in advance. It should last for weeks in the refrigerator in an airtight container. The intensity may decrease over time, but not the flavor.

FOR THE PUREE
1 cup fresh cloves of garlic, peeled and at room temperature
2 teaspoons salt

4 cups canola oil
½ cup bottled lemon juice from concentrate at room temperature
or: ½ cup freshly squeezed lemon juice, strained

To prepare the puree
Place the garlic and salt in a dry food processor fitted with a sharp metal blade. (Make certain that the food processor bowl, blade, lid, and utensils are completely dry before you begin, or the mixture may

separate while you are processing it.) Pulse the garlic until it is finely chopped and uniform in size. Use a dry flexible spatula to scrape down the sides of the bowl a few times.

Now start processing again, this time continuously as you slowly add ½ cup of the oil, pouring it in a thread-like stream and allowing it to emulsify with the garlic. Once it is combined, add 2 teaspoons lemon juice, one at a time. Slowly add a second ½ cup of oil in a thread-like stream, followed by 1 tablespoon lemon juice. Take your time while adding the oil, allowing it to properly emulsify with the garlic and lemon juice. Now slowly add a third ½ cup of oil followed by 2 tablespoons of lemon juice, one at a time. Slowly add a fourth ½ cup of oil (in a thread-like stream) followed by 2 tablespoons and 1 teaspoon lemon juice, one at a time. Slowly add 1 cup of oil followed by the remaining 2 tablespoons

of lemon juice, one at a time. Finally, add the last cup of oil slowly.

Continue to process until you have a uniform, thick garlic emulsion. Scrape down the sides of the bowl and continue to process another minute or two. The final consistency should be like fluffy mayonnaise.

Transfer the garlic puree to a container and refrigerate covered with a piece of paper towel overnight to prevent condensation. Cover with a lid the next day.

Selecting Garlic

Choose heads that are firm and fresh. Avoid ones that feel hollow or that have sprouted. Make certain the garlic is at room temperature before you begin this recipe.

Smoked Eggplant Dip

Baba Ghannouj (ba-ba gha-nooj)

Great-tasting baba ghannouj *has a subtle smoky flavor with just the right balance of lemon, tahini, and garlic. Offer it as part of a mezza (appetizer), on a dinner buffet, or take it along to a barbecue. The buttery flavor of the roasted "meaty" flesh of the eggplant complements most meals. It's also great as a snack served with warm pita bread.*

Specialty ingredients: Tahini, found at specialty markets or online.

Special equipment: A pestle (a garlic press will do).

Prepare ahead: You can prepare the dip up to 3 days in advance. Refrigerate covered until needed. The smoked eggplant can be prepared and frozen in a freezer bag for several weeks. Thaw and drain. Prepare the dip as directed.

FOR THE EGGPLANT DIP

1 medium eggplant at room temperature
  (about 1 pound)
1 large clove garlic
½ teaspoon salt
¼ cup freshly squeezed lemon juice
¼ cup plain yogurt
¼ cup tahini (mix well before using)

To smoke the eggplant

Remove any leaves from around the stem cap of the eggplant, leaving the stem attached. Pierce the eggplant several times with the tines of a fork and place it inside an unsealed plastic freezer bag. Place the freezer bag on a dish in the microwave on high for 5 minutes or until the eggplant begins to soften. Use tongs to remove the eggplant from the bag and lay it directly over a stovetop grate over a medium-high gas flame for about 3 minutes. Reserve the dish and the bag.

Gently turn the eggplant over and roast an additional 3 minutes. Remove it from the heat and return it to the dish. Drape the plastic bag over the eggplant and set it aside for about 15 minutes.

Remove the plastic and turn the eggplant over. Allow it to cool uncovered for 5 minutes, then hold the eggplant by the stem and gently peel the skin away from the flesh using a butter knife. Discard the skin. Cut and discard the stem, and transfer the flesh to a colander to drain any access liquid. (Remove any small speckles of blistered skin from the flesh before transferring it.)

*(**Alternative method**, if a stovetop gas flame is not available: Preheat the broiler on high. Prepare the eggplant as described above by placing it in the microwave. Then place the softened eggplant from the microwave on a foil-lined baking sheet. Set the tray directly under the broiler for 5 to 8 minutes or until the skin blisters. Turn the eggplant and return under the broiler for an additional 5 to 8 minutes. Transfer the eggplant to the dish, cool, and peel as described above.*

To prepare the eggplant dip

In a medium bowl, mash the garlic and salt to a pulp using a pestle. Add the smoked eggplant (it should be about 1 cup) and mash it with the pestle

until it is uniform in consistency and no large pieces remain. Add the lemon juice and mix well using a spatula. (Adding the lemon juice first lightens the overall color of the eggplant dip.) Add the yogurt and tahini and mix well.

Transfer the dip to a container and cover with a paper towel. Refrigerate for at least 4 hours or overnight. Cover with the lid once cooled.

(**Alternative method**, *if a stovetop gas flame is not available: Prepare the eggplant dip exactly as described above, but add ¼ teaspoon liquid smoke along with the yogurt and tahini. The rest of the procedure is the same as above.)*

To serve
Use the back of a spoon to spread the dip over a shallow dish so there is an outer raised lip around the perimeter, with a central "canal" around a raised mound in the center. Place a radish star or flower (see page 16) in the center on the raised mound. Garnish with a few sprigs of parsley and sprinkle the center and around the perimeter with paprika. Garnish with pomegranate seeds when they are in season (October through January). Pour extra-virgin olive oil within the central canal formed using the back of the spoon. Serve with warm pita bread or pita dippers, page 40.

Selecting Eggplants

Choose firm, smooth, glossy-skinned eggplants that are blemish free. Eggplants are very perishable, so store them in a plastic bag in the refrigerator and use them within a day or two. Eggplants that weigh approximately 1 pound work best for this recipe.

Spicy Red Pepper and Walnut Spread

SERVES 8 TO 10 (ABOUT 1 PINT)

Mouhamarra (moo-hum-ma-ra)

This flavorful spread is a great addition at any gathering. The spicy bite from the cayenne pepper combined with the sweet flavor of the roasted red bell pepper will both gratify and titillate your taste buds. Offer with toasted pita bread, crackers, or fresh vegetables. Your friends and family will love this one.

Specialty ingredients: Dibs ruman (pomegranate molasses), found at specialty markets or online.
Special equipment: A food processor.
Prepare ahead: You can prepare it several days in advance and refrigerate.

FOR THE SPREAD

½ cup coarsely chopped roasted red bell pepper
   (drained), store-bought or prepared fresh
¼ cup finely chopped yellow onion
2 cups finely ground walnuts
½ cup seasoned bread crumbs
½ teaspoon cayenne pepper
2 teaspoons ground cumin
2 teaspoons ground paprika
1 teaspoon salt
2 tablespoons dibs ruman
¼ cup tomato paste
½ cup extra-virgin olive oil

To prepare the spread

Place the bell pepper and onion in a food processor fitted with a metal blade and process to a pulp. Scrape down the sides with a spatula a couple of times. Add the remaining ingredients, and pulse several times until well combined. The spread should retain the texture of ground walnuts, with a paste-like consistency. Refrigerate for at least 2 hours prior to serving.

To serve

Spread over a flat serving dish and smooth out the top. Use the rounded top of the back of a spoon to make indentations in the spread, and the tines of a fork to make a border around the perimeter. Garnish with diced roasted red bell pepper, walnuts, and parsley.

Roasting fresh red bell peppers

Cut red bell peppers in half. Remove the ribs and seeds. Place the halves on a foil-lined baking sheet skin-side up. Place in the oven under the broiler set on high and broil until the skins blister. Remove the tray. Cover the peppers allowing them to steam for a few minutes. Peel and discard the blistered skins.

Spinach Triangles

Fatayer bi Sabanekh (fa-tie-yer bee sa-ban-nickh)

The key to great spinach triangles is thin pastry on the outside with lots of tangy spinach on the inside. They are offered at room temperature so you can avoid last-minute heating. You can add toasted pine nuts, golden raisins, or feta cheese to the filling to complement the tangy flavor. You can also use this filling when preparing the savory Greek pastry called spanakopita.

Special equipment: A 3-inch round cookie cutter and a pastry brush.

Prepare ahead: The baked triangles can be frozen for several weeks. Freeze uncovered on a plastic-lined baking sheet, then transfer to an airtight container. Reheat thawed triangles at 350°F for 5 to 7 minutes.

FOR THE DOUGH

1 recipe Basic Dough (see page 20)

FOR THE SPINACH FILLING

2 pounds frozen chopped spinach (thawed, drained, and squeezed dry)

2 cups diced yellow onion (¼ inch)

1 tablespoon salt

¼ teaspoon coarsely ground black pepper

⅓ cup and 3 tablespoons extra-virgin olive oil, divided

1 tablespoon lemon zest

¾ cup freshly squeezed lemon juice

To prepare the dough

Prepare the dough as described on page 20, and set it aside to rise.

To prepare the filling

Squeeze the thawed spinach over a colander with small perforations (to catch stray pieces). It is very

important to make sure that all the moisture has been hand-squeezed out of the spinach, otherwise the filling will be wet and the pastries may open while baking.

In a bowl, combine the spinach and onion. Just before you are ready to fill the pastries, add the salt, pepper, ⅓ cup olive oil, lemon zest, and lemon juice, and mix well. (Mixing the salt with the onions at the last minute prevents the onions from producing additional moisture in the filling.)

To prepare the triangles

Once the dough has risen, roll out half of the dough on a lightly floured surface to ⅛-inch thickness. Gently hold the rolled-out dough by the edges and lift it about 2 inches off the counter (this will allow any contraction in the dough to occur before

cutting). Cut the dough into 3-inch rounds using a cookie cutter; make one cut directly next to the other to maximize the number of rounds. Cover the rounds with plastic wrap to avoid drying.

Preheat the oven to 450°F. Foil-line a baking sheet, lightly brush it with olive oil, and set it within reach.

Pick up one round of dough at a time and flip it so that you are placing the filling on the underside (or whichever side seems stickier). Cradling the round of dough in one hand, place 2 tablespoons of filling in the middle of the round (this may seem like too much filling, but you need that amount so the triangles will be plump once they are baked). Use the tines of a fork to position and press the filling down into place, keeping the edges free of any stray pieces of filling. Form a triangle by raising three sides of the dough up and over the filling until they meet in the center. Press them closed.

Pinch each seam from the corner to the center, securing the filling inside the triangle. Remember to keep the seams free of filling. Repinch the seams so the pastry will not open while baking. Reshape the pastry into a triangle and place it on the greased foil-lined baking sheet. The triangle should resemble a three-sided pyramid with raised seams. Fill and close the rest of rounds of dough, placing the triangles side-by-side on the baking tray ¼ inch apart. Repeat with the second half of the dough.

Dip a pastry brush into the 3 tablespoons olive oil and generously dab the tops and sides of each triangle. Place the tray on the middle rack in the oven and bake for 18 to 20 minutes or until golden brown.

To serve
Serve slightly warm or at room temperature.

Thawing Spinach

To quickly thaw bagged frozen spinach in the microwave, pierce the plastic bag, then place the bag of spinach in the microwave for a few minutes until completely thawed. Drain and squeeze as directed.

{VARIATIONS}

Pine Nuts (*snobar*): Add 1 cup toasted pine nuts to the spinach filling. To toast pine nuts, preheat the oven to 350°F. Spread the nuts over a foil-lined baking sheet and bake in the center of the oven, shaking the pan occasionally, for 5 to 7 minutes or until golden brown.

Golden Raisins (*zbeeb*): Add 1 cup coarsely chopped golden raisins to the spinach filling.

Feta Cheese (*jibni*): Add 1 cup crumbled Bulgarian feta cheese to the spinach filling.

Garbanzo Bean Triangles with Beef Confit

ABOUT 3 DOZEN

Fatayer bi Hoummos (fa-tie-yer bee hum-moose)

These are so delicious, and the procedure is exactly the same as the previous recipe, except you will be filling the triangles with chopped garbanzo beans, shredded beef confit, and onions.

Specialty ingredients: Beef confit *(qawarma);* see recipe on page 136.

Special equipment: A food processor, a 3-inch round cookie cutter, and a pastry brush.

Prepare ahead: The baked triangles can be frozen for several weeks. Freeze uncovered on a plastic-lined baking sheet, then transfer to an airtight container. Reheat thawed triangles at 350°F for 5 to 7 minutes. **Note:** The beef confit needs to be prepared 1 day in advance, and the garbanzo beans need to soak overnight.

FOR THE DOUGH
1 recipe Basic Dough (see page 20)

FOR THE FILLING
1 cup dried garbanzo beans, soaked overnight
½ teaspoon baking soda
½ teaspoon and 1½ teaspoons salt, divided
1¾ cups diced yellow onion (¼ inch)
½ cup plain yogurt
¾ cup beef confit (without the rendered fat), broken into small pieces
½ cup and 3 tablespoons extra-virgin olive oil, divided
¼ teaspoon coarsely ground black pepper

To prepare the beef confit (the day before)
Prepare Beef Confit as described on page 136.

To soak the beans (overnight)
*Soak the beans in 4 cups water (or enough so they are submerged) with the baking soda and ½ teaspoon salt overnight at room temperature, uncovered. (**Note:** The baking soda will help soften the beans.)*

To prepare the dough
Prepare the Basic Dough as described on page 20, and set it aside to rise.

To prepare the filling
Drain the beans. Place them on a kitchen towel and thoroughly dry the excess water. Transfer the beans to a food processor fitted with a metal blade. Pulse several times until they are coarsely chopped (a little larger than grains of rice). Combine them in a bowl with the onions and mix well.

Just before you are ready to fill the pastries, add 1½ teaspoons salt, the yogurt, beef confit, ½ cup olive oil, and the pepper. Mix well. (Mixing the salt with the onions at the last minute prevents the onions from producing additional moisture in the filling.)

To prepare and serve the triangles
Follow the procedure in the previous recipe for Spinach Triangles (page 31). Serve warm.

Tabbouli Bites

This is a great way to offer tabbouli as a tray-passed appetizer or just to snack on around the pool or at a barbecue. There really isn't a traditional name for these delicious bites. I offered them at a reception years ago, and they continue to be a big hit.

Specialty ingredients: Bulgur wheat #1 (fine) can be found at specialty markets or online.

Prepare ahead: You can prepare the salad and hollow the tomatoes a day in advance and refrigerate separately. Dress and fill as directed. The bites can be filled up to 6 hours in advance and refrigerated covered until served.

Note: The yield may vary depending on the size of the cherry tomatoes you use.

FOR THE TABBOULI BITES

3 dozen cherry tomatoes (about 1 inch round)
1 recipe Parsley and Bulgur Wheat Salad, omitting the tomatoes (see page 58)

To prepare the tabbouli bites

Prepare the Parsley and Bulgur Wheat Salad omitting the diced tomatoes. Cover the salad and refrigerate for at least 2 hours prior to mixing.

Double-line a dish with paper towels and set it within reach. Cut the top off each cherry tomato (stem side), removing about ¼ inch. Discard the tops. Use a demitasse spoon to hollow the tomatoes, removing and discarding the center rib, the pulp, and seeds; do not remove the flesh and inner ribs from the walls of the tomatoes. Turn them upside down onto the paper towel–lined dish to allow the inner juices to drain. Cover with plastic wrap and refrigerate until ready to fill.

Dress the tabbouli just before filling the bites, using the same amount of dressing for tabbouli salad. Use a demitasse spoon to fill the bites, gently pressing the filling into the tomato with your fingertip.

To serve

Arrange the bites over green leaf lettuce with cut lemon.

Tangy Beef Fillo Rolls

2 DOZEN

Burak bi Lahm (bur-rack bee lah-him)

These light and flaky fillo rolls are absolutely delicious. The fillo forms a crisp delicate base around the savory yet sweet filling. They are so versatile making them the perfect choice as a tray passed hors d'oeuvres or an afternoon snack with a salad.

Specialty ingredients: Fillo dough, found in most grocery stores or specialty markets (my favorite brand is Apollo); Sumak and dibs ruman (pomegranate molasses), found at specialty markets or online.

Special equipment: A pastry brush.

Prepare ahead: Raw beef rolls can be frozen for several weeks. Freeze the rolls uncovered on a plastic-lined baking sheet, then transfer to an airtight container. Thaw and bake as directed.

FOR THE FILLING

1 tablespoon toasted pine nuts

¼ pound ground beef (80% lean)

¾ cup diced yellow onion (⅛ inch)

½ teaspoon salt

⅛ teaspoon coarsely ground black pepper

¼ teaspoon ground allspice

⅛ teaspoon ground cinnamon

1½ tablespoons freshly squeezed lemon juice

1½ teaspoons sumak

2½ teaspoons dibs ruman

(You can substitute ground lamb for the beef.)

FOR THE ROLLS

8 sheets of fillo dough (12 x 17 inches), at room temperature

½ cup melted butter

To prepare the filling

Preheat the oven to 350°F. Spread the pine nuts over a foil-lined baking sheet and toast in the center of the oven, shaking the pan occasionally, for 5 to 7 minutes or until golden brown. Cool the nuts before using.

Preheat a small skillet over medium-high heat. Add the ground meat and cook while breaking it into small, minced pieces. Once the meat is no longer pink, add the onions, salt, pepper, allspice, and cinnamon and sauté over medium-low heat until the onions are tender. Then add the lemon juice and simmer until the moisture is absorbed. Remove from the heat and mix in the sumak and dibs ruman. Cool uncovered prior to using.

To prepare the rolls

Preheat the oven to 350°F. Melt the butter over low heat.

On a flat surface (I use a large, plastic cutting board because it's easier to clean), butter and layer 2 sheets of fillo, placing them lengthwise, one at a time, one on top of the other. (The long 17-inch side of the fillo should be facing you from left to right.) Brush each sheet with butter by starting at the corners and edges and working your way to the center. Keep the rest of the fillo covered with plastic to prevent drying (see "Handling Fillo Dough" on page xiv).

Cut the stack of 2 fillo layers into 6 equal pieces. Start with a cut down the center (widthwise) from top to bottom; then make 2 equidistant cuts (lengthwise), from left to right, dividing the pastry into 6 equal strips, each about 4 inches wide by 8 inches long.

Place 1 full teaspoon of filling and 2 pine nuts about 1 inch in from the end of each strip of fillo, spreading the filling to 2 inches in length. Fold the

sides over to secure the filling. Roll from the bottom end, securing the filling inside as you roll up toward the opposite end. Each roll should be about 2 to 2½ inches long. Brush the outside of the rolls with melted butter to protect the fillo from drying. Place the rolls on a foil-lined baking sheet ½ inch apart, seam-side down so they don't unravel while baking. Repeat with the remaining fillo.

Bake the rolls in the center of the oven for 20 to 25 minutes or until golden brown. Cool 5 to 7 minutes prior to serving.

{VARIATIONS}

Tangy Chicken Fillo Rolls *(Burak bi Djeaj)*: Substitute ground chicken for the beef. The recipe and the procedure are the same as described above.

Feta Cheese Fillo Rolls *(Burak bi Jibni)*: See Feta Cheese Crescents on page 4 and follow the recipe for the filling. To prepare the rolls, follow the procedure above, placing a 1 teaspoon portion of cheese shaped into a 2-inch log at the end of each strip.

Thyme Pizzettas

Manakeesh bi Zahtar (mena-keesh bee zah-tar)

Traditionally offered at breakfast or brunch warm from the oven, these wonderful pizzettas are delicious to munch on any time of day. Enjoy them as a mid-afternoon treat with hummus or in the evening with a warm cup of your favorite tea. Pack them along for a snack on a hike or any outdoor activity; they are heat-resistant for several hours.

Specialty ingredients: Zahtar, sumak, and dibs ruman, found at specialty markets or online.

Special equipment: A 2½-inch round cookie cutter.

Prepare ahead: The topping can be prepared several days in advance and stored in the refrigerator. The baked pizzettas can be frozen for several weeks. Freeze them on a plastic-lined baking sheet, then transfer to an airtight container. Reheat thawed pastries for 3 to 5 minutes at 350°F.

FOR THE DOUGH

1 recipe Basic Dough (see page 20)

FOR THE ZAHTAR TOPPING

3 tablespoons toasted sesame seeds

½ cup plus 2 tablespoons zahtar

1½ tablespoons sumak

¼ teaspoon salt

¾ cup extra-virgin olive oil

2 teaspoons freshly squeezed lemon juice

2 teaspoons dibs ruman

¼ cup minced yellow onion

To prepare the dough

Prepare the dough as described on page 20 and set it aside to rise.

To prepare the zahtar topping

Preheat the oven to 350°F. Spread the sesame seeds over a foil-lined baking sheet and toast in the center of the oven, shaking the pan occasionally, for 5 to 7 minutes or until they are golden brown. Combine the remaining ingredients in a bowl and mix well. Mix in the toasted sesame seeds. Set aside covered for about 45 minutes, stirring periodically.

To prepare the pizzettas

Once the dough has risen, foil-line a baking sheet and set it aside. Preheat the oven to 450°F.

Roll out half of the dough on a lightly floured surface to ¼ inch thickness. Gently hold the rolled-out dough by the edges and lift it about 2 inches off the counter (this will allow any contraction in the dough to occur before cutting). Cut the dough into 2½-inch rounds using a cookie cutter; make one cut directly next to the other to maximize the number of rounds. Transfer the rounds to the baking sheet and place them 1 inch apart. Roll out the remaining dough.

Use your index and middle finger (close together) to open each piece of dough to 3 inches in diameter. Press down on the center of each pastry round with your fingertips; this will prevent them from puffing up like pillows while they bake. Slowly rotate your hand in a circular motion (bobbing your fingertips up and down) as you work your way toward the edge of the pastry, leaving a ¼-inch lip around the edge. (Dip your fingertips in flour if they begin to stick to the dough.)

Place 1 teaspoon of topping in the center of each pastry round. Use the tines of a fork to spread the topping over toward, but not over, the lip. Leave a small ¼-inch rim free of topping around the edge of the pastry. (If the topping seems thick and difficult to spread, thin it with some olive oil.)

Place on the middle rack of the oven. Bake at 450°F for 10 to 12 minutes. Remove the pizzettas once the edges begin to turn golden.

Red Pepper Pizzettas
Mankeesh bi Flaifli (mena-keesh bee flay-flee)

I always whip up a batch of these to serve along side thyme pizzettas; see the previous recipe. They are always a welcomed addition. While their flavors are distinctly different, they really complement one another and people seem to love them both.

Specialty ingredients: Kishk (which is a mixture of fermented milk, salt, and bulgar, dried and ground into a powder-like consistency with a tart flavor and sold as kashk powder in some markets), sumak, and dibs ruman, all found at specialty markets or online.

Note: The best kishk I have found is hand carried by friends or family from Lebanon. Store-bought kashk powders are good, but not like the ones you get from Lebanon.

Special equipment: A 2½-inch round cookie cutter.

Prepare ahead: The topping can be prepared several days in advance and stored in the refrigerator. The baked pizzettas can be frozen for several weeks. Freeze them on a plastic-lined baking sheet, then transfer to an airtight container. Reheat thawed pastries for 3 to 5 minutes at 350°F.

FOR THE DOUGH
1 recipe Basic Dough (see page 20)

FOR THE FLAIFLI TOPPING
¼ cup toasted sesame seeds
½ cup kishk
¼ teaspoon salt
⅛ teaspoon cayenne pepper
1½ teaspoons paprika
¾ teaspoons sumak
¾ cup extra-virgin olive oil
1½ teaspoons dibs ruman
1 tablespoon fresh lemon juice
½ cup minced yellow onion
5 tablespoons tomato paste

To prepare the dough
Prepare the dough as described on page 20 and set it aside to rise.

To prepare the flaifli topping
Preheat the oven to 350°F. Spread the sesame seeds over a foil-lined baking sheet and toast in the center of the oven, shaking the pan occasionally, for 5 to 7 minutes or until they are golden brown. Combine the remaining ingredients in a bowl and mix well. Mix in the toasted sesame seeds. Set aside covered for about 45 minutes, stirring periodically.

To prepare the pizzettas
Follow the procedure in the previous recipe for Thyme Pizzettas with one exception: place 1½ teaspoons of flaifli topping in the center of each pastry. The rest of the procedure remains the same.

Toasted Pita Dippers

4 DOZEN

Khibz Arabi Imhammas (khibz arrabee em-hum-mas)

These are great for dipping into Hummus (page 8), Smoked Eggplant Dip (page 28), Spicy Red Pepper and Walnut Spread (page 30), or any of your favorite dips. Drizzle olive oil over the toasted pitas and season with different herbs and spices, and they are ready to go.

Specialty ingredients: Sumak or zahtar, both found at specialty markets or online.

Prepare ahead: You can prepare these several days in advance and store them in an airtight container at room temperature.

FOR THE PITA DIPPERS
3 medium-sized pitas (about 6 inches each)
2 tablespoons extra-virgin olive oil
Seasonings (see variations below)

To prepare the pita dippers
Preheat the oven to 350°F. Cut each pita into quarters, then cut each quarter into quarters, yielding a total of 16 triangles per pita. (Do not separate the pita halves.)

Place the pita triangles side-by-side on a foil-lined baking sheet. Bake on the middle rack of the oven for about 15 to 20 minutes or until they are crisp and toasted all the way through. Different brands of pita vary in thickness; therefore, the baking time can vary as well. Remove and set aside to cool.

Gently transfer the cooled pita dippers to a large bowl. Drizzle olive oil over them and gently mix, coating the pita with the oil using your fingers. Sprinkle any one of the seasoning choices below over the pita and gently mix again.

*Once they are completely cooled, you can store them in a container with an airtight lid. (**Note:** If stored pita dippers seem stale the following day, they did not toast long enough in the oven. Make sure they crisp all the way through before removing them from the oven.)*

{VARIATIONS}

Paprika and Onion: Sprinkle 1 tablespoon granulated onion (not powdered) and 1½ teaspoons ground paprika over the baked pitas.
Zahtar: Sprinkle 2 tablespoons zahtar over the baked pitas.
Garlic Pepper: Sprinkle 2 teaspoons California-style (coarsely ground blend with red bell and black pepper) over the baked pitas.
Sumak: Sprinkle 2 tablespoons sumak over the baked pitas.
Rosemary: Sprinkle 1 tablespoon crushed rosemary over the baked pitas.
Italian: Sprinkle 2 tablespoons Italian seasoning over the baked pitas.

Opposite page: Paprika and Onion Toasted Dippers

40

Vegetable-Stuffed Grape Leaves

ABOUT 5 DOZEN

Warac Inab bi Zeyt (whar-raq ien-neb bee zeyt)

These stuffed grape leaves are a delicious, light, and healthy treat, with a tasty combination of vegetables and rice steamed in a savory lemon and olive oil broth. They are excellent for outdoor parties, the beach, or as a poolside snack.

Specialty ingredients: Grape leaves, which can be found at specialty markets or online packed brined in jars; or fresh, tender grape leaves off the vine.
Special equipment: Two 9-inch round cake pans.
Prepare ahead: The rolled filled grape leaves can be frozen (uncooked) for up to 2 months. Freeze on a plastic-lined tray uncovered, then store them in an airtight container. Thaw and cook as directed.
Note: The vegetable filling must be prepared 1 day in advance (to allow the rice to expand).

FOR THE FILLING

½ cup toasted pine nuts

1 cup converted (also called parboiled) rice

1¼ teaspoons and ¾ teaspoon salt, divided

¼ teaspoon coarsely ground black pepper

¾ cup and ⅓ cup freshly squeezed lemon juice, divided

⅓ cup and 1 tablespoon extra-virgin olive oil, divided

½ cup currants

¼ cup finely chopped fresh dill

2 cups finely chopped flat-leaf parsley; use green leafy parts and tender stems

1½ cups (peeled) finely chopped tomato

½ cup finely chopped green onion; use light and dark green parts

½ cup finely chopped yellow onion

¼ cup finely chopped fresh mint or 2 teaspoons dry mint flakes

About 3 cups boiling water

FOR THE GRAPE LEAVES

1 (16-ounce) jar grape leaves (Orlando brand if available)

To prepare the filling (prepare 1 day in advance)

Preheat the oven to 350°F. Spread the pine nuts over a foil-lined baking sheet and toast in the center of the oven, shaking the pan occasionally, for 5 to 7 minutes or until golden brown. Cool before adding them to the filling.

Combine the rice, 1¼ teaspoons salt, the pepper, ¾ cup lemon juice, and ⅓ cup olive oil in a bowl. Mix well. Add the currants, dill, parsley, tomato, both kinds of onion, and mint. Mix well. Cover well and refrigerate overnight.

To prepare the grape leaves

Drain the brine from the jar. Carefully remove the grape leaves one bunch at a time. Use scissors to cut off the stem at the base of each leaf. Discard the stems. Rinse the leaves in a bowl with hot running water for a minute or two. Then soak them in hot water for about 5 minutes, changing the water 3 times and removing as much of the brine from the leaves as possible. Drain the water, then drape the leaves over the edge of a colander. Set them aside to allow excess water to drain. (Cover and refrigerate until ready to roll.)

*(**Alternatively,** fresh grape leaves can be used. Select tender, new-growth leaves. Cut off the stem and rinse them well before rolling. Prepare as directed above.)*

Working With Grape Leaves

All leaves are not created equal; they vary in size. Most are in the medium-sized range (the desired size), while some are tiny and others large. Place smaller leaves together to create one, and cut larger ones down to size when necessary. If a leaf has a tear, patch it with a piece of another. The number of leaves varies from jar to jar.

To roll the grape leaves

Remove the filling from the refrigerator the following day and mix well. Transfer it to a fine-mesh strainer with a bowl underneath to catch any liquid that drains off. Keep the bowl under the strainer while you work. Reserve the drained liquid for later use.

To roll a grape leaf, take a leaf and place it flat on your work surface with the dull side (the side with raised veins) facing up and the stem end nearest to you. Place 1 level tablespoon of filling right above

the stem base and distribute it lengthwise (about 2½ inches). Fold the bottom of the leaf up and over the filling, then fold both sides (the right and left) of the leaf over the filling. Tuck and roll the leaf tightly and evenly up toward the tip of the leaf (just as you would roll a carpet), and set the rolled grape leaf aside (with the seam facing down so it will not unravel). Repeat until the filling is finished. The rolled grape leaves should be about 2½ inches long. Reserve the extra pieces of grape leaves for later use.

To cook the grape leaves

Preheat the oven to 400°F. Lower one rack to the lowest shelf of the oven. Brush olive oil over the bottom of two 9-inch round cake pans. Arrange some of the reserved leaves to cover the bottom of the pans to prevent sticking while the grape leaves cook. (If there are not enough grape leaves to line the bottom of the cake pans, peel a potato, and cut it into ¼-inch slices to line the bottom of the pan. You can also use rounds of sliced onion.)

Load the stuffed grape leaves, starting from the side of the pan. Place one grape leaf in at a time, seam-side down, end-to-end around the pan in concentric circles. Work your way toward the center, nestling one right next to the other. (Placing them close together will prevent them from unraveling while they steam.) About half of the grape leaf rolls should fit in a single layer in each cake pan (about 30 per pan).

Pour the reserved liquid from the grape leaf filling into a 1-quart measuring cup. Add ¾ teaspoon salt, ⅓ cup lemon juice, 1 tablespoon olive oil, and enough boiling water to bring the measure to 3 cups. Stir well and pour half the mixture over each pan of grape leaves. Cover and seal the top of each pan with aluminum foil.

Place the pans on a foil-lined baking sheet and bake on the lower rack of the oven for 1½ hours. Then set the grape leaves aside to cool for about 5 hours. (**Note:** I used to load rolled grape leaves into a pot with a dish on top to hold them in place and steam them on the stovetop. While adjusting the heat, the liquid would bubble and cause some of the leaves to wiggle loose and open. Therefore, I find this method of cooking them in the oven much easier.)

To serve

Arrange room-temperature grape leaves on a dish with lemon wedges and parsley. Reserve any cooking liquid to store leftovers.

Lamb-Stuffed Grape Leaves

ABOUT 5 DOZEN

Warac Inab bi Lahm (whar-ruck ien-neb bee lah-him)

Specialty ingredients: Grape leaves, which can be found at specialty markets or online packed brined in jars; or fresh, tender grape leaves off the vine.
Special equipment: Two 9-inch round cake pans.
Prepare ahead: The rolled filled grape leaves can be frozen (uncooked) for up to 2 months. Freeze on a plastic-lined tray uncovered, then store them in an airtight container. Thaw in the refrigerator and cook as directed.

FOR THE FILLING

1 pound coarsely ground lamb (from the leg)
1 cup converted (also called parboiled) rice
1½ teaspoon and 1 teaspoon salt, divided
½ teaspoon and ¼ teaspoon coarsely ground
  black pepper, divided
1 teaspoon and ½ teaspoon ground allspice,
  divided
½ teaspoon and ¼ teaspoon ground cinnamon,
  divided
½ cup melted butter
½ cup and ½ cup cold water, divided
1 tablespoon extra-virgin olive oil
¼ cup freshly squeezed lemon juice
1 (16-ounce) jar grape leaves (Orlando brand
  if available)
2¾ cups boiling water
(**You can substitute** coarsely ground beef—top
  round London broil—for the lamb.)

To prepare the filling

Combine the ground lamb, rice, 1½ teaspoons salt, ½ teaspoon pepper, 1 teaspoon allspice, ½ teaspoon cinnamon, the melted butter, and ½ cup of cold water in a bowl. Mix well, cover and refrigerate. After 30 minutes, remove from the refrigerator and add the second ½ cup of cold water. Mix well and begin rolling.

To prepare and roll the grape leaves

Follow the procedure as described in the previous recipe for Vegetable-Stuffed Grape Leaves; however, there is no need to transfer the meat filling to a strainer. Use 2 level teaspoons of filling per leaf.

To cook the grape leaves

Follow the procedure as described in the previous recipe for Vegetable-Stuffed Grape Leaves. Once the grape leaves are loaded in the pans, mix 1 teaspoon salt, ¼ teaspoon black pepper, ½ teaspoon allspice, ¼ teaspoon cinnamon, 2¾ cups boiling water, the olive oil, and lemon juice in a bowl. Stir well and pour half over each pan of grape leaves.

The rest of the procedure remains the same. Once you have removed the stuffed grape leaves from the oven, set them aside for a few minutes prior to serving.

To serve

Arrange warm grape leaves on a dish with lemon wedges and parsley. Reserve any cooking liquid to store and reheat leftovers.

Yogurt Cheese Canapés

Labni Canapé (leb-nee cana-pey)

2 DOZEN

These tasty canapés are so easy to prepare and are the perfect choice with cocktails or as a tray-passed hors d'oeuvre. The flavor of the fresh mint complements the tangy bite of the olives, and the cool yogurt cheese is so refreshing with the crisp cucumber.

Specialty ingredients: Yogurt cheese *(labni)*. You can prepare it fresh (see page 47), or buy it at a specialty market or online.

Special equipment: A 1½-inch round cookie cutter.

Prepare ahead: You can prepare the individual items a day in advance. Cover and refrigerate separately. You can assemble them up to 3 hours in advance. Refrigerate covered.

FOR THE YOGURT CHEESE CANAPÉS

1 small baguette (about a 12-inch baguette)

1 firm cucumber

24 small fresh mint leaves

½ cup yogurt cheese

12 small Spanish manzanilla olives,
   cut in half widthwise

Paprika

To prepare the yogurt cheese canapés

Slice the baguette into 24 rounds ¼ inch thick. Cut the cucumber into 24 slices ¼-inch thick. Use a 1½-inch round cookie cutter to cut an inner circle of bread from each round that is crust free. Cut the cucumber slices the same way so they will be a perfect fit once stacked over the discs of bread. Punch a small hole in the center of each cucumber slice large enough to set the small olive half on top of the hole.

Prepare 24 small fresh mint leaves that have been pre-rinsed and are completely dry (see Rinsing and Storing Produce, page xiv). Spread about 1 teaspoon of yogurt cheese over each disc of bread. Place the cucumber over the cheese. Set a half olive, pimento side facing up, in the hole in the cucumber. Insert the mint leaf under the olive, securing it in place. Cover with plastic wrap and refrigerate until ready to serve.

To serve

Arrange sprigs of fresh mint and sprinkle paprika along the edge of the serving dish.

Yogurt Cheese

Labni (leb-nee)

Traditionally, this yogurt cheese is offered in the morning with olives, fresh mint, olive oil, and an array of garden fresh vegetables with warm pita bread. Enjoy it for a snack or at mealtime rolled into a pita garden wrap (page 141). This combination is light, healthy, and delicious.

Special equipment: A cheesecloth.

Prepare ahead: The yogurt cheese can be pre-pared days in advance. It can be stored in an air-tight container in the refrigerator for several weeks. You can buy yogurt cheese (called *labni*, or some-times spelled *lebni*) at specialty markets.

FOR THE YOGURT CHEESE

1 quart plain yogurt (regular, reduced-fat, or
  fat-free)
½ teaspoon salt
1 tablespoon freshly squeezed lemon juice,
  strained

To prepare the yogurt cheese

Line a colander with a cheesecloth that has been folded in half to be doubly thick. Place a small bowl under the colander.

Add the salt and lemon juice to the yogurt and mix well. Pour the yogurt mixture into the cheesecloth-lined colander. Lift the edges of the cheesecloth up and over the yogurt, gently twisting the edges together to form a pouch. Rest the pouch of yogurt in the colander and set it aside at room temperature to drain. Empty the liquid in the bowl from time to time. Make sure the bottom of the colander is not touching the drained liquid.

After a few hours, begin twisting the edges of the cheesecloth, putting light pressure on the yogurt cheese inside the pouch; this will force additional moisture out. Repeat when necessary. After about 10 to 12 hours, check the thickness of the cheese. It should have the consistency of soft cream cheese. For thicker cheese, drain overnight. (Letting it drain overnight will also make it more tart.) Transfer the cheese to an airtight container and refrigerate.

Note: *Different brands of yogurt vary in the amount of moisture they contain. Some may drain in less time than others.*

Salads

(SALATA)

Great salads begin with fresh vegetables that have been rinsed and stored properly (see page xiv). I believe the key to crisp, crunchy salads is rinsing and storing the vegetables a day in advance to ensure that they are firm and cool before you begin chopping.

As in other parts of a Lebanese meal, you may find that the salads in this chapter incorporate many of the vegetables that you use daily in unexpected ways. Cabbage and Beet Salad dressed with a flavorful, garlic vinaigrette replaces traditional cabbage salads, or my unique Eggplant Salad, where buttery pieces of eggplant melt in your mouth and tangy pickled turnips tickle your tongue, tossed together with freshly chopped vegetables in an olive oil–vinegar dressing. Toasted pita croutons coated in olive oil and sumak replace ordinary croutons with a delightful effect. These salads are favorites around my home, and I know they will become favorites around yours, too!

Cabbage and Beet Salad 50
Dandelion Salad 51
Dandelion Salad with Yogurt 52
Eggplant Salad 52
Farmer's Salad with Tahini Dressing 55
Garbanzo Bean Salad 56

Lemon-Garlic Potato Salad 57
Parsley and Bulgur Wheat Salad 58
Pita Crouton Salad with Sumak Dressing . . . 60
Romaine Salad 62
Yogurt-Cucumber Salad 63

Opposite page: Eggplant Salad

Cabbage and Beet Salad

SERVES 4 (ABOUT 1 QUART)

Salata Malfoof ma Shamandar (sa-la-ta mel-foof ma sha-mun-dar)

This is a healthy alternative to traditional cabbage salads. The crisp texture of the cabbage with the sweet flavor of the beets is absolutely delicious. The debate over this salad is the dressing: vinegar or lemon juice? I prefer using apple cider vinegar in the dressing, while my mother prefers fresh lemon juice. Try it both ways. This is a great salad to take along to a barbecue or outdoor party.

Special equipment: A pestle (a garlic press will do).

Prepare ahead: You can prepare the salad up to 1 day in advance. Store covered in the refrigerator. Dress the salad as directed.

FOR THE SALAD

4 cups (lightly packed) thinly sliced green cabbage (⅛ inch)

1 (15-ounce) can sliced beets (drain and slice into ⅛-inch strips)

1 large clove garlic

½ teaspoon salt

2 tablespoons apple cider vinegar (or freshly squeezed lemon juice)

3 tablespoons extra-virgin olive oil

To prepare the salad

Combine the cabbage and beets in a medium-sized bowl; cover and refrigerate.

In a small bowl, mash the garlic and salt to a pulp using a pestle. Add the vinegar and oil. Mix well. Toss with the salad and refrigerate covered for about an hour prior to serving; this allows the flavors to develop.

Offer with kibbi trays (pages 99–104), or Eggplant Moussaka (page 138).

Selecting Cabbage

Choose heads that are firm and seem heavy for their size. Avoid light or discolored ones, as that means they have lost much of their moisture.

Dandelion Salad
Salata Hindbi ma Kishk (sa-la-ta hind-bee)

SERVES 4 (ABOUT 1 QUART)

Dandelion greens are one of the most nutritious leafy vegetables. Alone they have a slightly bitter flavor, but when they are mixed with red onions, kishk, and olive oil, they are absolutely delicious with a peppery bite.

Specialty ingredients: Dandelion greens found in supermarkets, health food stores, and farmers' markets; and kishk (or kashk powder), found at specialty markets or online.

Prepare ahead: You can cut the dandelion and onion several hours in advance. Refrigerate separately. Serve as directed.

FOR THE SALAD

4 cups (lightly packed) sliced dandelion (½ inch)
1½ cups diced red onion (¼ inch)
⅓ cup plus 1 tablespoon kishk
½ teaspoon salt
½ cup extra-virgin olive oil

To prepare the salad

Rinse the dandelion greens in a large bowl of cold running water several times. Shake off the excess water and place them on a kitchen towel to air-dry.

Cut the upper tender part of the dandelion greens widthwise into ½-inch slices. Add the red onion, kishk, salt, and olive oil. Mix well and serve.

Selecting Dandelion

Use tender young leaves, which are available in spring in most areas. As the season progresses, the leaves grow bigger and more tough and bitter.

Dandelion Salad with Yogurt

SERVES 4 (ABOUT 1 QUART)

Salata Hindbi ma Laban (sa-la-ta hind-bee ma leb-ban)

Specialty ingredients: Dandelion greens found in supermarkets, health food stores, and farmers' markets.

Prepare ahead: You can cut the dandelion several hours in advance and refrigerate. Serve as directed.

FOR THE SALAD

4 cups (lightly packed) sliced dandelion
  (½ inch)
1 large garlic clove
¾ teaspoon salt
1 cup yogurt
1 teaspoon tahini (optional)
2 tablespoons extra-virgin olive oil

To prepare the salad

Prepare the dandelion as described in the previous recipe for Dandelion Salad.

In a small bowl, mash the garlic and salt to a pulp using a pestle. Add the yogurt and the tahini; mix well. (**Note:** *The taste of garlic should be slight; add more to your taste.*)

You can leave the yogurt dressing out (covered) to allow it to come to room temperature. Mix with the yogurt dressing just before serving. Pour the olive oil over the top of the salad (do not mix) and serve.

Eggplant Salad

SERVES 4 (ABOUT 1½ QUARTS)

Salata Batinjan (sa-la-ta bet-tin-jan)

I composed this version of eggplant salad for a wedding reception with great approval from the newlyweds and their guests. It is it very colorful, and the individual flavors come together beautifully. The buttery texture of the eggplant with the crisp sumak croutons and tart flavor of the turnips is delicious.

Specialty ingredients: Pickled turnips and sumak, both found at specialty markets or online. Or you can prepare fresh Pickled Turnips (see recipe on page 17).

Special equipment: A candy/fry thermometer and a pestle (a garlic press will do).

Prepare ahead: The eggplant and the vegetables can be prepared up to 1 day in advance. Refrigerate separately. Serve as directed.

FOR THE SALAD

1 cup Pita Croutons (see recipe on page 60)

1 pound eggplant, room temperature

1 teaspoon salt

1½ cups diced tomato (½ inch); use firm red tomatoes

1½ cups cucumber (peel, quarter, and slice ¼-inch pieces)

½ cup radish (cut in half, slice ⅛ inch thick)

¼ cup diced green bell pepper (¼ inch)

½ cup coarsely chopped green onion; use light and dark green parts

½ cup diced pickled turnips (¼ inch), store-bought or homemade (see page 17)

½ cup coarsely chopped parsley; use green leafy parts and tender stems

2 cups canola oil (for frying)

FOR THE DRESSING

2 large cloves garlic

1 teaspoon salt

¼ cup apple cider vinegar

¼ cup extra-virgin olive oil

To prepare the salad

Prepare the pita croutons and set them aside until needed.

Cut the stem cap off the eggplant and peel it lengthwise, removing every other strip of skin for a striped appearance. Slice the eggplant widthwise into discs about 1 inch thick. Cut the smaller discs into 4 wedges and the larger discs into 6. See the photo on the previous page.

In a bowl, combine the pieces of eggplant with the salt. Mix well. Transfer the eggplant to a colander and set aside to drain for 30 minutes.

In a separate bowl, combine the tomato, cucumber, radish, bell pepper, onion, pickled turnips, and parsley. Mix well. Cover and refrigerate until needed.

Heat the canola oil in a small sauce pan over medium-high heat to 375°F, using a candy/fry thermometer to measure the temperature of the oil for accuracy. The oil should be about 1 inch deep. Fry about 6 pieces of eggplant at a time. Once evenly golden brown on all sides, remove the eggplant to a paper towel–lined plate. Fry the remaining pieces of eggplant. Make sure the temperature of the oil remains at 375°F so that the pieces of eggplant fry evenly.

Recycle the oil: See page xiv.

(**Alternatively**, you can bake the pieces of eggplant. Preheat the oven to 450°F. Mix the drained eggplant pieces with 1 tablespoon olive oil. Spread them over a baking sheet lined with foil and bake for 15 minutes on the middle rack.)

Set the cooked eggplant aside to cool, uncovered. After 30 minutes transfer the eggplant to the refrigerator to chill uncovered for 1 hour. Cover until needed.

To prepare the dressing

In a small bowl, mash the garlic and salt to a pulp using a pestle. Add the remaining ingredients for the dressing. Mix well and set aside covered until needed.

To serve

Add the croutons and dressing to the bowl with the prepared vegetables. Mix well. Gently fold in the eggplant, mix well, and serve at once.

Selecting Eggplant

Choose firm, smooth-skinned ones that are blemish free and that have a bright green stem cap. Eggplants are very perishable, so store them in a plastic bag in the refrigerator and use them within a day or two. Eggplants that weigh about 1 pound work well for this recipe.

Farmer's Salad with Tahini Dressing
Salata Felaheen (sa-la-ta fella-heen)

The word felaheen *refers to the farmer who tills the soil. What makes this salad so good is the nutty flavor of the tahini with the tart bite of the lemon and crushed garlic mixed in with the fresh, crisp vegetables. Enjoy this refreshingly different garden salad at a barbecue, a picnic, or take it to a potluck.*

Specialty ingredients: Tahini, which can be found in specialty markets or online.

Special equipment: A pestle (a garlic press will do).

Prepare ahead: The vegetables and dressing can be prepared 1 day in advance. Serve as directed.

FOR THE SALAD

2 cups diced tomato (½ inch); use firm red tomatoes

2 cups peeled and diced cucumber (½ inch)

1 cup radish (cut in half—tip to tail, sliced ⅛ inch half rounds)

½ cup coarsely chopped green onion; use light and dark green parts

¼ cup diced green bell pepper (¼ inch)

1 cup coarsely chopped flat-leaf parsley; use green leafy parts and tender stems

2 large cloves garlic

1 teaspoon salt

¼ cup tahini (mix well before using)

5 tablespoons freshly squeezed lemon juice

To prepare the salad

Combine the first 6 ingredients together in a bowl. Refrigerate covered until ready to serve.

In a small bowl, mash the garlic and salt to a pulp using a pestle. Add the tahini and lemon juice and whisk until creamy and smooth. Refrigerate covered until needed. Pour over the salad, mix well, and serve immediately.

Garbanzo Bean Salad

SERVES 4 (ABOUT 1 QUART)

Salata Hoummos Haab (sa-la-ta hum-moose hab)

This is such a healthy salad, and a great way to enjoy garbanzo beans, tossed with fresh garden vegetables in an aromatic dressing of garlic, lemon, and olive oil. The salad is delicious served with Grilled Chicken Kebabs (page 86), Lamb Kebabs (page 88), or Beef Fingers (page 84) at picnics, barbecues by the pool, or the beach.

Special equipment: A pestle (a garlic press will do).

Prepare ahead: You can prepare the vegetables up to 1 day in advance. Serve as directed. **Note:** As an alternative to using canned garbanzo beans, you can soak and cook dry beans as described on page 10. Once the beans are cooked, cool them completely before draining and using 1¾ cups of them in the salad. The other 1¾ cups can be frozen as directed.

FOR THE SALAD

1 (15- or 16-ounce) can garbanzo beans, drained

1 cup diced tomato (½ inch); use firm red tomatoes

1 cup peeled and diced cucumber (½ inch)

½ cup radish (cut in half—tip to tail, sliced ⅛ inch half rounds)

⅓ cup diced green bell pepper (¼ inch)

⅓ cup coarsely chopped green onion; use light and dark green parts

½ cup coarsely chopped flat-leaf parsley; use green leafy parts and tender stems

1 large clove garlic

1 teaspoon salt

4 tablespoons freshly squeezed lemon juice

3 tablespoons extra-virgin olive oil

To prepare the salad

Combine the first 7 ingredients in a mixing bowl. Refrigerate covered until ready to serve.

In a small bowl, mash the garlic and salt to a pulp using a pestle. Add the lemon juice and olive oil and mix well. Refrigerate covered until needed.

Toss the dressing with the salad and refrigerate about 1 hour prior to serving. For an extra crunch, add 1 cup pita croutons to the salad prior to serving (see the recipe for pita croutons on page 60).

Lemon-Garlic Potato Salad

SERVES 4 (ABOUT 1 QUART)

Salata Batata (sa-la-ta ba-ta-ta)

This is a great alternative to traditional potato salad. Offer this salad with grilled lamb, beef, chicken, or fish. It is also a great choice for occasions by the pool or outdoors. Since there is no dairy or mayonnaise in the dressing, you have less to be concerned about on warmer days.

Special Equipment: A pestle (a garlic press will do).

Prepare ahead: The potatoes and dressing can be prepared up to 1 day in advance. Cover and refrigerate separately. Serve as directed.

FOR THE SALAD

4 cups (about 2 pounds) peeled and diced red-skinned potato (½-inch cubes)

1½ teaspoons and 1 teaspoon salt, divided

2 large cloves garlic

½ cup coarsely chopped flat-leaf parsley; use green leafy parts and tender stems

3 tablespoons freshly squeezed lemon juice

3 tablespoons extra-virgin olive oil

To prepare the salad

Place a large pot with 6 cups water and 1½ teaspoons salt over high heat, covered, and bring to a rolling boil. Add the diced potatoes and return to a rolling boil, uncovered, for 5 minutes. Drain the water, then spread the potatoes evenly over a plastic-lined tray. Set them aside to cool uncovered for 1 hour, then cool an additional 2 hours in the refrigerator uncovered. (The potatoes must cool completely before mixing with the dressing; otherwise they may break into pieces.)

In a medium bowl, mash the garlic and 1 teaspoon salt to a pulp using a pestle. Add the parsley, lemon juice, and olive oil, and mix well. Use a spatula to gently fold in the cooled potatoes. Mix well and serve.

Selecting Potatoes

Choose firm, smooth potatoes with a bright red skin. Avoid ones that are soft and wrinkled or that have a green tint.

Parsley and Bulgur Wheat Salad

SERVES 4 (ABOUT 1 QUART)

Tabbouli (ta-boo-lee)

I have seen many versions of this salad. I was raised on this one, and it remains my favorite. The main ingredient is parsley, which is full of valuable nutrients, including vitamins K and C. I prefer using curly parsley, as I feel it yields a lighter salad. Prepare the parsley, green onion, and mint the day before, and you will end up with fresh tabbouli that is out-of-this-world good! Offer tabbouli at a barbecue, as the tart taste of the dressing combined with the rich flavor of the parsley and aromatic mint with wheat truly complements grilled meats, fish, and vegetables.

Specialty ingredients: Bulgur wheat #1 (fine), found at specialty markets or online.

Prepare ahead: For freshest vegetables, rinse and store them ahead of time (see page xiv). You can prepare the salad 1 day in advance. Refrigerate covered. Dress the salad as directed.

FOR THE SALAD

2½ cups (lightly packed) finely chopped curly parsley; use green leafy parts and tender stems

1 cup diced tomato (¼ inch); use firm red tomatoes

⅓ cup finely chopped green onion; use the green and white parts

2 tablespoons finely chopped fresh mint leaves

or: ½ tablespoon dried mint flakes

¼ cup bulgur wheat #1 (fine)

3 tablespoons freshly squeezed lemon juice

4 tablespoons extra-virgin olive oil

½ teaspoon salt

1/16 teaspoon sugar

1/16 teaspoon ground paprika

1/16 teaspoon ground black pepper

(For an extra-lemony flavor, add 1 teaspoon lemon zest.)

To prepare the vegetables (the day before)

Loosen the tie around the stems of parsley. Rinse the parsley several times in a bowl of cold water, changing the water until the water is clear of sand particles and debris. Dry the parsley by holding each bunch by the stems and shaking out the excess water. (I step outdoors to do this, giving each bunch several good swings. If stepping outdoors is not an option, you can give it a couple of good swings over the bathtub. You can also use a salad spinner if you have one.) Place the parsley on a dry kitchen towel (turning each bunch periodically), allowing it to air-dry (not wilt).

To store overnight, roll the air-dried bunches of parsley in a dry kitchen towel or paper towel and place them in a plastic bag in the refrigerator.

Rinse and store the fresh mint and green onions the day before as well (see Rinsing and Storing Produce, page xiv).

To prepare the tabbouli

It is essential to use a sharp 8- to 10-inch chef's knife to chop the parsley for tabbouli. (For larger amounts of tabbouli, you can use a food processor. The blade

must be sharp and the parsley must be air-dried, not wilted. Pulse the parsley in small batches, about 4 cups at a time depending on the size of your food processor. I use one that holds 12 cups.)

To prepare the salad, combine the first 5 ingredients in a bowl and mix well. Cover and refrigerate for at least 2 hours prior to serving (allowing the bulgur to expand). Add the next 6 ingredients and mix thoroughly just before serving.

To serve

Serve the tabbouli spooned on heart of romaine leaves (or tender cabbage leaves, fresh grape leaves off the vine, or endive spears), garnished with lemon wedges, tomato wedges, and sprigs of mint.

Selecting Parsley

Choose parsley with tightly curled leaves that are dark green with no wilting or yellowing.

Pita Crouton Salad with Sumak Dressing

SERVES 6 (ABOUT 2 QUARTS)

Fattoush (fettoush)

I believe it is the variety of vegetables and the shape and size of how each vegetable is cut combined with the dressing that make this salad so popular. It can be offered with a variety of entrees made with lamb, beef, poultry, or seafood. You can even add grilled chicken or shrimp to the salad, and it becomes a meal of its own.

Specialty ingredients: Sumak, found at specialty markets or online.

Prepare ahead: You can prepare the croutons in advance and store them in an airtight container for days. For freshest vegetables, rinse and store them ahead of time (see page xiv). The salad can be prepared 1 day in advance. Serve as directed.

FOR THE PITA CROUTONS

1 large pita bread (about 10 inches diameter)
or: 2 medium pita breads (about 6 inches diameter)
¼ cup extra-virgin olive oil
1 tablespoon sumak

FOR THE SALAD

2 cups (lightly packed) sliced romaine lettuce
1½ cups tomato (cut into wedges, slice each wedge into ½-inch triangles); use firm red tomatoes
¾ cup cucumber (quartered lengthwise, cut quarters into ¼ inch pieces)
½ cup radish (cut in half—tip to tail, sliced ⅛ inch half rounds)
⅓ cup diced green bell pepper (½ inch)
½ cup coarsely chopped green onion; use light and dark parts

¼ cup finely chopped fresh mint leaves or 1 teaspoon dried mint flakes
1 cup coarsely chopped flat-leaf parsley; use the green leafy parts and tender stems

FOR THE DRESSING

¼ cup extra-virgin olive oil
¼ cup apple cider vinegar
1 teaspoon salt
4 teaspoons sumak

To prepare the pita croutons

*Preheat the oven to 350°F. Cut the pitas into 1 x 1-inch squares. (**Note:** Do not separate the pita halves; the yield is about 2 cups of croutons.) Evenly spread the pitas over a foil-lined baking sheet and toast in the center of the oven, shaking the pan periodically for 15 to 18 minutes or until they are evenly golden brown. (Test a couple to make sure they are crisp all the way through, keeping in mind that different brands of pita vary in thickness; therefore the baking time can vary as well.)*

Once crisp, remove the pita squares from the oven. Transfer them to a container and add the olive oil and sumak. Mix well to coat the croutons with the mixture. Cool completely before storing. Store them covered at room temperature until needed. (If stored

croutons seem stale a day later, that means they did not toast long enough in the oven.)

To prepare the salad

Make certain all the vegetables have been rinsed well and are dry from excess moisture before you begin. Refrigerate the rinsed vegetables overnight if you can (see "Rinsing and Storing Produce," page xiv). Cut larger romaine leaves in half lengthwise along the rib; then slice widthwise into ¼-inch strips.

Place the tomato stem-side up and cut the tomato in half. Cut each half into 3 wedges (4 wedges for larger tomatoes). Slice each wedge widthwise into pieces ½ inch thick (the pieces will resemble triangles).

Peel the cucumber lengthwise, removing every other strip of skin for a striped appearance; then quarter lengthwise. Slice the quarters widthwise into ¼-inch pieces.

Cut each radish in half from tip to tail. Cut each half into ⅛-inch-thick half rounds.

Prepare the remaining vegetables as described above and mix together. Cover and refrigerate the salad for at least 2 hours or overnight prior to serving.

To serve

Toss the salad with the sumak croutons and dressing just before serving.

{VARIATIONS}

Red Onion: Add ½ cup thinly sliced red onion to the ingredients (my mother loves it this way).
Purslane: Add about 1 cup purslane (known as *bakli* in Arabic), available in summer months when you can find it at specialty markets or farmers' mar-

kets. Use the succulent leaves and tender tips.
Grilled Chicken or Shrimp: Add 3 cups chilled grilled chicken or grilled shrimp to the salad. Adjust the dressing to taste.

Romaine Salad
Salata Khus (sa-la-ta khus)

This "quick fix" salad is a last-minute favorite that delivers great flavor in no time. It is my version of Caesar salad without cheese and croutons. However, when in the mood, I throw in some pita croutons (page 60) and crumbled Bulgarian feta cheese.

Special equipment: A pestle (a garlic press will do).

Prepare ahead: You can slice the romaine lettuce early in the day and refrigerate it until needed. Or for extra-crisp romaine, after it has been rinsed and dripped dry, wrap it in a kitchen towel and place it in a plastic bag in the refrigerator overnight.

FOR THE SALAD

2 quarts (lightly packed) sliced romaine lettuce
1 large clove garlic
¾ teaspoon salt
3 tablespoons extra-virgin olive oil
3 tablespoons apple cider vinegar

To prepare the salad

Cut the romaine leaves widthwise into 1-inch strips. Wider leaves can be cut in half lengthwise along the rib so that the strips are not too long. Refrigerate covered until needed.

In a small bowl, mash the garlic and salt to a pulp using a pestle. Stir in the olive oil and vinegar. Mix with the salad and serve. You can add 1 cup Pita Croutons (page 60), and 1 cup crumbled Bulgarian feta cheese.

{VARIATION}

Tahini Dressing: Rather than mixing the lettuce with the dressing above, serve the salad with ⅓ cup Tahini Dressing (see recipe on page 55).

Yogurt-Cucumber Salad
Laban bi Khyar (leb-ban bee khyar)

SERVES 4 (ABOUT 1½ CUPS)

The cool texture of the cucumber and the aromatic scent of the mint swimming in the garlic-infused yogurt is so refreshing. This salad is excellent with kibbi trays (pages 99–103), Chicken with Spiced Rice (page 75), or Vegetable-Stuffed Cabbage Rolls (page 161), to name a few combinations. It is similar to the Greek version known as tzatziki, the Persian variety called must-o-kheyar, and the Indian version called raita.

Specialty ingredients: Tahini, found in specialty markets or online.

Special equipment: A pestle (a garlic press will do).

Prepare ahead: The yogurt can be prepared up to 1 day in advance and stored in the refrigerator. Add the cucumber as directed.

FOR THE SALAD

1 large clove garlic
½ teaspoon salt
1 cup plain yogurt (regular, reduced-fat, or fat-free)
½ teaspoon tahini (mix well before using)
1 tablespoon finely chopped fresh mint leaves
or: ¼ teaspoon dried mint flakes
1 cup cucumber (quartered and sliced ¼ inch)
(**You can omit** the tahini if you do not have it on hand. It serves as a binder.)

To prepare the salad

Place the garlic and salt in a medium bowl. Mash the garlic to a pulp using a pestle. Add the yogurt, tahini, and mint. Mix well. Cover and refrigerate until needed.

Peel the cucumber lengthwise, leaving every other peel of skin on the cucumber for a striped appearance. Quarter it lengthwise, then cut each quarter into pieces ¼ inch thick. Cover and refrigerate until

needed. Add the cucumber to the yogurt mixture just before serving.

Selecting cucumbers

Choose narrow, firm ones with a solid green color and without signs of yellowing or puffiness. English cucumbers are an excellent choice for this salad.

Roasted Lemon-Garlic Chicken

Main Dishes

(CHICKEN/LAMB/BEEF/FISH/VEGETARIAN)

I was not a stranger to the kitchen while growing up. I often helped my mother as we prepared what always seemed to be an incredible feast. The neighborhood kids always wanted to eat dinner at our house. Our kitchen was filled with foods, flavors, and aromas that were quite different than those they had experienced.

Today, I am still preparing these meals in my kitchen, and I am happy to report that my mother approves of them all. Enjoy such classic delights as Layered London Broil with Garlic Yogurt and Pita; a delicious melding of flavors and textures that begins with a layer of crisp pita croutons followed by a garlicky yogurt sauce with tender pieces of London broil and a scattering of toasted pine nuts and fresh plump pomegranate seeds on top, or Fire-Roasted Wheat with Lamb; steamed coarse green wheat with pearl onions and tender pieces of lamb; or pan-fried tilapia covered in a spicy sauce of jalapeño, ground pine nuts, and cilantro. This selection of recipes allows you to create and prepare a wide variety of robust meals packed with flavor that showcase the diverse, healthy, and nutritious cuisine of Lebanon.

Beef and Pine Nut–Stuffed Eggplants 66
Beef Tortellini in Cilantro Yogurt 68
Bulgur Pilaf with Chicken 71
Cardamom Chicken with Rice 72
Cardamom Lamb (or Beef) with Rice 74
Chicken and Spiced Rice with Toasted Nuts . . 75
Lamb (or Beef) and Spiced Rice with
   Toasted Nuts 77
Chicken Curry. 78
Cod Baked in Citrus Tahini. 81
Fire-Roasted Wheat with Lamb (or Beef). 83
Grilled Beef Fingers. 84
Grilled Chicken Kebabs 86
Grilled Lamb Kebabs 88
Grilled Lamb Rib Chops 90
Grilled Shrimp Kebabs 91
Grilled Vegetable Kebabs 92
Jute Mallow and Garlic-Cilantro Stew with
   Lamb (or Beef) 94
Kibbi Balls in Cilantro Yogurt 96

Kibbi Balls in Garbanzo-Tahini Sauce 98
Lamb (or Beef, or Chicken) Kibbi Tray 99
Pumpkin Kibbi Tray 102
Fish Kibbi Tray 103
Layered London Broil with Garlic Yogurt
   and Pita 105
Layered Chicken with Garlic Yogurt and Pita . 107
Lebanese Caraway Couscous with Chicken . 108
Lebanese Meatloaf 111
Raisin Couscous with Vegetable Stew 112
Raisin Couscous with Chicken and
   Vegetable Stew. 115
Raisin Couscous with Lamb (or Beef) and
   Vegetable Stew. 115
Red Snapper with Caramelized Cumin Rice . 116
Roast Leg of Lamb 119
Roasted Lemon-Garlic Chicken 121
Stuffed Squash and Grape Leaves 122
Stuffed Zucchini in Tomato Sauce 125
Tilapia with Jalapeño–Pine Nut Sauce 128

Beef and Pine Nut–Stuffed Eggplants

1 DOZEN

Shiekh el Mihshi (shaakh-ill-mih-shee)

These tender baby eggplants are stuffed with minced beef and pine nuts sautéed in a rich tomato, onion, and pomegranate sauce. The buttery texture of the eggplant coupled with the discreetly sweet yet tart flavor of the pomegranate makes this a special dish.

Specialty ingredients: Dibs ruman (pomegranate molasses), found at specialty markets or online.
Special equipment: A candy/fry thermometer.
Prepare ahead: The cooked stuffed eggplants can be refrigerated for several days or frozen in their sauce in an airtight container up to 2 months. Reheat and serve as directed.

FOR THE STUFFED EGGPLANTS

12 small eggplants (3 to 4 inches long)
1 teaspoon salt and ¾ teaspoon salt, divided
2 cups canola oil (for frying)
2 tablespoons extra-virgin olive oil
2 cups thinly sliced yellow onion (⅛ inch)
⅛ teaspoon coarsely ground black pepper
¼ teaspoon allspice
¼ teaspoon cinnamon
2½ cups boiling water
4 teaspoons dibs ruman
⅓ cup tomato paste
½ cup peeled and diced tomato (¼ inch)
¼ cup fresh pomegranate seeds (optional, when in season)

FOR THE MEAT FILLING

3 tablespoons toasted pine nuts
1 tablespoon extra-virgin olive oil
½ pound ground beef (80% lean)
1½ cups diced yellow onion (¼ inch)
1 teaspoon salt

¼ teaspoon coarsely ground black pepper
½ teaspoon ground allspice
¼ teaspoon ground cinnamon
(**You can substitute** ground lamb or ground chicken for the beef.)

To prepare the eggplants

Use a butter knife to remove the stem cap from the eggplants. Gently lift under the edge of the cap and pull it off with the stem. Peel the eggplants lengthwise, removing every other strip of skin for a striped appearance. Make a 2-inch slit lengthwise in each eggplant, about halfway into the flesh, to make a cavity for the stuffing.

Toss the eggplants in a bowl to coat them with 1 teaspoon salt. Let stand for 30 minutes, stirring periodically, then drain off the liquid.

To prepare the meat filling

Preheat the oven to 350°F. Spread the pine nuts over a foil-lined baking sheet and toast in the center of the oven, shaking the pan occasionally, for 5 to 7 minutes or until golden brown. Set aside.

Preheat the olive oil in a large skillet over medium-high heat, and cook the ground meat while breaking it into small minced pieces. Once the meat is no longer pink, reduce the heat to medium and stir in the onions, salt, and spices. Sauté until the onions are tender. Mix in the pine nuts, and remove from the heat. Transfer the filling to a dish. Cool slightly before stuffing the eggplants. Reserve the skillet.

To fry and stuff the eggplants

Preheat the canola oil in a small saucepan over medium-high heat to 375°F; use a candy/fry thermometer to keep the oil at the proper temperature to ensure that your eggplant will fry evenly. The oil should be about 1 inch deep. Fry about 3 eggplants at a time. Once the eggplants are evenly golden brown, remove them to a paper towel–lined dish.

Recycle the oil: *See page xiv.*

(Alternatively, *you can bake the eggplants. Preheat the oven to 450°F. Mix the drained eggplants with 3 tablespoons olive oil, and spread them over a foil-lined baking sheet, slit side up. Bake the eggplants on the middle rack in the oven for 20 minutes, then set the eggplants aside to cool, uncovered.)*

Once the eggplants have cooled, stuff the cavity of each one with 1 tablespoon meat filling. Set them aside loosely covered. Reserve any left over meat filling.

To cook the sauce and stuffed eggplants

Preheat the olive oil in the large skillet over medium-high heat. Add the sliced onions and ¾ teaspoon salt, and sauté the onions until they are limp and tender. Add the rest of the spices, the boiling water, dibs ruman, tomato paste, and diced tomato, stirring until the tomato paste has dissolved. Stir in any leftover meat filling.

Cover and cook the sauce over medium heat for about 5 minutes, then carefully add the stuffed eggplants, stuffed side facing up. Generously spoon

some sauce over the top of each eggplant. Cover and cook over medium heat for 5 to 7 minutes, then remove from the heat and let stand covered for 5 to 10 minutes prior to serving.

To serve

Serve over Basmati Rice with Toasted Noodles (page 134), warm pita bread, and a salad. Sprinkle ¼ cup fresh pomegranate seeds over the top when in season (October through January).

Selecting Eggplants

Use Italian or Indian eggplants. The Italian variety resembles the eggplants you are accustomed to seeing, but they are miniature. The Indian variety, also miniature, may be lighter in color and plump around the center. Either variety works well. Choose firm, smooth fruits that are blemish free. Eggplants are quite perishable, so store them in a plastic bag in the refrigerator and use them within a day or two.

Beef Tortellini in Cilantro Yogurt
Sheesh Barak (sheesh ba-rak)

Homemade tortellini cooked in a garlic-cilantro-laced yogurt sauce are easy to prepare and absolutely delicious. Offer this dish as a starter before a meal or as part of a buffet. Your friends and family will be intrigued by the delightful combination of flavors.

Specialty ingredients: Tahini, found at specialty markets or online.

Special equipment: A mortar and pestle (a garlic press will do), and a 2½-inch round cookie cutter.

Prepare ahead: The tortellini can be baked in advance and refrigerated for a couple of days or frozen for several weeks. Freeze baked tortellini on a plastic-lined baking tray, then store in an airtight container. Cook them directly from the freezer or refrigerator as described.

FOR THE DOUGH
1¼ cups unbleached flour
¼ teaspoon salt
6 tablespoons water

Measuring flour: See page xiv.

FOR THE FILLING
3 tablespoons toasted pine nuts
1 teaspoon melted butter
1 tablespoon extra-virgin olive oil
¼ pound ground beef (80% lean)
1 cup diced yellow onion (⅛ inch)
1 tablespoon freshly squeezed lemon juice
½ teaspoon salt
¼ teaspoon coarsely ground black pepper
½ teaspoon allspice
¼ teaspoon cinnamon

(**You can substitute** ground chicken or ground lamb for the beef.)

FOR THE YOGURT SAUCE
4 cups plain yogurt (regular, reduced, or fat-free)
2½ tablespoons cornstarch dissolved in 2 tablespoons cold water
½ teaspoon tahini (optional)
3 large cloves garlic mashed with 1 teaspoon salt
1 tablespoon butter
1 teaspoon ground coriander
⅓ cup finely chopped cilantro; use green leafy parts and tender stems
2 tablespoons freshly squeezed lemon juice

To prepare the dough
In a bowl, combine the flour, salt, and water. Mix and knead the dough, forming it into a flat disc. Wrap the dough in plastic wrap and set aside at room temperature to rest for 30 minutes.

To prepare the filling
Preheat the oven to 350°F. Spread the pine nuts over a foil-lined baking sheet and toast in the center of the oven, shaking the pan occasionally, for 5 to 7 minutes or until golden brown. Mix the melted butter with the nuts, then transfer to a paper towel–lined dish and set aside.

Preheat the olive oil in a small skillet over medium-high heat. Add the ground meat and cook, breaking it into small minced pieces. Once the meat is no longer pink, add the onion, lemon juice, salt, and spices. Reduce the heat to medium-low and cook uncovered until the onions are tender. Remove from the heat. Cool the filling completely before using.

To make the tortellini

Preheat the oven to 400°F. On a lightly floured surface, roll the dough out to ¹⁄₁₆-inch thickness. Gently hold the rolled-out dough by the edges and lift it about 2 inches off the counter (this will allow any contraction in the dough to occur before cutting). Cut the dough into 2½-inch rounds using a cookie cutter; cut the rounds one right next to the other to maximize the number of rounds. Cover them with plastic wrap to avoid drying. Lightly flour a foil-lined baking sheet and place it within reach.

To fill the tortellini, pick up one round of dough at a time and flip it so that you are placing the filling on the underside (or whichever side seems stickier). Cradling the round of dough in one hand place ½ tablespoon cooled filling and 3 pine nuts in the center of a the dough. Fold one side over to form a crescent shape and press well along the edges to secure the filling inside. Then wrap the crescent around your index finger and press the outer tips together, forming a ring shape.

Stand the ring-shaped tortellini on the tray, seam-side down. Repeat with the remaining rounds of dough, placing the tortellinis ½ inch apart on the baking sheet.

Bake the tortellinis on the middle rack in the oven, lightly shaking the tray occasionally, for 12 to 14 minutes, or until the edges brown. Remove and set aside.

To prepare the yogurt sauce

Rinse a medium-sized pot with cold water (this will help prevent the yogurt from sticking while it cooks). Pass the yogurt through a fine-mesh strainer into the rinsed pot. Add the dissolved cornstarch and the tahini. Mix well and set aside.

Mash the garlic to a pulp with the salt using a mortar and pestle. Melt the butter in a small skillet over medium heat. Add the garlic pulp and sauté until it begins to sizzle (not brown). Remove from the heat. Stir in the coriander. Add this mixture to the yogurt.

Place the yogurt mixture over high heat, uncovered, and cook, using a flat-edged heat-proof spatula to continually stir and scrape the bottom and sides of the pot to ensure the yogurt does not stick. Once it boils, check to make sure there aren't any lumps; use a whisk to evenly dissolve any lumps until the mixture is smooth. Add the baked tortellini, then the cilantro and lemon juice, and return the mixture to a boil, gently stirring with the flat-edged spatula to separate the tortellini from one another as they cook. Continue scraping the sides and the bottom of the pot. After 5 minutes, remove from the heat and set aside for 10 minutes, uncovered, prior to serving.

To serve

Serve the tortellini in a shallow serving bowl and garnish with lemon twists and sprigs of fresh cilantro. Serve over Basmati Rice with Toasted Noodles (page 134).

When reheating, if the yogurt sauce seems thick, use milk to thin it out. The consistency should be like that of cream soup.

{VARIATION}

Substitute fresh mint for the cilantro. Some specialty markets sell pre-made pasta especially prepared for *sheesh barak*. (**Alternatively,** you can substitute your favorite Italian style fresh tortellini from the grocery store.)

Bulgur Pilaf with Chicken

SERVES 4

Burghul Bidfeen ma Djeaj (burr-ghool bid-feen ma djeaj)

The earthy, robust flavor of the wheat combined with the garbanzo beans and pearl onions is a perfect match. It is so easy to prepare, versatile, and healthy too! It can be prepared with chicken, lamb, or beef. You can prepare the bulgur pilaf by itself and serve it with any of your favorite recipes. It's a great alternative to rice.

Special ingredients: Coarse bulgur #4, found in specialty markets or online.

Prepare ahead: You can prepare this dish up to 2 days in advance. Refrigerate until needed. Serve as directed.

FOR THE CHICKEN

For the chicken follow the recipe in Chicken and
　　Spiced Rice with Toasted Nuts (see page 75).

FOR THE BULGUR PILAF

3 tablespoons extra-virgin olive oil

1½ cups bulgur #4 (coarse)

1½ teaspoons and ¼ teaspoon ground caraway
　　seeds, divided

3 cups hot broth

1 cup canned garbanzo beans (drained)

1 cup frozen pearl onions (thawed)

To prepare the chicken

To prepare the chicken follow the procedure in Chicken and Spiced Rice with Toasted Nuts as described on page 75. Set aside.

To prepare the pilaf

Preheat the olive oil in a medium-sized pot over medium-high heat. Add the bulgur and mix until the grains are evenly coated. Add 1½ teaspoons ground caraway seeds, the hot broth, garbanzo beans, and pearl onions. Increase the heat to high. Once the mixture comes to a boil, reduce the heat to medium-low and simmer covered for 20 to 25 minutes or until all the moisture has been absorbed. Test a few grains of bulgur to make sure they are tender. If they are still crunchy, add a little boiling broth and continue to steam. Once tender, remove the bulgur from the heat and set aside covered for 15 minutes before serving.

To serve

Fluff the bulgur, using the tines of a fork, then transfer to a shallow serving dish. Arrange the pieces of meat around the bulgur and sprinkle them with ¼ teaspoon ground caraway.

Serve with Yogurt Cucumber Salad (page 63).

{VARIATION}

Bulgur Pilaf with Lamb (or Beef) (Burghul Bidfeen ma Lahm): For the lamb (or beef), follow the recipe and procedure for preparing the lamb (or beef) in Lamb (or Beef) and Spiced Rice with Toasted Nuts (see page 77); then follow the recipe and procedure above for the pilaf. Serve as described above.

Cardamom Chicken with Rice

SERVES 4

Djeaj ma Riz Boukhari (djeaj ma riz bou-khar-rhee)

Try to prepare this dish early in the morning or even the day before you are going to serve it. The flavors are enhanced as the meat marinates in the broth. The aroma that fills the air when this is cooking will make your mouth water. This dish is favored by people from the Gulf countries because it is similar to a dish they call kebsah.

Prepare ahead: You can prepare this dish up to 2 days in advance. Refrigerate until needed. Serve as directed.

FOR THE CHICKEN

1 whole chicken, about 4½ pounds, cut into 10 pieces

2 tablespoons apple cider vinegar

¼ cup extra-virgin olive oil

1½ cups diced yellow onion (¼ inch)

½ cup peeled and shredded carrot (use the large holes of a grater)

2¾ teaspoons salt

¼ teaspoon coarsely ground black pepper

¾ teaspoons ground allspice

½ teaspoon ground cinnamon

2 teaspoons ground cumin

1 teaspoon ground cardamom

⅛ teaspoon ground cloves

1/16 teaspoon ground nutmeg

5 cups boiling water

⅓ cup tomato paste

¾ cup peeled and diced tomato (½ inch)

(**You can substitute** about 3 pounds split chicken breast if you prefer all white meat. Cut each breast in half width-wise. The recipe and the procedure remain the same.)

FOR THE RICE

1 teaspoon extra-virgin olive oil

1 cup converted (also called parboiled) rice

2½ cups hot reserved broth

½ cup toasted slivered almonds

½ cup toasted golden raisins

2 tablespoons melted butter

To prepare the chicken

Cut the chicken into 10 pieces (see "Segmenting Chicken," page xv), leaving the skin on. Rinse in a bowl with 6 cups cold water and the vinegar to refresh the flavor of the chicken. Drain and set aside.

Preheat the olive oil in a large pot. Add the onions, carrots, salt, and spices, and sauté over medium-high heat for a couple of minutes. Add the pieces of chicken, and cook until the meat is no longer pink. Add the boiling water, tomato paste, and tomatoes. Stir well dissolving the tomato paste in the water. Increase the heat to high and bring the mixture to a rolling boil, uncovered, then reduce the heat to medium and simmer covered, stirring occasionally, for 25 minutes. Remove from the heat. Transfer the pieces of chicken to a flat tray and set aside to cool, uncovered. Reserve all of the broth.

After 15 minutes, remove and discard the skin and bones from the pieces of chicken. Do not remove the

center bone from the thigh or drumstick. Place the pieces of chicken in a container just large enough to hold them and cover with some of the reserved broth.

To prepare the rice

Preheat the olive oil in a medium pot over medium heat. Stir in the rice and coat the grains. Add 2½ cups hot reserved broth and increase the heat to high. Bring to a rolling boil; then reduce the heat to low and simmer, covered, for 15 minutes or until the broth has been absorbed. Then remove from the heat and set aside covered for 20 minutes. Fluff the rice, separating the grains with the tines of a fork, before serving.

Preheat the oven to 350°F. Spread the almonds and raisins over a foil-lined baking sheet, keeping them separate, and toast in the center of the oven, shaking the pan occasionally, for 5 to 7 minutes or until the almonds are golden and the raisins seem inflated. Remove from the oven and drizzle some of the melted butter over each, mixing well to incorporate the butter. Transfer to a paper towel–lined dish. Set aside to cool before using.

To serve

Warm the meat and rice. Arrange the rice on a platter with the pieces of meat around the perimeter of the rice. Scatter the room-temperature toasted nuts and raisins in the center. Garnish with sprigs of parsley and diced tomato around the edge of the platter. Serve with Jalapeño–Cilantro Salsa (page 144) as a condiment over the meat and rice, along with Pita Crouton Salad with Sumak Dressing (page 60).

Cardamom Lamb (or Beef) with Rice

SERVES 4

Lahm ma Riz Boukari (lah-him ma riz bou khar-rhee)

Prepare ahead: You can prepare this dish up to 2 days in advance. Refrigerate until needed. Serve as directed.

FOR THE LAMB (OR BEEF)

¼ cup extra-virgin olive oil

2 pounds lean lamb, from the leg, cut into
  1½ × 1½-inch pieces

or: 2 pounds beef (top round/London broil)

¼ cup freshly squeezed lemon juice

1½ cups diced yellow onion (¼ inch)

½ cup peeled and shredded carrot (use the
  large holes of a grater)

1 tablespoon salt

½ teaspoon coarsely ground black pepper

1¼ teaspoons ground allspice

¾ teaspoon ground cinnamon

1 tablespoon ground cumin

1½ teaspoons ground cardamom

¼ teaspoon ground cloves

⅛ teaspoon ground nutmeg

10 cups boiling water

⅔ cup tomato paste

¾ cup peeled and diced tomato (½ inch)

FOR THE RICE

Follow the recipe as described in the previous recipe for Cardomom Chicken with Rice.

To prepare the lamb (or beef)

Preheat the olive oil in a large pot over medium-high heat. Add the meat and fry until all of the moisture has evaporated and it is evenly browned (caramelized) on all sides. Add the lemon juice, onions, carrots, salt, and spices, and sauté for a minute. Add the boiling water, tomato paste, and the tomatoes. Stir well dissolving the tomato paste, in the water. Increase the heat to high and bring the mixture to a rolling boil, uncovered; then reduce the heat to medium and simmer covered, stirring occasionally, for about 1 hour and 15 minutes. At this point, test the meat with a fork. If it breaks apart easily, it's done; if not, continue to cook until tender. Once tender, remove from the heat and set aside covered. Reserve all of the broth.

To prepare the rice

Follow the procedure described in the previous recipe for Cardamom Chicken with Rice.

To serve

Serve as described in the previous recipe for Cardamom Chicken with Rice.

Chicken and Spiced Rice with Toasted Nuts

SERVES 4

Djeaj ma Riz Haswi (djeaj ma riz hush-wee)

The literal translation of this dish is "chicken with rice stuffing." However, most people prepare it this way. The spiced rice is simmered in chicken broth to draw out the individual flavors. Toasted nuts complete this dish. Prepare it in the morning or even the day before. The rich broth continues to tenderize the meat, enhancing the flavor.

Prepare ahead: You can prepare this dish up to 2 days in advance. Refrigerate the chicken and rice separately. Serve as directed.

FOR THE CHICKEN

1 whole chicken (about 4½ pounds)
2 tablespoons apple cider vinegar
4 teaspoons salt
1 cup diced yellow onion (1 inch)
1 rib celery (cut into 2-inch lengths)
1 (3 to 4 inch) stick cinnamon
½ teaspoon whole black peppercorns
1 teaspoon whole allspice berries
1 bay leaf
⅛ teaspoon ground cinnamon
(**You can substitute** 3 pounds split chicken breast if you prefer all white meat; the procedure remains the same.)

FOR THE SPICED RICE

1 tablespoon extra-virgin olive oil
¼ pound ground beef (80% lean)
2 tablespoons and 1 tablespoon butter, divided
½ teaspoon salt
¼ teaspoon coarsely ground black pepper
½ teaspoon ground allspice
¼ teaspoon ground cinnamon
⅛ teaspoon ground cloves
1/16 teaspoon ground nutmeg

1 cup converted (also called parboiled) rice
2½ cups hot reserved broth
¼ cup toasted pine nuts
¼ cup toasted slivered almonds
¼ cup toasted pistachios

To prepare the chicken

Rinse the whole chicken (or chicken breasts) in a large pot with 6 cups water and the vinegar to refresh the flavor of the chicken. Drain the water. Place the chicken, breast side facing up, in the same pot.

Add to the pot with the chicken 12 cups of water and the salt. Place over high heat, uncovered, and bring to a boil, stirring occasionally to ensure the chicken does not stick. Once it comes to a rolling boil, skim and discard any foam off the top. Add the next 6 ingredients and return to a boil, then reduce the heat to medium and simmer, covered, stirring occasionally, for 45 minutes. Remove from the heat and transfer the chicken to a flat tray to cool, uncovered. Pass the broth through a fine sieve and return it to the pot (reserve all the broth).

After the chicken has cooled (about 30 minutes), divide it into pieces. Remove the leg and thigh (keep them attached together as one piece, otherwise the meat will fall off the bone). Separate the whole breast from the back. Discard the back and

bones. Peel and discard all the skin from all the pieces of chicken. Break each half breast into 2 or 3 pieces lengthwise. Return the pieces of chicken to the reserved broth and sprinkle ⅛ teaspoon cinnamon over the top. Cover and set aside.

To prepare the rice

Preheat the olive oil in a medium pot over medium-high heat. Add the ground meat and cook while breaking it into small, minced pieces. Once it is browned, add 2 tablespoons butter, the salt, spices, and the rice. Mix well to coat the grains of rice.

Add 2½ cups hot reserved broth, increase the heat to high, and bring the mixture to a rolling boil, uncovered. Reduce the heat to low, cover, and simmer for 15 minutes or until the moisture is absorbed. Remove from the heat and set aside covered for 20 minutes. Fluff with a fork before serving.

Meanwhile, preheat the oven to 350°F. Spread the three kinds of nuts in separate rows on a foil-lined baking sheet and toast in the center of the oven, shaking the pan occasionally, for 5 to 7 minutes or until they turn golden brown. Drizzle 1 tablespoon melted butter evenly over the nuts and mix well, coating them with butter. Transfer them to a paper towel–lined dish to cool, uncovered. Set aside.

To serve

Heat the meat and the rice. Spread the rice over a platter, then arrange the pieces of meat around the perimeter of the rice. Scatter the room-temperature toasted nuts in the center. Sprinkle some cinnamon over the pieces of meat, and serve. Offer with Pita Crouton Salad with Sumak Dressing (page 60) or Yogurt-Cucumber Salad (page 63).

Lamb (or Beef) and Spiced Rice with Toasted Nuts

SERVES 4

Lahm ma Riz Haswi (lah-him ma riz hush-wee)

Prepare ahead: You can prepare this dish up to 2 days in advance. Refrigerate the lamb (or beef) and rice separately. Serve as directed.

FOR THE LAMB (OR BEEF)

2 tablespoons extra-virgin olive oil

2 pounds lean lamb (from the leg), cut into
1½ × 1½-inch pieces

or: beef (top round/London broil)

2 tablespoons freshly squeezed lemon juice

2 cups diced yellow onion (½ inch)

1 tablespoon salt

½ teaspoon coarsely ground black pepper

2 teaspoons ground allspice

1 teaspoon ground cinnamon

⅛ teaspoon ground cloves

1/16 teaspoon ground nutmeg

12 cups boiling water

FOR THE RICE

Follow the recipe as described in the previous recipe for Chicken and Spiced Rice with Toasted Nuts.

To prepare the lamb (or beef)

Preheat the olive oil in a large pot over medium-high heat. Add the meat and fry until all of the moisture has evaporated and the meat is evenly browned (caramelized) on all sides. Add the lemon juice, onions, salt, and spices. Cook and stir for about 1 minute.

Add the boiling water and increase the heat to high. Bring the mixture to a rolling boil. Reduce the heat to medium-low, cover, and simmer, stirring occasionally, for 1 hour and 15 minutes. Test the meat with a fork. If it breaks apart easily, it is done; if not, continue to cook until tender. Set aside. Reserve all of the broth.

To prepare the rice

Follow the procedure as described in the previous recipe for Chicken and Spiced Rice with Toasted Nuts.

To serve

Follow the serving suggestions as described in the previous recipe for Chicken and Spiced Rice with Toasted Nuts.

Chicken Curry

SERVES 6

Djeaj bil Curry (djeaj bill curry)

In the words of a good friend, "This recipe is absolutely sublime!" This flavorful dish is a combination of tender chunks of chicken sautéed with onions, celery, banana, and apples in a velvety curry sauce. An essential variety of condiments and Basmati Rice with Toasted Noodles complete this dish.

Special ingredients: Ca Ri Ni An Do D&D Gold Madras curry powder and Koon Chun plum sauce, found in specialty Asian markets or online. (These are the recommended brands to use; you can substitute others, but the flavor may vary.)

Prepare ahead: You can prepare the curry up to 2 days in advance. Refrigerate until needed. The flavors continue to develop. The condiments and the rice can also be prepared up to 2 days in advance. Refrigerate the rice and the mango chutney.

FOR THE CHICKEN

2 pounds trimmed boneless skinless chicken breast, cut into 1-inch pieces

1 tablespoon apple cider vinegar

2 tablespoons extra-virgin olive oil

FOR THE SAUCE

¼ cup and ¼ cup extra-virgin olive oil, divided

4 cups diced yellow onion (¼ inch)

2½ cups diced celery (¼ inch)

1½ cups diced green bell pepper (¼ inch)

1½ cups peeled and diced Granny Smith apple (½ inch)

2¼ teaspoons and 1 teaspoon salt, divided

1 tablespoon and 3 tablespoons curry powder, divided

¼ teaspoon table-grind black pepper

½ teaspoon allspice

¼ teaspoon cinnamon

1 cup diced banana (¼ inch), ripe but firm

5 tablespoons unbleached flour

4 cups warm milk

2 tablespoons tomato paste

FOR THE CONDIMENTS

1 cup coarsely chopped pecans, toasted

½ cup shredded coconut, toasted

1 cup peeled and diced fresh mango (¼ inch)

½ cup plum sauce

½ cup currants

FOR THE RICE

1½ recipes Basmati Rice with Toasted Noodles (page 134)

To prepare the chicken

In a bowl, rinse the chicken with 1 cup cold water and the vinegar to refresh the flavor of the chicken. Drain the water. Cut the chicken into 1-inch pieces. Preheat the olive oil in a large pot over medium-high heat. Add the chicken and cook until it is halfway done and no longer pink. Transfer it to a large bowl. Reserve the pot.

To prepare the sauce

Preheat ¼ cup olive oil in the reserved pot over medium-high heat. Add the onions, celery, bell pepper, apple, 2¼ teaspoons salt, 1 tablespoon curry, and the pepper, allspice, and cinnamon. Sauté for

several minutes, allowing the vegetables to soften a bit. Mix in the banana. Reduce the heat to medium and cook covered, stirring occasionally, for 5 minutes, then transfer the vegetable mixture to the large bowl over the meat.

Wipe the pot clean with paper towel. In the same pot, preheat ¼ cup oil over medium-high heat. Add 3 tablespoons curry powder, the flour, and 1 teaspoon salt. Whisk for a minute, allowing the mixture to sizzle but not stick. Slowly whisk in the warm milk. Increase the heat to high and continue whisking to avoid lumps and sticking. Once the mixture begins to bubble around the edges, reduce the heat to medium and continue to whisk as the sauce thickens, for about 2 minutes.

Reduce the heat to medium-low and add the tomato paste. Whisk occasionally, incorporating the tomato paste, and simmer for 4 minutes. Add the vegetable and meat mixture to the sauce, mix well, and increase the heat to high. Once the mixture begins to boil around the edges, reduce the heat to medium and cook uncovered, stirring occasionally, for 3 minutes, then remove from the heat and set aside covered. Serve hot.

To prepare the condiments
Preheat the oven to 350°F. Place the pecans on a foil-lined baking sheet and toast in the center of the oven, shaking the pan occasionally, for 5 to 7 minutes; then cool completely.

Place the coconut on a foil-lined baking sheet and toast in the center of the 350°F oven, shaking the pan occasionally, for 4 to 6 minutes; then cool completely.

Place the diced mango in a small bowl covered with plastic wrap in the microwave for 1½ minutes on high. Let it cool completely, uncovered, then mix with ½ cup plum sauce. The currants do not require any special preparation.

To prepare the rice

Follow the recipe and procedure for 1½ recipes Basmati Rice with Toasted Noodles, page 134. Set it aside until ready to serve.

To serve

Heat the curry and rice. Place the rice on a shallow platter with the curry in a bowl next to it. Arrange the condiments separately in bowls next to the curry. Your guests will enjoy layering the different flavors.

{VARIATIONS}

You can add to the variety of condiments offered with the curry items such as toasted peanuts, almonds, golden raisins, chopped apples, grapes, or bananas. Or substitute shrimp or roasted potato for the chicken, as below—or feature lamb or beef, as in the following recipe.

Lamb (or Beef) Curry (*Lahm bil Curry*): Substitute for the chicken, 2 pounds lamb or beef. See the recipe for Lamb (or Beef) and Spiced Rice with Toasted Nuts (page 77). Follow the recipe and the procedure to prepare the lamb (or beef). Once the meat is prepared, remove it with a slotted spoon to a small bowl and cover. Discard the broth. Refer to the previous recipe for Chicken Curry. Follow the recipe and procedure above for the sauce, condiments, and rice. Once the sauce has been prepared, add the meat to the sauce and bring the mixture to a slight boil. Serve as directed.

Shrimp Curry (*Aradis bil Curry*): Substitute for the chicken, 2 pounds 41/50 count shrimp, peeled and deveined. Preheat 2 tablespoons extra-virgin olive oil in a large pot over medium-high heat and sauté the shrimp, cooking it on all sides until it is opaque and seems halfway cooked. Transfer the shrimp to a large bowl, uncovered. Reserve the pot. Refer to the previous recipe for Chicken Curry. Follow the recipe and procedure for the sauce, condiments, and rice, and serve as directed.

Potato Curry (*Batata bil Curry*): Substitute for the chicken, 2 pounds peeled russet potato, diced into 1-inch cubes. Preheat the oven to 450°F. Mix the potatoes with ¼ cup extra-virgin olive oil, ½ teaspoon salt, and 1 tablespoon curry powder. Spread the potatoes over a foil-lined baking sheet, place on the middle rack of the oven, and roast them, shaking the pan occasionally, for 30 to 45 minutes or until golden brown. Transfer the potatoes to a large bowl, uncovered. Reserve the pot. Refer to the previous recipe for Chicken Curry. Follow the recipe and procedure for the sauce, condiments, and rice, and serve as directed.

Cod Baked in Citrus Tahini

SERVES 6

Tajin (ta-jin)

In this dish, fresh fillet of cod is baked in a citrus-infused tahini sauce with sautéed onions, topped with toasted almonds and pine nuts. The flaky texture and mild flavor of the fish complement the nutty taste of the tahini with citrus. A squeeze of fresh lemon over the individual servings pops the flavor.

Specialty ingredients: Tahini, found in specialty markets or online.

Special equipment: A 9½-inch pie plate.

Prepare ahead: You can prepare this up to 1 day in advance. After baking, cool, then refrigerate covered. For best results, serve slightly warm.

FOR THE FISH

1 pound fresh cod fillet (skinless)

2 tablespoons and ⅓ cup freshly squeezed lemon juice, divided

½ teaspoon and ½ teaspoon and ¾ teaspoon salt, divided

1 cup extra-virgin olive oil

½ cup tahini (mix well before using)

¾ cup freshly squeezed orange juice

⅓ cup water

¼ cup blanched slivered almonds

¼ cup pine nuts

1 tablespoon melted butter

3 cups thinly sliced yellow onion (⅛ inch)

2 tablespoons finely chopped parsley

8 lemon wedges

(**You can substitute** any mild fresh white fillet of fish for the cod.)

To prepare the fish

Rinse the fillets under cold running water, then drain and pat dry. Cut the fillets widthwise into 3- to 4-inch lengths and transfer them to a dish. Drizzle 2 tablespoons lemon juice over the fish fillets, then sprinkle with ½ teaspoon salt.

*Preheat the olive oil in a medium-sized skillet over high heat. The oil should be about ¼ inch deep. Reduce the heat to medium-high. Test the oil by lowering one end of the fish in the oil; when it sizzles, place 2 to 3 pieces of fish in the pan and fry 1½ to 2 minutes per side. Make certain the fish is cooked through but still moist before removing. (The thickness of the fillet may require more or less frying time.) Remove with a slotted spoon to a paper towel–lined dish. Fry the remaining pieces of fish. (**Alternatively**, the fillets can be baked in a preheated 450°F oven for 8 to 10 minutes or until cooked through.)*

Check the pieces of fish and remove any small bones. Set the fish aside, loosely covered with foil. Drain and reserve the oil from the skillet. Reserve the skillet.

To prepare the cod baked in citrus tahini

Combine the tahini, ⅓ cup lemon juice, the orange juice, water, and ½ teaspoon salt in a bowl. Use an electric mixer or whisk to beat until smooth, like the consistency of thin pancake batter. Set it aside.

Preheat the oven to 350°F. Spread the almonds and pine nuts over a foil-lined baking sheet and toast in the center of the oven, shaking the pan occasionally, for 5 to 7 minutes or until golden brown. Remove the tray from the oven. Mix the melted butter with the nuts. Transfer them to a paper towel–lined dish. Set aside to cool.

Lightly brush the sides and bottom of a 9½-inch pie plate with some of the reserved oil and set it aside.

Preheat the skillet with ¼ cup of the reserved oil over medium-high heat. Add the onions and ¾ teaspoon salt. Reduce the heat to medium and cook until the onions are limp and tender (if they begin to brown, reduce the heat). Transfer the onions to the greased pie plate, spreading them evenly over the bottom. Arrange the pieces of fish over the onions. Pour the tahini sauce over the fish and onions. Make sure the sauce gets in between the pieces of fish; use the tines of a fork to gently press the fish under the sauce.

Bake the fish on the middle rack of the 350°F oven for 30 minutes, then set aside uncovered for at least 1 hour prior to serving.

To serve

Scatter toasted pine nuts and almonds over the top of the baked fish and sprinkle chopped parsley around the border. Offer with lemon wedges to squeeze over individual servings. Serve slightly warm or at room temperature.

Fire-Roasted Wheat with Lamb (or Beef)

SERVES 4

Freekeh ma Lahm (free-keh ma lah-him)

Freekeh is green fire-roasted coarse-grained wheat. It is harvested while young so it retains more protein and vitamins than most other grains. Fire-roasting gives it a rich, smoky flavor. It is delicious with lamb, beef, chicken, or vegetarian style, and it is a great alternative to rice, pasta, or potatoes.

Specialty ingredients: Freekeh, found at specialty markets or online.

Prepare ahead: You can prepare this dish up to 2 days in advance. The rich broth continues to tenderize the meat while enhancing the flavor.

FOR THE LAMB (OR BEEF)

2 tablespoons extra-virgin olive oil

2 pounds lean lamb, from the leg, cut into 1½ x 1½-inch pieces

or: 2 pounds beef (top round/London broil)

2 tablespoons freshly squeezed lemon juice

2 cups diced yellow onion (½ inch)

4 teaspoons salt

½ teaspoon coarsely ground black pepper

1 teaspoon ground allspice

½ teaspoon ground cinnamon

⅛ teaspoon ground cloves

1/16 teaspoon ground nutmeg

12 cups boiling water

FOR THE FIRE-ROASTED WHEAT

2 tablespoons extra-virgin olive oil

2 cups freekeh

4½ cups hot reserved broth

2 cups frozen pearl onions

To prepare the lamb (or beef)

Preheat the olive oil in a large pot over medium-high heat. Add the meat and fry until all of the moisture has evaporated and it is evenly browned (caramelized) on all sides. Add the lemon juice, onions, salt, and spices, and sauté for about 1 minute. Add the boiling water, increase the heat to high, and bring the mixture to a rolling boil. Reduce the heat to medium-low, cover, and simmer, stirring occasionally, for 1 hour and 15 minutes. Test the meat with a fork. If it breaks apart easily then it's done; if not, continue to cook until tender. Set aside. Reserve all of the broth.

To prepare the fire-roasted wheat

Preheat the olive oil in a large pot over medium heat. Add the wheat and stir, coating the grains. Add the hot reserved broth and the frozen pearl onions. Increase the heat to high and bring to a rolling boil. Reduce the heat to medium-low, cover, and

simmer 20 to 25 minutes or until the broth has been absorbed. If it seems dry, add a little more broth. Remove from the heat and set aside for 15 minutes before serving.

To serve

Arrange the wheat on a platter and the pieces of meat around the perimeter. Sprinkle some cinnamon over the pieces of meat. Serve with Farmer's Salad (page 55).

{VARIATION}

Fire-Roasted Wheat with Chicken *(Freekeh ma Djeaj)*: For the chicken, follow the recipe and procedure for preparing the chicken in Chicken and Spiced Rice with Toasted Nuts (page 75). Prepare the fire-roasted wheat as described above. Serve as directed above.

Grilled Beef Fingers

7 FINGERS

Kefta Mishwi (kef-ta mish-wee)

I grew up eating this delicious combination of ground beef, parsley, and onions. The traditional shape of kefta is like a hot dog with tapered ends. Growing up, my parents used to shape them into patties and serve them with fried potatoes. That was our version of hamburgers and fries.

Special equipment: A gas grill, (a charcoal or electric grill will do).

Prepare ahead: The fingers can be prepared early in the day, refrigerated covered, and grilled the same day. Or they can be frozen raw for several weeks. Freeze on a plastic-lined baking sheet, then store in an airtight container. Thaw overnight in the refrigerator and grill as directed.

FOR THE FINGERS

1 pound ground beef (80%)

¾ cup minced yellow onion, squeezed dry

½ cup finely chopped flat-leaf parsley, use green leafy parts and tender stems

1 tablespoon balsamic vinegar

1 teaspoon salt

½ teaspoon coarsely ground black pepper

½ teaspoon ground allspice
¼ teaspoon ground cinnamon
⅛ teaspoon ground cloves
¹⁄₁₆ teaspoon ground nutmeg
(**You can substitute** ground lamb for the beef.)

To prepare the fingers

Place all the ingredients in a bowl. Mix well with your hands, using massage-like strokes, working the onions and parsley into the beef.

Divide the mixture into ⅓-cup portions. On a flat surface (I use a plastic cutting board—it has good traction and is easy to clean), roll each portion

into a finger about 6 inches long and tapered at both ends. Cover with plastic and refrigerate until needed. Grill the same day.

To grill the fingers

Preheat the grill on medium-high heat. Grill the fingers for about 3 minutes while rolling them back and forth. Make sure they are cooked through but still moist before removing from the heat. Wrap the fingers in foil, allowing them to steam for 3 to 5 minutes prior to serving. **Note:** *Grilling times vary between grills.*

To serve

Offer with Hummus (page 8), warm pita bread, and Parsley and Bulgur Wheat Salad (page 58).

{VARIATION}

Cut each ⅓-cup portion in half and make 14 cocktail-size fingers. Load them on 3-inch cocktail picks after they are grilled, and offer as a tray-passed appetizer with hummus dip. Alternatively, you can divide the mixture into 4 equal portions for burgers.

Grilled Chicken Kebabs

4 SKEWERS

Sheesh Tawook Mishwi (sheesh ta-wook mish-wee)

This simple marinade infuses chicken with great flavor. The chunks of grilled chicken are so moist and tender. This tasty combination of yogurt, fresh ginger, lemon, and spices will become one of your favorite ways to marinate chicken.

Special equipment: A gas grill (a charcoal or electric grill will do), and 4 (8-inch) metal or bamboo skewers. (I prefer reusable metal skewers.)

Prepare ahead: The marinade can be prepared several days in advance and refrigerated. The chicken skewers can be refrigerated for several hours prior to grilling. Grill the same day, as directed.

FOR THE CHICKEN

¼ cup plain yogurt

1 tablespoon lemon zest

¼ cup freshly squeezed lemon juice

¼ cup minced yellow onion

1 packed tablespoon peeled and grated fresh
   ginger (use the large holes of a grater)

¼ cup ketchup

1 teaspoon salt

¼ teaspoon coarsely ground black pepper

½ teaspoon ground allspice

¼ teaspoon ground cinnamon

1¼ pounds trimmed boneless skinless chicken
   breast, cut into 1½ x 1½-inch pieces (about
   20 pieces)

1 tablespoon apple cider vinegar

8 pieces zucchini, whole round slices ¾ inch
   thick (select narrow zucchini)

1 teaspoon olive oil

To prepare the chicken and zucchini

Combine the first 10 ingredients in a bowl; mix well and set aside. Rinse the chicken in 1 cup cold water with the vinegar to refresh the flavor of the chicken, then drain.

Cut the chicken into 1½ x 1½-inch pieces. Add the chicken to the marinade and mix well. Cover and refrigerate for at least 6 hours or overnight prior to loading them on the skewers.

Cut the zucchini and coat with the oil just before loading the skewers.

Load each skewer by piercing 1 piece of chicken with the skewer followed by a slice of zucchini. Load 3 more pieces of chicken followed by a slice of zucchini, with a final piece of chicken at the end. Pour any remaining marinade over the skewers.

To grill the chicken

Preheat the grill on medium-high heat. Grill for about 3 to 3½ minutes on one side. Flip the skewers and grill an additional 3 to 3½ minutes. Make sure the meat is cooked through but still moist before removing from the heat. Wrap the skewers in foil and allow them to steam for 4 to 6 minutes prior to serving. (If you use disposable wooden skewers, soak them for a couple of hours prior to loading the meat. Make

sure the chicken is close together on the skewer to avoid open spaces on the skewer that may catch fire.) **Note:** *Grilling times vary between grills.*

To serve

Offer the kebabs with Robust Garlic Puree (page 26) and Pita Crouton Salad with Sumak Dressing (page 60) or Garbanzo Bean Salad (page 56).

{VARIATION}

You can use this marinade on split breasts or a whole cut-up chicken.

Grilled Lamb Kebabs

Sheesh Kebab Mishwi (sheesh ka-bob mish-wee)

This marinade is easy to prepare and enhances the flavor of the lamb. The garlic complements the flavor of the meat, while the fresh lemon juice lightens the overall taste. The tender morsels of grilled lamb with tiny specks of grilled garlic surrounding the pieces make this absolutely delicious.

Special equipment: A gas grill, (a charcoal or electric grill will do), 4 (8-inch) bamboo or metal skewers (I prefer reusable metal skewers), and a pestle (a garlic press will do).

Prepare ahead: The lamb skewers can be refrigerated for several hours prior to grilling. Grill the same day, as directed.

FOR THE LAMB

1¼ pounds lean lamb, cut into 1½ × 1½-inch pieces (about 20 pieces)

3 large cloves garlic

½ teaspoon salt

¼ cup grated onion (use the large holes of a grater), squeezed dry

2 tablespoons freshly squeezed lemon juice

1 tablespoon balsamic vinegar

¼ teaspoon coarsely ground black pepper

½ teaspoon ground allspice

¼ teaspoon ground cinnamon

2 small onions, each cut into 4 wedges

(**You can substitute** lean tender beef for the lamb.)

To prepare the lamb

Cut the lamb into 1½ × 1½-inch pieces. In a small bowl, mash the garlic and salt to a pulp using a pestle. Add the lamb and the rest of the ingredients (except the onion wedges) to the bowl. Cover and refrigerate for at least 4 hours prior to loading them on skewers.

Load each skewer by piercing 1 piece of lamb with the skewer followed by an onion. Load 3 more pieces of lamb followed by an onion, with a final piece of lamb at the end.

Pour any remaining marinade over the skewers.

To grill the lamb

Preheat the grill to medium-high heat. Grill for about 3½ to 4 minutes on one side. Flip the skewers and grill an additional 3½ to 4 minutes. Make sure the meat is cooked through but still moist before removing from the heat. Wrap the skewers in foil, allowing them to steam for 4 to 6 minutes prior to serving. (If you use disposable wooden skewers, soak them for a couple of hours prior to loading the meat. Make sure the meat is close together on the skewer to avoid open spaces on the skewer that may catch fire.) **Note**: *Grilling times vary slightly between grills.*

To serve

Offer with Hummus (page 8), warm pita bread, and Cabbage and Beet Salad (page 50).

Grilled Lamb Kebabs

Grilled Lamb Rib Chops

8 RIB CHOPS

Castaleta Mishwi (kess-ta-let-ta mish-wee)

The meat on these grilled rib chops is so tender and delicious, it's like butter. The marinade of balsamic vinegar coupled with fresh lemon, onion, and spices gives the chops great flavor. They are especially appetizing served on a bed of fresh herbs.

Special equipment: A mortar and pestle (a garlic press will do) and a gas grill, (a charcoal or electric grill will do).

Prepare ahead: The rib chops can be marinated early in the day. Cover and refrigerate. Grill the same day as directed.

FOR THE RIB CHOPS

1½ pounds lamb rib rack, cut into 8 rib chops (1-inch-thick chops)

3 large cloves garlic

½ teaspoon salt

½ cup grated yellow onion (use the large holes of a grater), squeezed dry

2 tablespoons freshly squeezed lemon juice

3 tablespoons balsamic vinegar

1 tablespoon spicy mustard

½ teaspoon coarsely ground black pepper

¼ teaspoon ground allspice

⅛ teaspoon ground cinnamon

(**You can substitute** lamb loin chops.)

To prepare the rib chops

Spread the rib chops in a single layer in a flat casserole dish just large enough to hold them. In a mortar or small bowl, mash the garlic and salt to a pulp using a pestle. Add the remaining ingredients and mix well. Rub the marinade over both sides of the rib chops. Cover and refrigerate for several hours. (Flip once while marinating.)

Preheat the grill on medium-high heat. Grill for 1½ to 2 minutes on one side. Flip the rib chops and grill an additional 1½ to 2 minutes for medium-rare. Make sure they are cooked through but still moist before removing from the heat. Wrap the rib chops in foil and allow them to steam for 4 to 6 minutes prior to serving. **Note:** *Grilling times vary between grills.*

To serve

Offer with Basmati Rice with Cumin, Lentils, and Onion (page 135) and Yogurt Cucumber Salad (page 63).

{VARIATION}

Substitute other herbs or spices in the marinade such as chopped parsley, basil, cumin, or thyme.

Grilled Shrimp Kebabs

4 SKEWERS

Sheesh Aradis Mishwi (sheesh array-dis mish-wee)

This light marinade for shrimp is easy to prepare and delicious. The delicate flavor of the fresh cilantro and lemon enhance the succulent taste of the shrimp. Bright and colorful red bell peppers and snow peas add to the subtle flavors. Your guests will enjoy the simple pleasures of shrimp prepared this way.

Special equipment: A gas grill, (a charcoal or electric grill will do), and 4 (8-inch) bamboo or metal skewers. (I prefer 8-inch reusable metal skewers.)
Prepare ahead: The shrimp skewers can be refrigerated for several hours prior to grilling. Grill the same day, as directed.

FOR THE SHRIMP

20 shrimp (16–20 or 21–25 count), peeled and deveined
¼ cup grated yellow onion (use the large holes of a grater), squeezed dry
2 tablespoons finely chopped cilantro
2 teaspoons lemon zest
2 tablespoons freshly squeezed lemon juice
1 tablespoon extra-virgin olive oil
8 blanched snow peas, each about 4 inches long
8 pieces red bell pepper, cut into 1-inch squares

To prepare the shrimp

*Combine the shrimp and the rest of the ingredients in a bowl. (**Note:** Do not add more than 1 tablespoon olive oil, as it may catch fire when grilling, leaving a black residue on the shrimp.) Mix well and refrigerate covered for a couple of hours prior to loading them on the skewers.*

Load each skewer by piercing through the U-shaped back of 1 shrimp, followed by a piece of bell pepper.

Slide these over to the opposite end of the skewer. Pierce another shrimp together with a snow pea wrapped over the back of the shrimp. The skewer will go through the snow pea, then the shrimp, and out the other side, securing the snow pea to the shrimp's back. Add a third shrimp in the center, followed by another shrimp with a snow pea wrap, followed by a piece of bell pepper, and a final shrimp at the end. Pour any remaining marinade over the skewers.

To grill the shrimp

Preheat the grill on medium-high heat. Grill for about 1½ to 2 minutes on one side. Flip the skewers and grill an additional 1½ to 2 minutes. Make sure the shrimp are cooked through but still moist before removing them from the heat. Wrap the skewers in foil and allow them to steam for 2 to 4 minutes prior to serving. *(If you use disposable wooden skewers, soak them for a couple of hours prior to loading the shrimp. Make sure the shrimp are close together on the skewer to avoid open spaces on the skewer that may catch fire.)* **Note:** *Grilling times vary between grills.*

To serve

Offer with Basmati Rice with Green Onions (page 134) and Garbanzo Bean Salad (page 56), or with Lemon-Garlic Potato Salad (page 57).

{VARIATION}

Substitute other herbs for the cilantro such as dill, chives, or parsley.

Selecting Shrimp

Try not to use shrimp smaller than 21–25 count to the pound, as they tend to dry out. Shrimp that are smaller would be any size above 25. As the number of shrimp increase in amount per pound, they decrease in size.

Grilled Vegetable Kebabs

8 SKEWERS

Sheesh Khoudra Mishwi (sheesh khud-dra mish-wee)

Grilled vegetables are always a great addition at a barbecue or as a side dish with the main meal. The colors are vibrant, and the individual flavors are delicious. They are easy to prepare and complement many meals. Mix and match seasonal vegetables as you like.

Special equipment: A gas grill, (a charcoal or electric grill will do), and 8 (8-inch) bamboo or metal skewers. (I prefer reusable metal skewers.)

Prepare ahead: The vegetable skewers can be refrigerated for several hours prior to grilling. Grill the same day, as directed.

FOR THE VEGETABLES

½ pound peeled carrots, cut into 1 x 1-inch pieces (about 15 pieces)

½ pound green zucchini, cut into 1 x 1-inch pieces (about 15 pieces)

½ pound yellow squash, cut into 1 x 1-inch pieces (about 15 pieces)

½ pound red bell pepper, cut into 1 x 1-inch squares (about 24 pieces)

2 tablespoons finely chopped fresh thyme **or** 1 teaspoon dry thyme

2 tablespoons extra-virgin olive oil

4 small onions, each cut into 4 wedges

To prepare the vegetables

*Place the carrot pieces in a small saucepan over high heat with enough water to cover them. Bring to a boil uncovered for 5 minutes. Drain and place them in a bowl with the other ingredients (except the onion wedges—they may fall apart) and mix well. (**Note:** Do not add more than 2 tablespoons*

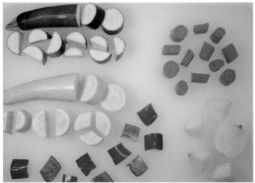

To grill the vegetables

Preheat the grill on medium-high heat. Grill 1½ to 2 minutes on one side. Flip the skewers and grill an additional 1½ to 2 minutes. Remove from the grill and wrap the skewers in foil, allowing them to steam for 3 to 5 minutes prior to serving. (If you use disposable wooden skewers, soak them for a couple of hours prior to loading the vegetables. Make sure the vegetables are close together on the skewer to avoid open spaces on the skewer that may catch fire.) **Note:** *Grilling times vary between grills.*

To serve

Offer the kebabs with grilled meats, fish, or any of your favorite dishes. You can also grill the vegetables in a grill basket and serve them as a side dish.

olive oil, as it may catch fire when grilling, leaving a black residue on the vegetables.) Cover and refrigerate for several hours prior to loading them on the skewers. Store the onions separately until ready to load the skewers.

Load the vegetables on the skewers, mixing the colors for contrast.

Jute Mallow and Garlic-Cilantro Stew with Lamb (or Beef)

SERVES 6

Mloukhiyeh bi Lahm (mloo-khee-yee bee lah-him)

My parents had a sunny spot in the yard where these jute plants (mloukhiyeh) grew in the summer. After they were cut, rinsed, and all the water had dried, we would carefully pick the leaves off the stem. My mother would chop them and prepare this exceptional dish of jute mallow steamed with fresh garlic and cilantro in a rich broth, offered with tender chunks of seasoned lamb, red onions, toasted pita, and aromatic basmati rice.

Specialty ingredients: Frozen chopped (not whole leaf) mloukhiyeh (also known as jute or Jew's mallow), found at specialty markets or online.

Special equipment: A mortar and pestle (a garlic press will do).

Prepare ahead: This dish can be prepared up to 2 days in advance. Refrigerate all the ingredients separately (except the pita chips) until needed. Heat and serve as directed. Prepare the onion topping the same day you are using it.

FOR THE LAMB (OR BEEF)

Follow the recipe for lamb (or beef) as prepared for the Lamb (or Beef) with Spiced Rice and Toasted Nuts (page 77).

FOR THE JUTE MALLOW STEW

4 cups reserved broth

2 (14-ounce) packages frozen chopped mloukhiyeh

¼ cup garlic cloves with ½ teaspoon salt, mashed

2 tablespoons butter

1 teaspoon ground coriander

½ cup finely chopped cilantro; use green leafy parts and tender stems

3 tablespoons freshly squeezed lemon juice

FOR THE RICE

1½ recipes plain Basmati Rice (page 132).

FOR THE PITA CHIPS

2 large pita breads (about 10 inches diameter)

or: 4 medium pita breads (about 6 inches diameter)

FOR THE ONION TOPPING

2 cups diced red onion (¼ inch)

1 cup diced yellow onion (¼ inch)

½ teaspoon salt

½ cup red wine vinegar

2 tablespoons apple cider vinegar

To prepare the lamb (or beef)

Follow the procedure for lamb (or beef) as prepared for the Lamb (or Beef) with Spiced Rice and Toasted Nuts (page 77). Set aside until needed.

To prepare the jute mallow stew

Place 4 cups of reserved broth and the frozen mloukhiyeh in a large pot over medium heat, uncovered. Slowly melt the mloukhiyeh into the broth, stirring occasionally.

Mash the garlic to a pulp with the salt using a mortar and pestle. Melt the butter in a separate small skillet over medium heat. Add the garlic pulp and sauté until the garlic begins to sizzle (not brown). Remove from the heat.

Add the ground coriander to the skillet. Mix well with the garlic and add them to the mloukhiyeh stew, followed by the cilantro and lemon juice. Continue to cook the stew over medium heat, uncovered, stirring frequently, for about 5 minutes, or until the mloukhiyeh has melted and it begins to bubble around the edges. If it begins to boil, slightly reduce the heat. Small bubbles of foam will rise to the surface. Skim as much of this off as possible to reduce the viscosity of the stew. Remove the stew from the heat and set aside uncovered (it will retain a greener color uncovered).

To prepare the rice

Follow the recipe and the procedure to prepare the plain Basmati Rice (page 132). Set it aside until needed.

To prepare the pita chips

Cut the pitas into 1-inch squares (about 4 cups). **Do not** separate the pita halves.

Preheat the oven to 350°F. Spread the pita squares over a foil-lined baking sheet and bake in the center of the oven, shaking the tray occasionally, for 18 to 20 minutes, or until golden brown. (Keep in mind that different brands of pita vary in thickness; therefore the baking time can vary.) Test a couple to make sure they are crisp. Transfer them to an airtight container. Cool completely before covering.

To prepare the onion topping
Combine all the ingredients. Mix well and serve the same day.

To serve
Place the warm mloukhiyeh stew in a bowl. Place the warm meat with some broth in a shallow platter and sprinkle with cinnamon. Place the warm rice on a separate platter. Put the toasted pita chips and onion topping in separate serving dishes.

Provide shallow soup dishes for your guests to layer their individual plates. Traditionally, the pita chips go on the bottom of the dish, followed by some rice and pieces of meat. Pour some jute mallow stew over that and top with the vinegar and onion.

> ## Cooking jute mallow
>
> This green leafy vegetable is like okra in that it has viscous properties. Remove as much of the foam that forms on top while it is cooking to reduce the viscosity.

{VARIATION}

Jute Mallow and Garlic-Cilantro Stew with Chicken (*Mloukhiyeh bi Djeaj*): Substitute chicken for the lamb (or beef), following the recipe and procedure for preparing the chicken in Chicken and Spiced Rice with Toasted Nuts (page 75). The rest of the recipe and procedure for the jute mallow stew, rice, pita chips, and onion topping remain the same as described in the recipe above. Serve as directed above.

Kibbi Balls in Cilantro Yogurt

1 DOZEN

Kibbi Labaniyeh (kib-bee leb-ban-nee-yee)

The layering of flavors in this dish will intrigue you. It is so versatile that it can be served as a soup, as a starter to a meal, or as part of a buffet. What makes this taste so delicious is the duet of flavors created by the cilantro-laced garlic yogurt and the enticing onion, red bell pepper, sumak, and walnut filling in the kibbi balls.

Specialty ingredients: Tahini, found at specialty markets or online. Some specialty markets sell pre-made kibbi balls. They should be raw or steamed and frozen.

Special equipment: A mortar and pestle (a garlic press will do).

Prepare ahead: This dish can be prepared up to 2 days in advance and refrigerated. You can prepare the raw kibbi balls days to weeks in advance and freeze them until needed. Cook them directly from the freezer as described below.

FOR THE KIBBI BALLS
1 dozen Lamb Kibbi Balls, using filling #2 (see recipe on page 24)
Yogurt sauce, as prepared to accompany Beef Tortellini in Cilantro Yogurt (see page 68)

To prepare the kibbi balls

Follow the recipe and the procedure to prepare the Lamb Kibbi Balls on pages 24–26. Once the kibbi has been prepared (using lamb, beef, or chicken), follow the procedure to open, fill, and close the kibbi balls, using filling #2. You do not need to fry them for this recipe. You only need 1 dozen for this recipe.

To prepare the yogurt sauce

Follow the recipe and the procedure to prepare the yogurt sauce on page 68. Cook the yogurt sauce as directed, adding raw or frozen kibbi balls to the sauce instead of tortellini.

When reheating to serve, if the yogurt sauce seems thick, use milk to thin it out. The consistency should be like a light cream soup.

To serve

Place the yogurt sauce with kibbi balls in a shallow serving bowl and garnish with lemon twists and sprigs of fresh cilantro. Serve with Basmati Rice with Toasted Noodles (page 134).

{VARIATION}

You can substitute fresh mint for the cilantro in the sauce.

Kibbi Balls in Garbanzo-Tahini Sauce

1 DOZEN

Kibbi Arnabiyeh (kib-bee ar-na-bee-yee)

The nutty flavor of the citrus-infused tahini sauce combined with tender steamed onions and garbanzo beans makes for a unique taste sensation. The delicately flavored kibbi balls filled with minced meat and pine nuts sautéed with the creamy garbanzo-tahini sauce will have you coming back for more.

Specialty ingredients: Tahini, found at specialty markets or online.

Prepare ahead: This dish can be prepared up to 2 days in advance and refrigerated. You can prepare the raw kibbi balls days to weeks in advance and freeze them until needed. Cook them directly from the freezer as described below.

FOR THE KIBBI BALLS

1 dozen Lamb Kibbi Balls, using filling #1
   (recipe on page 24)

FOR THE GARBANZO-TAHINI SAUCE

2 tablespoons extra-virgin olive oil
3 cups sliced yellow onion (¼-inch)
1¾ teaspoons salt
3 cups boiling water
1 cup tahini (mix well before using)
¾ cup freshly squeezed grapefruit juice
¼ cup freshly squeezed orange juice
3 tablespoons freshly squeezed lemon juice
1 cup canned garbanzo beans, drained

For the kibbi balls

Follow the recipe and the procedure to prepare the Lamb Kibbi Balls as on pages 24–26 (using lamb, beef, or chicken). Once the kibbi has been prepared, follow the procedure to open, fill, and close the kibbi balls, using filling #1. You do not need to fry them for this recipe. You only need 1 dozen for this recipe.

To prepare the garbanzo-tahini sauce

Preheat the olive oil in a large pot over medium-high heat. Add the onions and salt, reduce the heat to medium, and cook the onions until they are tender but not browned. Add the boiling water, tahini, and the citrus juices. Use a whisk to blend the mixture until it is smooth and creamy.

Add the garbanzo beans, increase the heat to high, and bring the tahini sauce to a boil. Add the kibbi balls and return the mixture to a boil, then reduce the heat to medium-high and cook uncovered for 5 to 7 minutes, gently stirring the mixture from time to time using a flat-edged, heat-proof spatula.

Remove the sauce from the heat and set aside for 15 to 20 minutes, allowing the tahini to cool a bit prior to serving. The consistency should be like a thick cream soup. You can thin the mixture by adding more lemon juice or water.

To serve

Serve slightly warm with Basmati Rice with Toasted Noodles (page 134) and Pita Crouton Salad with Sumak Dressing (page 60).

Lamb (or Beef, or Chicken) Kibbi Tray

ONE 9-INCH TRAY (4 SERVINGS)

Kibbi bi Saniyeh (kib-bee bee sa-nee-yee)

Kibbi is a mixture of spiced meat, onion, and bulgur wheat ground together and made into a variety of shapes and sizes. The most common forms are kibbi bi saniyeh, *which is traditionally baked in a round tray and served in wedges, and* kibbi kebab, *(page 24) kibbi balls. As children, we would devour kibbi balls with ketchup. Traditionally, kibbi is served with Yogurt Cucumber Salad (page 63) or Cabbage and Beet Salad (page 50). That's not to say there aren't other ways to enjoy kibbi, as we still do with ketchup and fries.*

Specialty ingredients: Bulgur wheat #1 (fine), found in specialty markets or online.

Special equipment: A meat grinder and an 9-inch round cake pan that is 2 inches deep.

Prepare ahead: The kibbi tray can be prepared and frozen raw for several weeks in airtight plastic. Bake as directed without thawing. Baked trays can be refrigerated for several days or frozen for several weeks. Reheat thawed trays at 350°F for 15 to 20 minutes. **Note:** The bulgur must soak overnight.

FOR THE KIBBI

1¼ cups bulgur wheat #1 fine (soak overnight)

1½ teaspoons salt

¼ teaspoon coarsely ground black pepper

½ teaspoon ground allspice

¼ teaspoon ground cinnamon

½ pound lean lamb (from the leg), cut into 1-inch pieces

¾ cup diced yellow onion (½ inch)

⅓ cup extra-virgin olive oil

(You can substitute beef [top round London broil] or boneless/skinless chicken breast in place of the lamb.)

FOR THE KIBBI FILLING

1½ tablespoons toasted pine nuts

½ tablespoon melted butter

1 tablespoon extra-virgin olive oil

¼ pound ground lamb

¾ cup diced yellow onion (¼ inch)

½ teaspoon salt

⅛ teaspoon coarsely ground black pepper

¼ teaspoon ground allspice

⅛ teaspoon ground cinnamon

(You can substitute ground beef or chicken for the ground lamb.)

To prepare the kibbi (soak overnight)

Combine the bulgur with 1 cup water in a bowl. Stir well. Cover the bowl with plastic wrap, sealing it around the edges. Refrigerate overnight to allow the bulgur to expand. (This will make it easier to work with once it is ground.)

To prepare the kibbi filling

Preheat the oven to 350°F. Spread the pine nuts over a foil-lined baking sheet and toast in the center of the oven, shaking the tray occasionally, for 5 to 7 minutes or until golden brown. Mix the melted butter with the nuts. Transfer to a paper towel–lined dish. Set aside.

Preheat the olive oil in a small skillet over medium-high heat. Add the ground meat and cook, breaking it into small, minced pieces. Once the meat is no longer pink, reduce the heat to medium-low and stir in the onions, salt, and spices. Sauté until the onions are tender, then set aside to cool.

To prepare the kibbi (the following day)
Remove the soaked bulgur from the refrigerator and set it aside. Combine the salt, pepper, allspice, and cinnamon in a bowl. Pass the meat and onion (mixed together) through a meat grinder fitted with a fine-cutting plate, and add to the bowl with the seasonings. Mix well.

Add the soaked bulgur to the seasoned meat mixture. Using massage-like strokes, work the bulgur into the meat until it is evenly combined. Pass the mixture through the same meat grinder fitted with the fine-cutting plate, and once again use massage-like strokes to combine the ground mixture. Shape it into a ball and set it aside.

To prepare the kibbi tray
Grease the sides and bottom of a 9-inch round cake pan that is 2 inches deep with some olive oil and set it aside.

Set a small bowl of cold water within reach. Cut the ball of kibbi in half. Between 2 pieces of plastic wrap, roll one half of the kibbi into a 9-inch circle. Flip it into the bottom of the pan. Dip your fingers in the water and gently press and smooth the kibbi, distributing it evenly along the bottom of the pan.

Place the filling over the kibbi. Use the tines of a fork to evenly distribute the filling up to, but not touching, the sides of the pan. Distribute the pine nuts over the filling. Roll the other half of the kibbi the same way and place it in the pan over the filling. Dip your hand in the water and press down, firmly securing the filling in the center and allowing any air pockets to escape. Use your fingers to smooth out the kibbi evenly until the surface is level.

Preheat the oven to 400°F. Dip the tip of a butter knife into the water and cut the pan of kibbi into four wedges. Score the top of each wedge, making a pattern of squares or diamonds. Dip the tip of the knife in the water and re-cut the kibbi into wedges, (this will allow the oil to seep in between the wedges prior to baking).

Insert the tip of the knife around the rim of the pan, loosening the kibbi from the sides. Pour ⅓ cup olive oil over the top of the kibbi and rotate the pan, *evenly distributing the oil over the top and down the sides.*

Place the pan on the middle rack in the oven and bake 35 to 40 minutes or until the kibbi is browned around the edges, then remove from the oven and set aside to cool for 10 minutes.

To serve

Offer the kibbi warm, using each wedge as a serving. Alternatively, cut each wedge into 2 or 3 pieces. Offer with Cabbage and Beet Salad (recipe on page 50) or Yogurt Cucumber Salad (page 63).

Preparing kibbi

It is important to get the moisture-to-bulgur ratio correct. Sometimes you may have to toss in a little extra bulgur if the kibbi mixture seems too damp, and at other times you may need to dip your hands in water to introduce additional moisture.

Several recipes for kibbi recommend using a food processor to prepare the kibbi. I have not had good results using that method. I find it does not grind the bulgur wheat the same way a meat grinder does.

Pumpkin Kibbi Tray

ONE 9-INCH TRAY (4 SERVINGS)

Kibbi bi Saniyeh Luctine (kib-bee bee sa-nee-yee luck-teen)

Traditionally kibbi trays are prepared from lamb, beef, or chicken (see the previous recipe). This recipe provides you with an excellent alternative that truly delivers taste and flavor. Whenever I serve this variety of kibbi, my friends and family are always surprised to learn that it is vegetarian.

Specialty ingredients: Bulgur wheat #1 fine, and dibs ruman, both found in specialty markets or online.

Special equipment: A food processor, a meat grinder, and one 9-inch round cake pan that is 2 inches deep.

Prepare ahead: The tray can be prepared and frozen raw for several weeks in plastic wrap. Bake as directed without thawing. Baked trays can be refrigerated for several days or frozen for several weeks. Reheat thawed trays at 350°F for 15 to 20 minutes. **Note:** The kibbi must soak overnight to allow the bulgur to expand.

FOR THE KIBBI

1¼ cups diced yellow onion (½ inch)
1 (15-ounce) can 100% pure pumpkin puree
1½ cups bulgur wheat, #1 fine
⅓ cup all-purpose flour
1¼ teaspoons salt
½ teaspoon coarsely ground black pepper
½ teaspoon ground allspice
¼ teaspoon ground cinnamon
⅓ cup of extra-virgin olive oil

FOR THE FILLING

2 tablespoons extra-virgin olive oil
3 cups lightly packed sliced yellow onion (¼ inch)
½ cup coarsely chopped walnuts

¾ teaspoon salt
¼ teaspoon coarsely ground black pepper
1 tablespoon freshly squeezed lemon juice
2 tablespoons dibs ruman

To prepare the pumpkin kibbi (soak overnight)

Place the onion in a food processor fitted with a metal blade and process to a pulp. Combine the onion pulp in a bowl with the pumpkin, bulgur, flour, salt, and spices. Mix well, then pat down the kibbi mixture. Cover the bowl with plastic wrap, sealing it around the edges, and refrigerate overnight (this will allow the bulgur to absorb the moisture).

To prepare the filling

Preheat the olive oil in a large skillet over high heat. Add the onions, walnuts, salt, pepper, and lemon juice, and stir well. Reduce the heat to medium-low and cook until the onions are limp and tender, then remove from the heat. Stir in the dibs ruman. Cool the filling before using.

To prepare the kibbi tray (the following day)

Remove the pumpkin kibbi mixture from the refrigerator and pass it through a meat grinder fitted with a fine-cutting plate. Shape the mixture into a ball. Grease the sides and bottom of a 9-inch round cake pan that is 2 inches deep with olive oil and set aside.

Set a small bowl of cold water within reach. Cut the ball of kibbi in half. Between 2 pieces of plastic wrap, roll one half into a 9-inch circle and flip it into the bottom of the pan. Dip one hand in the water and gently press and smooth the kibbi, distributing it evenly along the bottom of the pan. Add the filling to the pan. Use the tines of a fork to distribute the filling up to, but not touching, the sides of the pan. Roll the other half of the kibbi the same way and place it in the pan over the filling. Dip your hand in the water and press down, firmly securing the filling in the center and allowing any air pockets to escape. Use your fingers to smooth out the kibbi evenly until the surface is level.

Preheat the oven to 400°F. See the photos on page 101 for cutting and scoring the kibbi. Dip the tip of a butter knife into the water and cut the pan of kibbi into four wedges. Score the top of each wedge, making a pattern of squares or diamonds. Dip the tip of the knife in the water and re-cut the kibbi into wedges (this will allow the oil to seep in between the wedges prior to baking).

Insert the tip of the knife around the rim of the pan, loosening the kibbi from the sides. Pour ⅓ cup olive oil over the top of the kibbi and rotate the pan, evenly distributing the oil over the top and down the sides.

Place on the middle rack in the oven and bake the kibbi 35 to 40 minutes or until golden around the edges, then remove from the oven and set aside to cool for 30 minutes.

To serve

Offer slightly warm or at room temperature, using each wedge as a serving. Alternatively, cut each wedge into 2 or 3 pieces. Serve with Pita Crouton Salad with Sumak Dressing (page 60).

Fish Kibbi Tray

ONE 9-INCH TRAY

Kibbi bi Saniyeh Samak (kib-bee bee-sa-nee-yee sem-mek)

This unique and delicious kibbi tray differs from the meat and pumpkin variety (see the previous two recipes), in that it has only one layer of kibbi over the filling. Usually kibbi trays consist of two layers of kibbi with the filling in the center. The traditional way of making this variety is to layer the filling on the bottom of the tray with one layer of kibbi on top. I believe the intricate flavors found in this kibbi tray will delight your taste buds.

Specialty ingredients: Bulgur wheat #1 fine.
Special equipment: A meat grinder and a 9-inch round cake pan.
Prepare ahead: You can bake the kibbi fish tray in advance and refrigerate it covered for several days. Serve slightly warm. **Note:** The bulgar must soak overnight.

FOR THE KIBBI
1 cup bulgur wheat #1 fine (soak overnight)

½ pound fresh (or previously frozen) cod fillet, cut into 1-inch pieces (pat dry with paper towel)

1 teaspoon salt

¼ teaspoon coarsely ground black pepper

¼ cup flour

½ cup diced yellow onion (½ inch)

¼ cup finely chopped cilantro

1 tablespoon orange zest

1 tablespoon lemon zest

¼ cup extra-virgin olive oil

FOR THE FILLING

2 tablespoons extra-virgin olive oil

3 cups lightly packed sliced yellow onion (¼ inch)

½ cup coarsely chopped walnuts

¾ teaspoon salt

¼ teaspoon coarsely ground black pepper

½ teaspoon ground coriander

2 tablespoons freshly squeezed orange juice

2 tablespoons freshly squeezed lemon juice

¼ cup coarsely chopped cilantro; use green leafy parts and tender stems

To prepare the kibbi (soak overnight)

Combine the bulgur with ½ cup water in a bowl. Stir well. Cover the bowl with plastic wrap, sealing it around the edges. Refrigerate overnight to allow the bulgur to expand.

To prepare the filling

Preheat the olive oil in a large skillet over medium-high heat. Add the onions, walnuts, salt, pepper, and coriander, and stir well. Reduce the heat to medium-low and cook until the onions are limp and tender. Add the citrus juices and the cilantro and cook until the liquid is absorbed. Remove from the heat and set aside.

To prepare the kibbi tray (the following day)

Remove the soaked bulgur from the refrigerator and set it aside. Combine the salt, pepper, flour, and both zests in a mixing bowl. Pass the fish, onion, and cilantro (mixed together) through a meat grinder fitted with a fine-cutting plate into the bowl and mix well. Add the soaked bulgur and ¼ cup cold water. Using massage-like strokes, work the bulgur into the fish until it is evenly combined. Pass the mixture through the same meat grinder fitted with the fine-cutting plate, and once again use massage-like strokes to combine the ground mixture. Shape it into a ball and set it aside.

Preheat the oven to 400°F. Grease the sides and bottom of a 9-inch round cake pan with some olive oil. Evenly distribute the filling over the bottom of the pan and set it aside.

Set a small bowl of cold water within reach. Between 2 pieces of plastic wrap, roll the kibbi ball into a 9-inch circle. Flip it over the filling. Dip your hand in the water and gently press the kibbi, distributing it evenly until the surface is smooth and even. Cut and score the kibbi, following the procedure for kibbi trays on page 101. Pour ¼ cup olive oil over the top of the kibbi and rotate the pan, evenly distributing the oil over the top and down the sides.

Place on the middle rack in the oven and bake for 30 to 35 minutes or until golden brown around the edges, then remove from the oven and set aside to cool for 30 minutes.

To serve

Offer slightly warm or at room temperature with a salad of your choice.

Layereɒ Lonɒon Broil with Garlic Yogurt anɒ Pita

SERVES 4

Fatteh ma Lahm (fet-tee ma lah-him)

This dish is composed of several layers. It begins with toasted pita chips followed by tender morsels of London broil with garbanzo beans and onions. Garlic yogurt is next, followed by toasted pine nuts on top. While the individual layers can be prepared in advance, this dish needs to be assembled just before serving.

Specialty ingredients: Clarified butter (see page 196) and tahini, found in specialty markets or online.

Special equipment: A pestle (a garlic press will do).

Prepare ahead: Prepare clarified butter in advance as described on page 196. You can prepare this dish up to 2 days in advance. Refrigerate the garbanzo, onion, and London broil mixture and the garlic yogurt sauce. The other items do not need refrigeration. Keep all the items separate and covered. Serve as directed.

FOR THE LONDON BROIL

2 tablespoons extra-virgin olive oil

1 pound lean top round London broil, cut into 1-inch pieces

1 tablespoon freshly squeezed lemon juice

1 cup diced yellow onion (½ inch)

1½ teaspoons salt

¼ teaspoon coarsely ground black pepper

½ teaspoon ground allspice

½ teaspoon ground cinnamon

⅛ teaspoon ground cloves

¹⁄₁₆ teaspoon ground nutmeg

5 cups boiling water

(**You can substitute** lean lamb from the leg or lamb shanks for the beef.)

FOR THE PITA CROUTONS

1½ large pita breads (about 10 inches diameter)

or: 3 medium pita breads (about 6 inches diameter)

2 tablespoons melted clarified butter

FOR THE PINE NUTS

⅓ cup toasted pine nuts

3 tablespoons melted clarified butter

½ cup fresh pomegranate seeds, when in season

FOR THE GARBANZO BEANS AND ONIONS

¼ cup extra-virgin olive oil

4 cups diced yellow onion (¼ inch)

1 teaspoon salt

¼ teaspoon coarsely ground black pepper

½ teaspoon allspice

¼ teaspoon cinnamon

1 (15- or 16-ounce can) garbanzo beans, drained

FOR THE GARLIC-YOGURT SAUCE

2 large cloves garlic

1 teaspoon salt

2 cups plain yogurt (regular, reduced-fat, or fat-free)

1 teaspoon tahini (optional)

To prepare the London broil

Preheat the olive oil in a large pot over medium-high heat. Add the meat and cook until all of the moisture has evaporated and it is evenly browned (caramelized) on all sides. Add the lemon juice, onions, salt, and spices, and sauté for about 1 minute, then add the boiling water. Bring the mixture to a rolling boil, then reduce the heat to medium-low, cover, and simmer, stirring occasionally. After 1 hour and 15 minutes test the meat with a fork. If it breaks apart easily, then it is done; if not, continue to cook until tender. Remove the pieces of meat and onion to a dish, cover, and set aside. Reserve ½ cup broth for later use.

To prepare the pita croutons

Preheat the oven to 350°F. Cut the pitas cut into 1-inch squares (do not separate the pita halves). Spread the croutons over a foil-lined baking sheet and bake in the center of the oven, shaking the tray occasionally, for 20 to 25 minutes or until they are golden brown. Test a couple of the croutons to make sure they are crisp. Pour the melted clarified butter over them and mix well. Set them aside on the baking sheet.

To prepare the pine nuts

Preheat the oven to 350°F. Spread the pine nuts over a foil-lined baking sheet and toast in the center of the oven, shaking the tray occasionally, for 5 to 7 minutes or until they are golden brown, then transfer them to a small microwavable bowl. Add the melted clarified butter. Set aside.

To prepare the garbanzo beans and onions

Preheat the olive oil in a large skillet over medium-high heat. Add the onions, salt, and spices, and mix well. Add the garbanzo beans. Reduce the heat to medium and cook, uncovered, until the onions are tender. Add the ½ cup reserved broth and the pieces

of meat and onion. Increase the heat to high and cook for about a minute or until most of the liquid is absorbed. Remove from the heat, cover, and set aside.

To prepare the garlic-yogurt sauce
In a bowl, mash the garlic and salt to a pulp using a pestle. Stir in the yogurt and tahini. Refrigerate until needed. Bring to room temperature before using.

To serve
Heat the garbanzo, onion, and meat mixture. Warm the toasted pita croutons in the oven.

Spread the warm pita croutons over the bottom of a flat dish or platter. Pour the heated garbanzo, onion, and meat mixture over the pita layer, then spoon the room-temperature garlic-yogurt sauce over the meat layer. Reheat the butter and pine nut mixture and drizzle it over the yogurt. Sprinkle pomegranate seeds over the top, when in season (October through January). Serve at once.

{VARIATION}
You can omit the London broil and serve this dish without meat. Just double the recipe for the garbanzo beans and onions. You can also substitute chicken for the London broil as described in the next recipe.

Layered Chicken with Garlic Yogurt and Pita
SERVES 4

Fatteh ma Djeaj (fet-tee maa djeaj)

Specialty ingredients: Clarified butter (see page 196) and tahini, found in specialty markets or online.

Special equipment: A pestle (a garlic press will do).

Prepare ahead: Prepare clarified butter in advance as described on page 196. You can prepare this dish up to 2 days in advance. Refrigerate the garbanzo, onion, and chicken mixture and the garlic yogurt sauce. The other items do not need refrigeration. Keep all the items separate and covered. Serve as directed.

FOR THE CHICKEN

1 whole chicken (about 4½ pounds)
2 tablespoons cider vinegar
1 tablespoon salt
1 cup diced yellow onion (1 inch)
1 rib celery, cut into 2-inch lengths
1 (3- to 4-inch) stick cinnamon
½ teaspoon whole black peppercorns
1 teaspoon whole allspice berries
1 bay leaf

FOR THE PITA CROUTONS, PINE NUTS, GARBANZO BEANS AND ONIONS, AND YOGURT SAUCE

Follow the previous recipe for Layered London Broil with Garlic Yogurt and Pita (see page 105).

To prepare the chicken

Rinse the chicken in a large pot with 6 cups water and the vinegar to refresh the flavor of the chicken. Drain the water. Place the back side of the chicken facing down in the same large pot. Add 10 cups of water and the salt, place over high heat, and bring to a rolling boil, uncovered. Skim all the foam from the top. Add the rest of the ingredients for the chicken to the pot, and return to a boil. Reduce the heat to medium, cover, and simmer, stirring occasionally to ensure the chicken does not stick, for 45 minutes.

Remove from the heat and transfer the chicken to a tray to cool, uncovered, for 30 minutes. Reserve ½ cup of the broth.

When the chicken has cooled, remove all the skin and bones. Pull the chicken into bite-sized pieces, cover, and set aside until needed.

To prepare the pita croutons, pine nuts, garbanzo and onion, and yogurt sauce

Follow the procedure for Layered London Broil with Garlic Yogurt and Pita as described in the previous recipe.

To serve

Offer as described for Layered London Broil with Garlic Yogurt and Pita in the previous recipe.

Lebanese Caraway Couscous with Chicken

SERVES 4

Moughrabiyeh ma Djeaj (mough-ra-bee-yee ma djeaj)

Lebanese couscous consists of larger dried beads made from flour, salt, and water, like pasta. These flavorful beads are steamed in a rich broth, then mixed with pearl onions and garbanzo beans. Freshly ground caraway and cinnamon complete this dish.

Specialty ingredients: *Moughrabiyeh,* found in specialty markets or online.

Prepare ahead: This dish can be prepared up to 2 days in advance. Refrigerate the items separately until needed. Serve as directed.

FOR THE CHICKEN

3 pounds split chicken breast

2 tablespoons apple cider vinegar

4 teaspoons salt

1 cup diced yellow onion (1 inch)

1 rib celery (cut into 2-inch lengths)

1 (3- to 4-inch) stick cinnamon

½ teaspoon whole black peppercorns

1 teaspoon whole allspice berries

1 bay leaf

⅛ teaspoon ground cinnamon

⅛ teaspoon each of ground caraway and cinnamon for garnish

(**You can substitute** a 4½ pound whole chicken for the split chicken breast if you want legs and thighs; the procedure remains the same.)

FOR THE GARBANZO BEAN–ONION SAUCE

2 cups diced yellow onion (1 inch)

1½ cups water

¼ teaspoon salt

½ teaspoon and ⅛ teaspoon ground caraway, divided

¼ teaspoon and ⅛ teaspoon ground cinnamon, divided

1 cup frozen pearl onions

1 (15- or 16-ounce) can garbanzo beans, drained

2 cups reserved broth

FOR THE LEBANESE COUSCOUS

2 tablespoons extra-virgin olive oil

1½ cups moughrabiyeh (Lebanese couscous)

¼ teaspoon salt

1½ teaspoon ground caraway

½ teaspoon ground cinnamon

3 cups hot reserved broth

1 tablespoon butter

To prepare the chicken

Rinse the chicken in a large pot with 6 cups water and the vinegar to refresh the flavor of the chicken. Drain the water. Pour 12 cups of water over the chicken (breast meat facing up) and add the salt to the pot. Place over high heat, uncovered. Stir occasionally to ensure the chicken does not stick.

Once it comes to a rolling boil, skim any foam from the top. Add the onion, celery, cinnamon stick, whole peppercorns, whole allspice berries, and the bay leaf to the pot. Return to a boil. Reduce the heat to medium-low, cover, and simmer, stirring occasionally, for 45 minutes. Remove from the heat and transfer the chicken to a flat tray to cool uncovered (about 30 minutes). Pass the broth through a fine-mesh sieve and return it to the pot. Reserve all of the broth.

Peel and discard all the skin and bones from the chicken. Separate each breast lengthwise into 2 or 3 pieces and return them to the broth. (If using whole chicken, separate each leg and thigh as one piece and do not de-bone.) Add ⅛ teaspoon ground cinnamon over the chicken broth. Mix well, cover, and set aside until needed.

To prepare the garbanzo bean–onion sauce

In a medium-sized saucepan over high heat, bring the diced onions, water, salt, ½ teaspoon caraway, and ¼ teaspoon cinnamon to a boil. Reduce the heat to medium-low, cover, and simmer for 30 minutes. Then remove the cover and increase the heat to high, and cook, stirring frequently, until most of the liquid evaporates. Remove from the heat.

Use a whisk to mash the onions to a pulp. Add the pearl onions, garbanzo beans, and 2 cups of the reserved broth to the saucepan. Place over high heat and bring to a boil. Reduce the heat to medium-low, cover, and simmer for 5 minutes, then remove from the heat and add ⅛ teaspoon caraway and ⅛ teaspoon cinnamon. Mix well and set aside until needed.

To prepare the Lebanese couscous

Preheat the olive oil in a large pot over medium-high heat. Add the Lebanese couscous and cook,

stirring constantly, evenly browning the couscous beads. Once the couscous beads begin to turn reddish brown, add the salt, caraway, and cinnamon. Mix well. Add 3 cups of hot reserved broth and the butter.

Increase the heat to high and bring to a boil, then reduce the heat to medium-low, cover, and simmer. After 15 minutes try a few beads to see if they are tender and the broth has been absorbed. If they are not tender and all the broth has been absorbed, add additional broth (¼ cup at a time) and continue to cook until tender. Remove from the heat.

Use a slotted spoon to transfer half of the cooked garbanzo bean and pearl onion mixture from the sauce over the cooked couscous. Gently fold it into the couscous. Cover and set aside for 30 minutes, allowing the flavors to mingle and the couscous to expand.

To serve

Heat the couscous, meat, and garbanzo–onion sauce. Place the couscous on a flat platter and surround it with pieces of meat. Sprinkle ground caraway and cinnamon over the meat. Serve the garbanzo–onion sauce on the side. Serve with a salad of your choice, perhaps Farmer's Salad (page 55).

{VARIATION}

Lebanese Caraway Couscous with Lamb (or Beef) (*Moughrabiyeh ma Lahm*): Prepare the lamb (or beef) as described in the recipe for Lamb (or Beef) with Spiced Rice and Toasted Nuts (page 77). Prepare and serve the garbanzo–onion sauce and couscous as described above for Lebanese Caraway Couscous with Chicken.

Lebanese Meatloaf

SERVES 4

Kefta bil Saniyeh (kef-ta bill sa-nee-yee)

This is an easy and delicious alternative to traditional meatloaf and can be prepared a couple of days in advance. As the meat and potatoes marinate in the sauce, the flavors are enhanced. This recipe comes in handy for a quick Sunday evening dinner.

Special equipment: A 9 x 13 x 2-inch baking dish.

Prepare ahead: You can bake the meatloaf a couple of days in advance. Refrigerate covered. Reheat at 350°F until heated through. Serve as directed.

FOR THE MEATLOAF

2 russet baking potatoes (about ½ pound each), peeled and cut lengthwise into 8 equal spears

3 cups (lightly packed) thinly sliced yellow onion (¼ inch)

2 tablespoons and ½ tablespoon extra-virgin olive oil, divided

½ teaspoon and 1½ teaspoon salt, divided

1½ pounds ground beef (80% lean)

1 cup minced yellow onion

½ cup finely chopped flat-leaf parsley; use green leafy parts and tender stems

2 egg whites

1½ tablespoons balsamic vinegar

¾ teaspoon coarsely ground black pepper

¾ teaspoon ground allspice

¼ teaspoon cinnamon

$^{1}/_{16}$ teaspoon cloves

$^{1}/_{16}$ teaspoon nutmeg

8 ounces frozen peas (about 2 cups)

1 cup peeled and diced tomato (½ inch)

1 (29-ounce) can tomato sauce

(**You can substitute** ground lamb in place of the ground beef.)

111

To prepare the meatloaf

Preheat the oven to 450°F. Place the potato spears, sliced onions, 2 tablespoons olive oil, and ½ teaspoon salt on a foil-lined baking sheet. Mix well and spread evenly over the tray. Roast the potatoes and onions on the middle rack in oven, shaking the pan occasionally, for 25 minutes.

Grease the bottom of a 9 x 13 x 2-inch baking dish with ½ tablespoon olive oil and set it aside. Combine the ground beef, minced onion, parsley, egg whites, vinegar, 1½ teaspoons salt, and spices in a bowl. Mix well. Transfer the meat mixture to the center of the greased baking dish. Shape it lengthwise into a loaf about 3 inches wide and 12 inches long.

Once the potatoes and onions are done, remove them from the oven and set them aside. Reduce the oven temperature to 375°F. Divide half the onions and potatoes on either side of the meatloaf. Sprinkle the frozen peas and the diced tomato over the potato spears. Pour the tomato sauce evenly over the top of the meatloaf and vegetables. Cover the baking dish with aluminum foil and seal it around the edges. Place it on the middle rack of the oven and bake for 45 minutes, then remove the foil (reserve for later use) and continue to bake uncovered for another 15 minutes.

Remove the meatloaf from the oven. Spoon sauce from the sides over the top of the meatloaf and gently mix sauce around the sides of the meatloaf, blending the liquid bottom layer into the thicker upper layer of tomato sauce. Set aside and cover (with the foil) for 15 minutes prior to slicing and serving.

To serve

Transfer the meatloaf to a shallow serving platter and slice into ½-inch slices. Arrange the onion, potato, and pea mixture to either side and garnish with sprigs of fresh parsley. Serve basmati rice on the side (see page 132).

Raisin Couscous with Vegetable Stew

SERVES 6

Couscous ma Khudra (couscous ma khud-dra)

Tiny couscous granules are made from semolina, just like pasta. They are steamed with golden raisins, chopped parsley, and cinnamon. The addition of garbanzo beans completes this light, delicious, and colorful dish. A rich stew of green zucchini, yellow squash, onions, and carrots is offered on the side.

Prepare ahead: You can prepare this up to 2 days in advance and refrigerate. As the vegetables marinate in the sauce, their flavor is enhanced. Serve as directed.

FOR THE COUSCOUS

2⅓ cups couscous

¾ teaspoon and ¼ teaspoon salt, divided

¼ teaspoon and ⅛ teaspoon cinnamon, divided

½ cup golden raisins

Opposite page: Raisin Couscous with Vegetable Stew

¼ cup finely chopped flat-leaf parsley; use
   green leafy parts and tender stems
¼ cup extra-virgin olive oil
2⅓ cups boiling water
1 (15- or 16-ounce can) garbanzo beans, drained

FOR THE STEW

1½ pounds carrots, peeled and cut into
   1 x 1-inch pieces (about 30 pieces)
2 tablespoons extra-virgin olive oil
2½ cups diced yellow onion (¼ inch)
2 teaspoons salt
¼ teaspoon coarsely ground black pepper
½ teaspoon ground allspice
¼ teaspoon ground cinnamon
4 cups boiling water
1½ pounds yellow squash, cut into 1 x 1-inch
   pieces (about 30 pieces)
1½ pounds green zucchini, cut into 1 x 1-inch
   pieces (about 30 pieces)
1 (6-ounce can) tomato paste
2 cups firm peeled and diced red tomatoes
   (½ inch)

To prepare the couscous

*Combine the couscous, ¾ teaspoon salt, ¼ tea-
spoon cinnamon, the raisins, parsley, and olive oil
in a bowl. Mix well. Pour the boiling water over the
mixture and mix well. Cover and set aside.*

*Place the drained garbanzo beans, ¼ teaspoon
salt, ⅛ teaspoon cinnamon, and 1 cup water in a
saucepan over high heat. Bring to a rolling boil and
cook, uncovered, for 2 minutes. Drain the water and
add the beans to the couscous mixture, using your
hands (careful, it's hot) to gently separate the grains
as you mix in the beans. Cover and set aside.*

To prepare the stew

*Place the carrots in a medium saucepan with 3 cups
water over high heat. Bring to a boil and cook, uncovered, for 5 minutes. Drain, cover, and set aside.*

*Preheat the olive oil in a large pot over medium-high
heat. Add the onions, salt, and spices. Cook and stir
for about 2 minutes, uncovered. Add the squash and
zucchini and cook an additional minute or two.*

*Add the boiling water, tomato paste, carrots, and
tomatoes. Stir well, dissolving the tomato paste in
the water, then increase the heat to high. Once the
mixture comes to a rolling boil, reduce the heat to
medium and simmer uncovered for about 4 minutes,
then remove from the heat and set aside for 5 minutes uncovered prior to serving.*

To serve

*Platter the warm couscous and stew separately.
Place a bowl of the stew in the center of a flat platter. Spread the couscous on the platter around the
bowl and serve.*

Selecting squash and zucchini

Choose ones that are firm and narrow with smooth
skin. Avoid thick ones that seem soft, as they may
be porous and full of seeds.

Raisin Couscous with Chicken and Vegetable Stew

SERVES 6

Couscous ma Djeaj (couscous ma djeaj)

Prepare ahead: You can prepare this up to 2 days in advance and refrigerate. As the chicken and vegetables marinate in the sauce, their flavor is enhanced. Serve as directed.

FOR THE CHICKEN

1 recipe Raisin Couscous with Vegetable Stew (see the previous recipe)

2 pounds trimmed boneless skinless chicken breast, cut into 1-inch pieces

1 tablespoon cider vinegar

2 tablespoons extra-virgin olive oil

2 cups diced yellow onion (¼ inch)

2 teaspoons salt

¼ teaspoon coarsely ground black pepper

½ teaspoon ground allspice

¼ teaspoon ground cinnamon

4 cups boiling water

To prepare the chicken

Prepare the Raisin Couscous and Vegetable Stew as described in the previous recipe; set aside.

Rinse the chicken in 1 cup cold water with the vinegar to refresh the flavor of the chicken. Drain and cut into 1-inch pieces.

Preheat the olive oil in a large skillet over medium-high heat. Add the onions, salt, and spices, and sauté for about 2 minutes. Add the chicken and continue to cook. Once the meat is no longer pink, add the boiling water, cover, and cook over medium heat for 15 minutes. Use a slotted spoon to transfer the chicken and onions to the prepared vegetable stew. Discard the chicken broth.

To serve

Serve as described in the previous recipe for Raisin Couscous with Vegetable Stew.

Raisin Couscous with Lamb (or Beef) and Vegetable Stew

SERVES 6

Couscous ma Lahm (couscous ma lah-him)

Prepare ahead: You can prepare this up to 2 days in advance and refrigerate. As the lamb (or beef) and vegetables marinate in the sauce, their flavor is enhanced. Serve as directed.

FOR THE LAMB (OR BEEF)

1 recipe Raisin Couscous with Vegetable Stew (see page 112)

2 tablespoons extra-virgin olive oil

2 pounds lean lamb (from the leg), cut into
   1-inch pieces

or: 2 pounds top round London broil

2 tablespoons freshly squeezed lemon juice

2 cups diced yellow onion (½ inch)

2 teaspoons and 1 teaspoon salt, divided

½ teaspoon coarsely ground black pepper

1 teaspoon ground allspice

½ teaspoon ground cinnamon

⅛ teaspoon ground cloves

1/16 teaspoon ground nutmeg

2 large garlic cloves

10 cups boiling water

To prepare the lamb (or beef)

Prepare the Raisin Couscous and Vegetable Stew as described on page 114; set aside.

Preheat the olive oil in a large pot over medium-high heat. Add the meat and fry until all of the moisture

has evaporated and the meat is evenly browned (caramelized) on all sides. Stir in the lemon juice, onions, 2 teaspoons salt, and spices and sauté for about 1 minute.

Using a mortar and pestle, mash the garlic with 1 teaspoon salt to a pulp, and add it to the mixture. Add the boiling water, increase the heat to high, and bring the mixture to a rolling boil, uncovered. Reduce the heat to medium-low and simmer covered, stirring occasionally, for about 1 hour and 15 minutes. Test the meat with a fork. If it breaks apart easily, then it is done; if not, continue to cook until tender. Use a slotted spoon to transfer the meat and onions to the prepared vegetable stew. Discard the meat broth.

To serve

Serve as described for Raisin Couscous with Chicken and Vegetable Stew (page 115).

Red Snapper with Caramelized Cumin Rice   SERVES 4
Sayadiyeh (sayeh-dee-yee)

The subtle flavors in this recipe are going to surprise you. Moist pieces of red snapper are laid on a bed of rice steamed in a rich broth prepared with caramelized onions and cumin. Toasted almonds and cumin-laced onion sauce complete this dish.

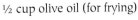

Special equipment: A food processor or a blender.
Prepare ahead: This dish can be prepared 4 to 5 hours in advance. Store loosely covered in a cool dry place. Serve as directed.

FOR THE RED SNAPPER WITH CARAMELIZED CUMIN RICE

1½ pounds fresh red snapper filet, skinless

2 tablespoons freshly squeezed lemon juice

¾ teaspoon and 1 teaspoon and ¼ teaspoon
   salt, divided

½ cup olive oil (for frying)

4 cups sliced yellow onion (⅛ inch)

1½ teaspoons and ⅛ teaspoon ground cumin, divided

4 cups boiling water

1 cup converted (also called parboiled) rice

1 tablespoon butter and 1 tablespoon melted butter, divided

½ cup toasted slivered almonds

(**You may substitute** tilapia, cod, halibut, or any mild-flavored fish.)

To prepare the fish

Rinse the fillets under cold running water, drain, and pat dry. Cut each fillet widthwise into 3- to 4-inch lengths and transfer to a dish. Drizzle lemon juice over the top, then sprinkle with ¾ teaspoon salt.

*Preheat a medium skillet over high heat with the olive oil (or enough oil so that it is about ¼ inch deep). Reduce the heat to medium-high. Test the oil by lowering one end of the fish in the oil; when it sizzles, place 2 to 3 pieces of fish in the pan and fry about 1½ to 2 minutes per side. Make certain the fish is cooked through but still moist before removing. (The thickness of the filets may require more or less frying time.) Remove with a slotted spoon to a dish double-lined with paper towels. Fry the remaining pieces of fish. (**Alternatively**, the fillets can be baked in a preheated oven 450°F for 8–10 minutes or until cooked through.)*

Check the pieces of fish and remove any small bones. Set aside uncovered for 15 minutes, then transfer the pieces of fish to a foil-lined baking sheet. Reserve ½ cup small pieces of fish and set them aside for later use. Loosely drape waxed paper over the fish and set aside in a cool, dry place until needed. Drain and reserve the oil and the skillet.

To prepare the cumin-onion broth

Preheat the same skillet over medium-high heat with ¼ cup of the reserved oil. Add the onions and 1 teaspoon salt, and sauté the onions until they are caramelized and evenly a deep reddish color. Reduce the heat to medium, and stir in the cumin.

Carefully add the boiling water (**caution**: it may splatter) and simmer uncovered for 3 minutes, then drain the mixture through a fine-mesh sieve. Reserve the broth and onions separately.

Place the reserved onions in a food processor or blender, and pulse until coarsely pureed. Set aside.

To prepare the rice and almonds

Preheat 1 tablespoon of the reserved oil in a medium-sized pot over high heat. Add the rice and stir, coating the grains. Add 2½ cups of the reserved broth and bring to a rolling boil. Add 1 tablespoon butter. Reduce the heat to low, cover, and simmer for 15 minutes, or until the liquid has been absorbed.

Remove the rice from the heat, stir in the ½ cup reserved pieces of fish and half of the pureed onions, and set aside covered. After 30 minutes, fluff the rice with a fork and set aside, covered, until needed.

Preheat the oven to 350°F. Spread the almonds over a foil-lined baking sheet and toast in the center of the oven, shaking the pan occasionally, for 5 to 7 minutes or until golden brown. Drizzle 1 tablespoon melted butter over the nuts and mix well. Transfer to a paper towel–lined dish. Set aside to cool.

To prepare the cumin-onion sauce

Place the remaining half of the pureed onions in a small saucepan with 1 cup of water (or left over reserved broth) over high heat and bring to a rolling boil. Remove from the heat and season to taste with about ¼ teaspoon salt and ⅛ teaspoon cumin. Set aside.

To serve

This dish is best offered slightly warm or room temperature. Heat the fish uncovered in the oven at 300°F until warm. Warm the rice over medium heat. Arrange the rice in a shallow serving platter with the fish around the perimeter of the rice. Sprinkle the toasted almonds in the center. Offer the warm cumin-onion broth on the side.

Roast Leg of Lamb
Fakhed Ghannem (fakh-eid ghun-num)

SERVES 6 TO 8

The aroma of herbs and spices that fills the air while this marinated leg of lamb is roasting will entice you to take a bite before it's done. A favorite around the holidays, this makes an excellent centerpiece for any occasion.

Special equipment: A roasting pan and rack, a basting brush, and kitchen twine.

Prepare ahead: You can marinate the leg of lamb 1 day in advance. The leg can be roasted 4 to 5 hours in advance; however, it is best right out of the oven. Serve as directed.

FOR THE LAMB
4 tablespoons finely minced garlic
¾ cup finely minced yellow onion
¼ cup yogurt
1 teaspoon lemon zest
2 tablespoons freshly squeezed lemon juice
2 tablespoons balsamic vinegar
2 tablespoons Dijon mustard
¼ cup ketchup
½ teaspoon table-grind black pepper
½ teaspoon ground allspice
¼ teaspoon ground cinnamon
1 (4–4½-pound) boneless leg of lamb
1 teaspoon and 1 teaspoon kosher salt, divided
Kitchen twine
2 cups boiling water

To prepare the leg of lamb

In a bowl, combine the first 11 ingredients for the marinade. Mix well. Add the leg of lamb and rub the marinade all over the lamb. Cover and refrigerate for at least 6 hours or overnight.

Remove the leg from the refrigerator and let it stand for about ½ hour to allow it to come to room temperature. Add 1 teaspoon of salt, rubbing it evenly over the leg.

Preheat the oven to 450°F. Shape the lamb into a cylinder (fatty side facing up) while tucking any loose pieces in and under the roast. Try to keep the roast uniform in size from one end to the other so it will bake evenly. Use individual pieces of twine to tie around the roast at 2-inch intervals (see "Tying a Roast," page xv). Tighten the twine just enough so it presses firmly against the meat but is not cutting into it.

Place the leg on the rack (fatty side facing up) in the roasting pan. Pour any remaining marinade over the leg and sprinkle the top surface of the meat with

1 teaspoon salt. Add the boiling water to the roasting pan. Tent loosely with foil and place the roast in the center of the oven for 30 minutes. Then remove the pan from the oven and reduce the heat to 300°F. Baste the leg before returning it, again loosely tented with foil, to the oven, for 1 hour more.

After one hour, remove the foil tent, increase the oven temperature to 400°F, and baste the leg of lamb again, then return it to the oven for 10 to 15 minutes to brown.

Remove the pan from the oven and let the roast rest for 10 to 15 minutes before carving, allowing the juices to redistribute. (The leg should be medium-rare at this stage; bake longer for medium to well done.) Strain the sauce.

To serve

Transfer the roast to a shallow serving platter and carve into slices. Surround the roast with fresh sprigs of mint and sliced tomato wedges. Offer the sauce in a dish on the side. Alternatively, surround the lamb with grilled vegetables (page 92).

Roasted Lemon-Garlic Chicken

SERVES 4

Djeaj bil Furrin (djeaj-bill-fur-rin)

This recipe is easy to prepare and delivers a lot of flavor. A combination of fresh lemon juice, garlic, onions, and olive oil set the stage for this dish. The aroma that fills the air as the chicken bakes will captivate your taste buds.

Special equipment: A pestle (a garlic press will do).

Prepare ahead: You can roast the chicken several hours in advance, although it is best right out of the oven. Reheat at 425°F for 15 to 20 minutes or until heated through. **Note:** The chicken should marinate for 2 days for full flavor.

FOR THE CHICKEN

1 whole chicken—about 4½ pounds, cut into
   10 pieces
2 tablespoons apple cider vinegar
5 large cloves garlic
1½ teaspoons salt
¼ cup cloves garlic (cut in half lengthwise)
1 tablespoon lemon zest
½ cup freshly squeezed lemon juice
2 lemons (cut each into 6 wedges)
2 tablespoons extra-virgin olive oil
½ cup grated yellow onion (use the large holes
   of a grater)
¼ teaspoon table-grind black pepper
Lemon wedges, sprigs of parsley, and paprika
   (for garnish)
(**You can substitute** 3 pounds split chicken
   breast if you prefer all white meat. Cut each
   breast in half width-wise).

To prepare the chicken

Cut the chicken into 10 pieces (see "Segmenting Chicken," page xv). In a large bowl, rinse the pieces of chicken in 6 cups cold water with the vinegar to refresh the flavor of the chicken. Drain and set aside.

Place the 5 large cloves of garlic in the same large bowl with the salt, and use a pestle to mash it to a pulp. Add the remaining ingredients (not the garnish) and mix well. Add the chicken and fully coat the pieces. Cover and refrigerate for 2 days (after the first day, stir the mixture and transfer the pieces on top to the bottom to evenly marinate).

Preheat the oven to 450°F. Place the pieces of chicken, skin-side up, in an ovenproof baking dish just large enough to hold them. Place the legs and thighs toward the outer edge of the dish and the breasts and wings toward the center. Wedge the pieces of lemon and garlic between the pieces of chicken. Pour the remaining marinade over the top. Bake on the middle rack of the oven for 40 to 45 minutes, basting the chicken a couple of times.

To brown the chicken, place under the broiler until golden brown. Keep a watchful eye, as it will brown quickly under the broiler. Remove from the oven and let stand for 10 minutes prior to serving.

To serve

Garnish with fresh lemon wedges and sprigs of parsley, and lightly sprinkle paprika around the perimeter of the dish.

{VARIATIONS}

Roasted Lemon-Ginger Chicken: You can substitute ¼ cup grated fresh ginger for the garlic.

Grilled Lemon-Garlic (or Ginger) Chicken: Grill the chicken over medium heat while basting several times with the marinade. Once cooked through, remove to a foil pouch and let steam for about 10 minutes prior to serving. This marinade also works well with boneless skinless chicken breast on the grill. Use about 3 pounds trimmed boneless/skinless breasts.

Stuffed Squash and Grape Leaves

SERVES 4

Cousa Mihshi Warac Inab (koosa mihh-shee war-rac ein-nab)

This dish of squash and grape leaves stuffed with ground lamb and rice steamed together in a rich flavorful tomato broth is a perfect choice for a Sunday meal with family and friends. One of the wonderful things about this meal is that you can prepare it in advance and refrigerate it until you are ready to serve it.

Special equipment: A zucchini corer and kitchen twine.

Prepare ahead: You can prepare this up to 2 days in advance. Refrigerate until needed. You can freeze the cooked squash and grape leaves for several weeks. Submerge them in the tomato broth, then freeze. Thaw in the refrigerator. Reheat in the microwave or on the stove until warm all the way through. Serve as directed.

FOR THE STUFFED SQUASH AND GRAPE LEAVES

½ pound coarsely ground lamb, from the leg

½ cup converted (also called parboiled) rice

¾ teaspoon salt

¼ teaspoon coarsely ground black pepper

½ teaspoon ground allspice

¼ teaspoon ground cinnamon

¼ cup melted butter

2 tablespoons and 2 tablespoons tomato paste, divided

¼ cup and ¼ cup cold water, divided

6 yellow squash (about 2 inches wide at the base and 4 to 5 inches long)

1 (8-ounce jar) grape leaves (Orlando brand if available), or about 18 grape leaves

1 large yellow onion (slice into ¼-inch rounds)

1 (29-ounce can) tomato sauce

2 cups beef broth

Kitchen twine

(**You can substitute** coarsely ground beef for the lamb, or zucchini for the squash.

To prepare the stuffed squash and grape leaves

For the filling, combine the ground lamb, rice, salt, pepper, allspice, cinnamon, butter, 2 tablespoons

tomato paste, and ¼ cup cold water in a bowl. Mix well, cover, and refrigerate for 30 minutes.

In the meantime, prepare the squash. Use room-temperature vegetables, as they are easier to hollow and less likely to crack. Rinse the squash using a vegetable brush to remove finely embedded particles. Turn the squash upside down and shave the light brown tip off the bottom.

Cut each squash into a 4-inch length by removing the top portion. Holding the squash in one hand, carefully insert a zucchini corer lengthwise into the cut top of the vegetable. Go deep enough to reach about ¼ to ½ inch away from the bottom, being careful not to pierce through the bottom or sides. Keep a ¼-inch thick wall around the squash as you gently turn the corer, removing and discarding the

insides. (**Alternatively**, you can squeeze the excess liquid from the insides of the squash and incorporate the pulp into the Mini Dill Omelets on page 14, as traditionally done in my family.)

Prepare the grape leaves by following the procedure on pages 43–44, for Vegetable-Stuffed Grape Leaves. Set them aside.

Remove the filling from the refrigerator, add the second ¼ cup of cold water, and mix well. Start filling the squash by placing small portions of filling into the hollowed cavity. Tap the base of the squash against the counter, forcing the filling to the bottom. Use your fingertip to push it down. Fill each squash to the top, leaving the last ¼ inch without filling. This will allow space for the rice to expand while it cooks. Set the squash aside.

Roll the grape leaves with the remaining filling by following the procedure described for Vegetable-Stuffed Grape Leaves (page 43), with one exception: use 2 teaspoons of filling for each grape leaf. Once the grape leaves are rolled, arrange them into 2 equal stacks. Line them 4 in a row, side by side, with 3 above those and 2 on top. Use kitchen twine to tie each stack into a bundle. Gently tie the string tight enough around the stack to keep them secure within the bundle, yet allowing them room to expand as they cook.

Selecting Squash

Pick squash that are firm and straight, as curved ones are harder to core.

To cook the stuffed squash and grape leaves

Select a medium-sized pot just large enough to hold the squash standing in an upright position and the 2 bundles of grape leaves by their sides. Line the bottom of the pot with the slices of onion.

Stand the squash upright in the pot. Place the bundles of grape leaves next to the squash in such a way that they are securing the squash in an upright position. Dissolve 2 tablespoons tomato paste with the tomato sauce and the broth; then add it to the pot. Cover and place it over medium-high heat. Once it comes to a boil, reduce the heat to medium-low and cook, covered, for 1 hour. Spoon hot broth over the tops of the squash and the grape leaves periodically while they are cooking. Remove the pot from the heat and set it aside covered for 30 minutes prior to serving.

To serve

Cut and discard the twine from around the bundles of grape leaves. Arrange the squash and the grape leaves in a shallow platter with the sauce and onions poured around the sides. Offer with Pita Crouton Salad with Sumak Dressing (page 60) and warm pita bread.

Stuffed Zucchini in Tomato Sauce

6 ZUCCHINI

Kablama bi Banadora (kab-blaa-ma bee ban-na dour-ra)

I believe these zucchini stuffed with minced beef, onions, and toasted pine nuts simmered in a rich tomato sauce will quickly become one of your favorite dishes. Serve them over basmati rice (page 132), couscous (page 112), or bulgur pilaf (page 71), and one of your favorite salads.

Special equipment: A zucchini corer.

Prepare ahead: You can prepare this dish up to 2 days in advance and refrigerate. The flavors continue to develop as it marinates in the rich tomato sauce. Serve as directed.

FOR THE FILLING

2 tablespoons toasted pine nuts

1 tablespoon extra-virgin olive oil

½ pound ground beef (80%)

1½ cups diced yellow onion (½ inch)

1¼ teaspoons salt

¼ teaspoon coarsely ground black pepper

½ teaspoon allspice

¼ teaspoon cinnamon

(**You can substitute** ground lamb or ground chicken for the beef.)

FOR THE STUFFED ZUCCHINI

6 zucchini, room temperature (about 1¼ inches wide at the base and about 4 to 5 inches long)

1 (29-ounce can) tomato sauce

1 cup peeled and coarsely chopped tomato

(**You can substitute** yellow squash for the zucchini.)

To prepare the filling

Preheat the oven to 350°F. Spread the pine nuts over a foil-lined baking sheet and toast them in the center of the oven, shaking the pan occasionally, for 5 to 7 minutes or until golden brown. Set aside.

Preheat the olive oil in a large skillet over medium-high heat. Add the ground meat and cook while breaking it into small, minced pieces. Once the meat is no longer pink, reduce the heat to medium-low. Add the onions, salt, and spices, and sauté until the onions are tender. Mix the pine nuts with the filling and transfer it to a dish. Set aside to cool. Reserve the skillet.

To prepare the stuffed zucchini

Use room-temperature vegetables, as they are easier to hollow and less likely to crack. Rinse the zucchini using a vegetable brush to remove finely embedded particles. Turn the zucchini upside down and shave the light brown tip off the bottom. Cut each zucchini into a 4-inch length by removing the top portion.

Holding the zucchini in one hand, carefully insert a zucchini corer lengthwise into the cut top of the squash. Go deep enough to reach ¼ to ½ inch away from the bottom, careful not to pierce through the bottom or sides. Keep a ¼-inch-thick wall around the vegetable as you gently turn the corer,

Stuffed Zucchini in Tomato Sauce

removing and discarding the insides. **(Alternatively,** *you can squeeze the excess liquid from the insides of the zucchini and incorporate the pulp into the Mini Dill Omelets on page 14, as traditionally done in my family.)*

Place the hollowed zucchini on a dish and seal it with plastic wrap. Place the dish in the microwave on high for 3 minutes. Remove the dish and set it aside, allowing the zucchini to steam for 5 minutes, then remove the plastic wrap and turn the zucchini upside down so that all the liquid can drain out. (Careful, they are hot!)

Combine the tomato sauce and the chopped tomato in the large skillet. Cover and cook over medium-high heat for 8 minutes, stirring periodically. In the meantime, stuff the zucchini: Pack the filling into the hollowed cavities and use your finger to push it down. Make sure the filling gets all the way down into the base and fill each to the top. Give them one final press to make sure the filling is packed in well. **(Caution:** *Do not press so hard that you burst the zucchini.)*

Once the tomato sauce has cooked for 8 minutes, reduce the heat to low. Stir in any leftover filling, then place the stuffed zucchini in the skillet. Cover and let them simmer over low heat for 30 minutes.

Selecting Zucchini

Pick squash that are firm and straight, as curved ones are harder to core.

Turn the zucchini periodically and spoon sauce over them. (Do not bring to a boil, because the filling may shake out.)

To serve
Serve over Basmati Rice with Toasted Noodles (page 134) and your favorite salad.

{VARIATION}

Stuffed Zucchini in Cilantro Yogurt (Kablama bi Laban): Prepare the stuffed zucchini as described above. Rather than cooking them in tomato sauce, follow the recipe and procedure for the yogurt sauce in the Beef Tortellini in Cilantro Yogurt recipe (page 68). Once the yogurt sauce has been prepared, place the stuffed zucchini in the sauce and simmer uncovered over low heat for 10 to 15 minutes (do not bring to a boil, because the filling may shake out). Serve as described above for Stuffed Zucchini in Tomato.

Tilapia with Jalapeño–Pine Nut Sauce

SERVES 4

Samakeh Harrah (sema-key harr-ra)

Moist tilapia fillets are arranged in the shape of a fish, then coated in a flavorful sauce of sautéed onions, garlic, and jalapeño combined with fresh cilantro, lemon, and ground pine nuts. The aroma that fills the air while preparing this sauce is amazing. This dish will both impress and delight your dinner guests.

Specialty ingredients: Tahini, found in specialty markets or online.
Special equipment: A food processor.
Prepare ahead: You can prepare the sauce up to 2 days in advance. The fish should be prepared the same day. You can assemble the fish 3 to 4 hours before serving. Store loosely covered in a cool, dry place. Serve as directed.

FOR THE SAUCE

½ cup tahini (mix well before using)
¼ cup and 1 tablespoon freshly squeezed lemon juice, divided
½ teaspoon and ½ teaspoon salt, divided
2 tablespoons extra-virgin olive oil
1 cup minced yellow onion
¼ cup minced garlic
1 tablespoon minced jalapeño (seeded)
1½ tablespoons ground coriander
1½ teaspoons ground cumin
⅛ teaspoon cayenne pepper
1 cup boiling water
1 cup finely ground pine nuts
1 cup finely chopped cilantro; use green leafy pats and tender stems

FOR THE FISH

1½ pounds tilapia fillet
2 tablespoons freshly squeezed lemon juice
¾ teaspoon salt

½ cup olive oil (for frying)
(**You can substitute** any smaller fillets of similar firm mild fish such as orange roughy or Dover sole for the tilapia.)

To prepare the sauce

Combine the tahini, ¼ cup lemon juice, ½ cup water, and ½ teaspoon salt in a bowl and whisk until smooth; set aside.

Preheat the olive oil in a medium skillet over medium-high heat. Add the onion, garlic, jalapeño, ½ teaspoon salt, coriander, cumin, and cayenne pepper. Reduce the heat to medium-low and sauté until the onions are tender. Add the boiling water, increase the heat to high, and cook until all the moisture is absorbed. Reduce the heat to medium and stir in the ground pine nuts and the tahini sauce. Add the cilantro and 1 tablespoon lemon juice and mix to combine all the ingredients. Reduce the heat to medium-low and simmer uncovered for 4 minutes (do not let the mixture boil, or the tahini may separate). Then remove from the heat, and set aside uncovered. Cool to room temperature before using.

To prepare the fish

Rinse the fillets under cold running water, drain, and pat dry. Transfer to a tray. Drizzle the lemon juice over the fillets, then sprinkle with salt.

Preheat the ½ cup olive oil (or enough oil so it is about ¼ inch deep) in a medium skillet over medium-high heat. Test the oil by lowering one end of the fish in the oil; if it sizzles, place 2 to 3 pieces of fish in the pan and fry about 1 to 1½ minutes per side. (Make certain the fish is cooked through but still moist before removing.) Remove with a slotted spoon to a paper towel–lined dish. Fry the remaining pieces of fish. (**Alternatively,** the fillets can be baked. Preheat the oven to 450°F. Brush a foil-lined baking sheet with oil. Bake the fillets for 7 to 10 minutes or until cooked through.)

Set the fish aside loosely covered with foil. Cool to room temperature before using.

To serve

Arrange the cooled pieces of fillet in the shape of a fish on a flat platter. Layer a few pieces of the fillet toward the center to make the fish appear thicker, and spread sauce in between the layers, securing them in place. Coat the outer pieces with about ¼

inch of sauce, covering any exposed fillet. Smooth the surface of the sauce using a flexible spatula.

Cut strips of carrot and arrange them forming a decorative tail, dorsal, and side fins. Use the tip of a radish for the eye. Thinly slice cucumber half-moons and arrange them (3 rows deep) behind the eye to resemble scales. Garnish the perimeter of the dish with half slices of lemon and sprigs of cilantro. Sprinkle finely chopped cilantro around the edges of the platter.

Store in a cool, dry area (up to 3 to 4 hours) loosely draped with waxed paper until ready to serve. Although this dish is traditionally offered at room temperature, you may decide otherwise.

{ VARIATION }

You can prepare the sauce separately and serve it as a dip with crackers, fresh vegetable crudités, or Toasted Pita Dippers (page 40). You can substitute walnuts for the pine nuts; however, the sauce will be grayish in color.

Side Dishes

(VEGETARIAN/CHICKEN/LAMB/BEEF)

Never underestimate the addition of a great side dish. From pureed lentils with toasted onions to Jalapeño Cilantro Salsa or Fava Beans with Garlic and Lemon, a good side dish can really complement and even enhance a meal. The versatility of several of these recipes gives you the option of preparing them vegetarian style or with chicken, beef, or lamb to turn it into a main course. Choose from healthy vegetables, like okra or Fordhook lima beans prepared in a rich tomato and cilantro sauce with olive oil, or tangy sautéed spinach with lemon and olive oil topped with caramelized onions. Many of the recipes can be prepared a day or two in advance, and since most of them are offered at room temperature they can be transferred to their platters in advance.

Basmati Rice 132
Basmati Rice with Green Onions 134
Basmati Rice with Toasted Noodles 134
Basmati Rice with Cumin, Lentils,
    and Onion 135
Beef Confit. 136
Eggplant Moussaka. 138
Fava Beans with Garlic and Lemon 139
Garden Wraps. 141
Green Beans in Tomato and Olive Oil 142
Lamb (or Beef) with Green Beans in Tomato
    and Olive Oil 143
Jalapeño-Cilantro Salsa. 144
Lentils with Caramelized Onions 145
Fordhook Lima Beans with Cilantro 146
Lamb (or Beef) and Fordhook Lima
    Beans with Cilantro 148
Chicken and Fordhook Lima Beans
    with Cilantro. 149

Roasted Onion-Cumin Potato Spears 150
Scrambled Eggs with Beef Confit
    and Potatoes. 151
Spinach with Caramelized Onions 152
Spinach with Minced Lamb and
    Pine Nuts 154
Stewed Okra and Cilantro in Olive Oil 155
Stewed Okra and Lamb (or Beef)
    with Cilantro. 156
Stewed Okra and Chicken with Cilantro. . . 157
Stuffed Vegetables. 158
Vegetable-Stuffed Cabbage Rolls 161
Cabbage Rolls with Lamb
    (or Beef) 164
Lentil Noodle Stew 165
Lentil Soup with Ruby Swiss Chard
    and Lemon 166
Miniature Meatball Soup 168
Mixed Bean Stew. 169

Opposite page: Miniature Meatball Soup

Basmati Rice

SERVES 4

Riz Basmati (riz-bus-ma-tee)

The fragrance that fills the air while preparing this rice is heavenly. This long-grained rice is well known for the perfume-like aroma it releases as it steams. This basic recipe and those that follow provide five delicious combinations of basmati rice.

Specialty ingredients: Basmati rice, preferably Indian or Pakistani, found at specialty markets or online.

Prepare ahead: You can prepare this up to 3 days in advance. Refrigerate covered. Serve as directed.

FOR PLAIN BASMATI RICE

1 cup basmati rice

2 cups water

½ teaspoon salt

1 tablespoon butter

To prepare plain basmati rice

Rinse the rice in a fine-mesh strainer under cold running water for about 15 seconds. Drain well.

Stir the rice, water, salt, and butter together in a medium saucepan and bring to a boil over high heat, uncovered. Once it comes to a rolling boil, reduce the heat to medium-low and simmer covered for 10 minutes, or until all the moisture is absorbed. Remove from the heat and set aside, covered. After 20 minutes fluff with a fork, separating the grains. Serve warm.

Preparing basmati rice pilafs

For best results, do not exceed 3 cups of rice in a pot at one time. When preparing 2 or 3 cups, increase the cooking time and slightly increase the cooking temperature. Make certain all of the water is completely absorbed before removing the pot from the heat. Let stand covered for at least 40 minutes prior to fluffing with a fork.

When preparing any of the following seasoned basmati rice dishes, after folding the additional ingredients into the plain basmati rice, let the pilaf stand covered for about 30 minutes to allow the flavors to develop.

{VARIATION}

Basmati Rice with Saffron (Riz Basmati ma Zafaron): Follow the recipe and procedure above to prepare the plain basmati rice, except add ½ teaspoon saffron threads with the water, salt, and butter. Serve warm.

Basmati Rice combinations

Basmati Rice with Green Onions

SERVES 4

Riz Basmati ma Bussel Ukhdar (riz bus-ma-tee ma-bus-sul ukhh-dar)

FOR THE BASMATI RICE WITH GREEN ONIONS

1 recipe plain Basmati Rice (page 132)

2 tablespoons extra-virgin olive oil

½ cup coarsely chopped green onion; use light and dark green parts

2 tablespoons finely chopped dill

¼ teaspoon salt

To prepare the basmati rice with green onions

Prepare the plain Basmati Rice as described on page 132 and set it aside for 20 minutes prior to folding in the onion-dill mixture.

Preheat the olive oil in a small skillet over medium heat. Add the onion, dill, and salt. Reduce the heat to medium-low and cook until the onions are tender. Pour the mixture over the prepared rice, and gently fold it into the rice using a flexible spatula. Set aside covered. Serve warm.

Basmati Rice with Toasted Noodles

SERVES 4

Riz Basmati ma Shireeyee (riz bus-ma-tee ma shy-ree-yee)

Special ingredients: Angel hair nests (not angel hair pasta) can be found in specialty markets or online, while cut *fideo-fideo cortado* (not coiled) sometimes called cut *fideo-fideos cortos* (not coiled), can be found in most grocery stores in the pasta section.

FOR THE BASMATI RICE WITH TOASTED NOODLES

1 recipe plain Basmati Rice (page 132)

2 tablespoons extra-virgin olive oil

½ cup angel hair nests, broken into pieces (not angel hair pasta)

or: cut *fideo-fideo cortado* (not coiled)

¼ teaspoon salt

½ cup boiling water

To prepare the basmati rice with toasted noodles

Prepare the plain Basmati Rice as described on page 132 and set it aside for 20 minutes prior to folding in the toasted noodles.

*Preheat the olive oil in a small skillet over medium-high heat. Add the noodle pieces and salt and pan-roast the noodles, stirring constantly. Once they begin to brown, reduce the heat to medium-low. Keep pan-roasting the noodles until they are reddish in color. Carefully add ½ cup boiling water (**caution:** it will splatter). Increase the heat to high and cook until most of the water is absorbed. Remove from the heat, cover, and set aside for 10 minutes, then gently fold the toasted noodles into the rice using a flexible spatula. Set aside covered. Serve warm.*

Basmati Rice with Cumin, Lentils, and Onion

SERVES 4

Riz Basmati ma Adas (riz bus-ma-tee ma ud-dus)

FOR THE BASMATI RICE WITH CUMIN, LENTILS, AND ONION

1 recipe plain Basmati Rice (page 132)

¼ cup lentils

3 cups water

¼ teaspoon and ½ teaspoon salt, divided

3 tablespoons extra-virgin olive oil

½ cup diced yellow onion (¼ inch)

¼ cup golden raisins

¼ cup coarsely chopped green onion; use light and dark green parts

¾ teaspoon cumin

To prepare the basmati rice with cumin, lentils, and onion

Prepare the plain Basmati Rice as described on page 132, and set it aside for 20 minutes prior to folding in the cumin-lentil-onion mixture.

Meanwhile, place the lentils, water, and ¼ teaspoon salt in a medium saucepan over high heat, uncovered. Bring to a rolling boil, then reduce the heat to medium-high and cook uncovered for 10 to 12 minutes or until the lentils are tender. Drain the lentils and set them aside, uncovered.

Preheat the olive oil in the same medium saucepan over medium heat. Add the yellow onion and ½ teaspoon salt, and sauté until the onions are tender. Add the raisins and cook them until they seem inflated. Then add the green onions, cumin, and drained lentils. Mix together for about a minute. Pour this mixture over the prepared rice, and gently fold it into the rice using a flexible spatula. Serve lightly warm or at room temperature.

Beef Confit

Qawarma (ka-war-ma)

Confit is one of the oldest ways to preserve food. If you have never tried this variety of confit, then you are in for a real treat. Delicious and versatile, these spicy cubes of beef are used in recipes ranging from scrambled eggs with beef confit and potatoes (page 151) to garbanzo bean triangles with beef confit (page 33). Traditionally they were prepared in rendered lamb fat; however, I have substituted rendered beef fat (it is easier to find).

Specialty ingredients: Beef fat from your local meat market.

Special equipment: A candy/fry thermometer.

Prepare ahead: Beef confit should keep in the refrigerator up to 4 months. The rendered beef fat can be prepared days to weeks in advance. Store in a well-sealed container and refrigerate until ready to use. **Note**: The beef cubes must marinate overnight.

FOR THE BEEF CONFIT

2 pounds lean top-round London broil

2 tablespoons salt

1 tablespoon coarsely ground black pepper

2 teaspoons allspice

¾ teaspoon cinnamon

¼ teaspoon white pepper

FOR THE RENDERED FAT

3½ pounds coarsely ground beef fat (yields about 2½ cups rendered fat)

To marinate the beef (overnight)

Weigh the beef after removing all the fat and fibers to ensure you begin with 2 pounds lean beef. Dice into ¾-inch cubes. Keep the cubes consistent in size so they will cook evenly. Combine them with the salt and spices in a bowl, mixing well to coat the cubes evenly. Cover and refrigerate overnight.

To render the beef fat

Place the ground fat in a large pot over medium-high heat, uncovered. Once the fat begins to sizzle, stir periodically. When it is boiling and no longer pink, reduce the heat to medium-low and simmer uncovered, stirring periodically, for 25 to 30 minutes. At first the rendered fat will appear cloudy as steam rises from the pot, but eventually it will begin to clear as the moisture evaporates.

Once the rendered fat appears clear with very little steam rising from the pot, remove the pot from the heat. Pass the cooked fat through a fine-mesh strainer. Discard the cooked pieces of fat and reserve the approximate 2½ cups of rendered fat.

To prepare the beef confit (the following day)

Heat 2½ cups rendered fat in a medium pot, uncovered, over medium-high heat (to 300°F; use a candy/fry thermometer to measure the temperature for accuracy). Meanwhile remove the marinated beef cubes from the refrigerator and mix them well. If liquid has formed overnight, drain and discard it.

Once the temperature reaches 300°F, transfer the beef cubes to the pot and stir with the oil. The temperature will drop with the addition of the cold beef cubes. Adjust the heat to medium-low (or lower, if

necessary), bringing the temperature to 200°–225°F. Simmer uncovered, stirring periodically and making certain the beef cubes are submerged beneath the fat as they simmer. (**Note:** *The temperature should not exceed 225°F; otherwise the beef will cook too fast and will not be as tender.*)

After about 1 hour, remove a few beef cubes. Cut them with a fork; they should break apart easily. If not, continue to simmer until tender.

Transfer the beef cubes to a sterilized heat-proof container just large enough to hold them. Pour the rendered fat over them. Make sure the beef cubes are submerged beneath the rendered fat. Set aside

uncovered to cool for several hours until the fat has solidified. Transfer the confit to the refrigerator to chill uncovered for several hours before covering (to avoid condensation).

When using the beef confit in recipes, melt, drain, and discard the rendered fat, using only the beef cubes.

To serve

Offer with fried or scrambled eggs and warm pita bread, or in your favorite quiche recipe, or Mini Beef Confit Omelets (page 15) (always drain the rendered fat from the confit and use only the cubes in recipes).

Eggplant Moussaka

SERVES 6

Mousaka'a Batinjan bi Zeyt (em-suc-ka'a bet-tin-jan bee zate)

This side dish, richly flavored with sautéed onions and garlic with fresh tomato and buttery eggplant, is excellent for picnics, lunches, or as an afternoon snack. It is prepared in olive oil, which makes it ideal for outdoor events. On a warm evening you can offer this dish last minute without heating.

Special equipment: A candy/fry thermometer.

Prepare ahead: You can prepare this dish up to 3 days in advance. Refrigerate covered. The flavors continue to develop as it marinates. Serve as directed.

FOR THE EGGPLANT MOUSSAKA

1½ pounds eggplant, room temperature

1 teaspoon and 1 teaspoon salt, divided

2 tablespoons and 1 tablespoon extra-virgin olive oil, divided

1 cup packed sliced yellow onion (¼ inch)

¼ cup cloves of garlic (cut in half lengthwise)

½ cup frozen pearl onions, thawed

⅔ cup canned garbanzo beans, drained

⅛ teaspoon coarsely ground black pepper

2 tablespoons finely chopped fresh mint

or: 1 teaspoon dry mint flakes

2 cups boiling water

⅓ cup tomato paste

¾ cup peeled and diced tomato (1 inch)

2 cups canola oil (for frying)

To prepare the eggplant

Cut the stem cap off. Peel the eggplant lengthwise, removing every other strip of skin for a striped appearance. Slice the eggplant widthwise into discs about 1 inch thick. Cut the smaller discs into 4 wedges and the larger discs into 6 (see page 53, Eggplant Salad, for photo).

Combine the pieces of eggplant with 1 teaspoon salt in a bowl, mixing well to coat the pieces. Transfer the eggplant to a colander and set aside to drain for 30 minutes.

To prepare the moussaka

Preheat a large skillet with 2 tablespoons olive oil over medium-high heat. Add the sliced onions, garlic, and 1 teaspoon salt, and sauté until the onions are limp and tender. Add the pearl onions, garbanzo beans, pepper, and mint and cook for a minute, then stir in the boiling water and tomato paste. Once the tomato paste has dissolved, reduce the heat to medium and cook covered for 5 minutes. Then remove from the heat, stir in the tomato, and set aside, covered.

In a small saucepan, heat the canola oil over medium-high heat to 375°F (use a candy/fry thermometer to measure the temperature of the oil for accuracy). The oil should be about 1 inch deep. Fry about 6 pieces of eggplant at a time until evenly golden brown on all sides, then remove to a paper towel–lined plate. Fry the remaining pieces of eggplant. Make sure the temperature of the oil remains at 375°F so that the pieces of eggplant fry evenly.

Recycle the oil: See page xiv.

(**Alternatively,** you can bake the pieces of egg-plant. Preheat the oven to 450°F. Mix the drained eggplant pieces with 1½ tablespoons olive oil. Spread them over a baking sheet lined with foil and bake for 15 minutes on the middle rack.)

Arrange the cooked eggplant pieces in the skillet over the tomato mixture, and gently fold them into the mixture. Place the skillet over high heat. Once it comes to a boil around the edges, reduce the heat to medium and cook, covered, for 5 to 7 minutes, then remove from the heat.

Gently stir in 1 tablespoon olive oil, and set aside covered. Serve at room temperature.

Fava Beans with Garlic and Lemon
Foul Moudammus (fool moo-dum-mus)

SERVES 4

This delicious combination of warm fava beans mixed with fresh garlic and lemon juice is traditionally offered at breakfast, brunch, or with mezza finger foods. Lemon and garlic seem to draw the deep flavor out of the beans. Adjust the garlic, lemon, and salt to your taste.

Special ingredients: Canned fava beans (*foul mou-dammas*), found in specialty markets or online.
Special equipment: A pestle (a garlic press will do).
Prepare ahead: You can prepare the beans a couple of days in advance and refrigerate until needed. Serve as directed.

FOR THE FAVA BEANS
1 (15-ounce) can of fava beans, drained
1 large clove garlic
½ teaspoon salt
3 tablespoons freshly squeezed lemon juice

2 tablespoons and 1 tablespoon extra-virgin olive oil, divided
¼ cup canned garbanzo beans, drained
2 tablespoons coarsely chopped flat-leaf parsley

To prepare the fava beans
Place the drained fava beans in a medium sauce-pan with 1 cup water over high heat and bring to a rolling boil. Reduce the heat to medium-low and cook, covered, for 5 minutes.

While the beans cook, place the garlic and salt in a bowl and mash to a pulp using a pestle. Add the lemon juice and 2 tablespoons olive oil to the bowl. Mix well.

Remove the beans from the heat and drain. Fold the beans into the garlic mixture. Mix well, lightly mashing a few of the beans to thicken the sauce. Set aside covered for about 10 minutes, allowing the flavors to develop.

To serve

Serve slightly warm or at room temperature. Transfer the beans to a shallow bowl and top the center with the drained garbanzo beans. Sprinkle parsley and drizzle 1 tablespoon olive oil over the beans. Offer a plate of tomato wedges, spring onions, sliced cucumber, and warm pita bread on the side.

Fava Beans with Garlic and Lemon

Garden Wraps

Arous Jneini (a-roos jnay-nee)

The literal translation of arous *is "bride" and* jneini *is "garden." Long ago in various villages, they did not like the bride to appear too thin, so they would wrap her in layers to make her appear full and robust. That is exactly what these delicious pita wrap sandwiches are; they are full and robust. Fresh pita bread is wrapped around layers of yogurt cheese, crisp vegetables, olives, and fresh mint. Be sure to use very fresh pita breads, so they are soft and pliable.*

Specialty ingredients: Yogurt cheese (*labni*); you can prepare it fresh (page 47) or find it at specialty markets or online.

FOR THE WRAPS

2 large fresh pita breads (10 to 12 inches diameter)

½ cup yogurt cheese (*labni*)

24 Moroccan olives (pitted) or Kalamata olives (pitted)

12 slices cucumber (¼-inch rounds)

½ cup diced tomato (½ inch)

20 fresh mint leaves

1 tablespoon extra-virgin olive oil

To prepare the wraps

Place the pita breads on a flat surface. Spread half of the labni cheese down the center (from top to bottom) of each round. Dividing the remaining ingredients between the 2 wraps, layer the olives over the labni cheese, followed by the cucumber, tomato, and mint leaves. Drizzle the oil over the vegetables. Fold the base up and over the filling about 2 inches to secure the filling from falling out of the bottom, then roll the pita from left to right, forming a cylinder with the filling inside. Wrap a paper napkin around the bottom, and enjoy!

{VARIATIONS}

You can fill vegetarian pita wraps with Crispy Bean & Herb Patties (page 2), lettuce, and pickled turnips (page 17) drizzled with tahini sauce (page 7). For meat wraps, fill them with Grilled Beef Fingers (page 84), lettuce and tomato, and hummus (page 8); or grilled chicken (page 86), lettuce and tomato, and Robust Garlic Puree (page 26).

Green Beans in Tomato and Olive Oil

SERVES 6

Loubi bi Zeyt (loo-bee bee zeyt)

This easy-to-make dish is a delicious way to offer green beans. Since it is served at room temperature, it is a great choice for outdoor parties, or as an afternoon snack with warm pita bread.

Prepare ahead: You can prepare this dish up to 3 days in advance. Refrigerate covered. The flavors continue to develop as it marinates. Serve as directed.

FOR THE BEANS

2 tablespoons and 1 tablespoon extra-virgin olive oil, divided
2 cups diced yellow onion (¼ inch)
⅓ cup cloves of garlic (cut in half lengthwise)
1¾ teaspoons salt
1 pound fresh green beans (cut into 1-inch lengths)
¼ teaspoon coarsely ground black pepper
¼ teaspoon sugar
3 cups boiling water
½ cup tomato paste
1 cup peeled and diced tomato (1 inch)
(**You can substitute** frozen cut green beans for fresh; they can be added without thawing.)

To prepare the beans

Preheat 2 tablespoons olive oil in a large pot over medium-high heat. Add the onions, garlic, and salt, and sauté for about 2 minutes. (If the onions start to brown, slightly reduce the heat.) Stir in the beans, pepper, and sugar. Add the boiling water and tomato paste and stir well to dissolve the tomato paste, then add the tomatoes.

Increase the heat to high and bring the mixture to a rolling boil uncovered, then reduce the heat to medium and simmer covered for 30 minutes, stirring periodically. (If the beans begin to stick, slightly reduce the heat.) Test a few beans to make sure they are tender. If so, mix in 1 tablespoon olive oil and remove from the heat. Set aside to cool covered.

To serve

Offer at room temperature with warm pita bread.

Lamb (or Beef) with Green Beans in Tomato and Olive Oil

SERVES 4

Loubi bi Lahm (loo-bee bee lah-him)

Prepare ahead: You can prepare this dish up to 3 days in advance. Refrigerate covered. The flavors continue to develop as it marinates. Serve as directed.

FOR THE LAMB (OR BEEF)

1 recipe Green Beans in Tomato and Olive Oil
  (see previous recipe)
2 tablespoons extra-virgin olive oil
1 pound lean lamb (from the leg), cut into
  1-inch cubes
or: 1 pound lean beef (top round/London broil)
1 tablespoon freshly squeezed lemon juice
1 cup diced yellow onion (½ inch)
1½ teaspoons salt
½ teaspoon coarsely ground black pepper
½ teaspoon allspice
¼ teaspoon cinnamon
4½ cups boiling water
½ cup tomato paste

To prepare the lamb (or beef)

Prepare the Green Beans in Tomato and Olive Oil as described in the previous recipe; set it aside.

Preheat the olive oil in a medium-sized pot over medium-high heat. Add the lamb (or beef) and fry until all of the moisture has evaporated and the meat is evenly browned (caramelized) on all sides. Stir in the lemon juice, onion, salt, and spices. Add the boiling water and tomato paste, stirring to dissolve the tomato paste.

Increase the heat to high. Once the mixture comes to a rolling boil, reduce the heat to medium and simmer covered for about 1 hour and 15 minutes, stirring periodically. (If the mixture begins to stick, slightly reduce the heat.) Test the meat with a fork. If it breaks apart easily, then it is done; if not, continue to cook until tender.

Use a slotted spoon to transfer the meat to the cooked beans and stir to combine. Reserve the leftover sauce from the meat to serve on the side.

To serve

Offer warm with Basmati Rice with Toasted Noodles (page 134), and Pita Crouton Salad with Sumak Dressing (page 60).

Jalapeño-Cilantro Salsa

ABOUT 2 CUPS

Douggous (doog-goos)

This flavorful combination of jalapeño, cilantro, garlic, tomatoes, and fresh lemon juice accompanies several dishes. Offer it with Cardamom Chicken with Rice (page 72) or with your favorite fish recipe. Once you try the salsa, you will find many other ways to use it.

Special equipment: A pestle (a garlic press will do).

Prepare ahead: The salsa can be prepared up to 1 day in advance. Refrigerate covered.

FOR THE SALSA

1 large clove garlic

¼ teaspoon salt

2 cups diced tomato (¼ inch), firm red tomatoes

1 teaspoon minced jalapeños; remove ribs and seeds

2 tablespoons freshly squeezed lemon juice

¼ cup finely chopped cilantro; use green leafy parts and tender stems

Handling Jalapeños

Wash your hands well after mincing jalapeños or other hot peppers (especially after handling the ribs and seeds, which have the most heat), and do not rub your eyes, nose, or mouth. Wear gloves if you have them.

To prepare the salsa

In a small bowl, mash the garlic and salt into a pulp using a pestle. Add the remaining ingredients and mix well. Transfer to an airtight container. Cover and refrigerate for at least 2 hours to allow the flavors to develop prior to serving.

Lentils with Caramelized Onions
Mujaddara (moo-jud-dar-ra)

Lentils are wonderful disc-shaped pulses that have a mild earthy flavor and are high in fiber and protein. The caramelized onions enhance the rich texture and color of the pureed lentils. This dish is served at room temperature, making it ideal for picnics, an afternoon snack with warm pita bread, or even at the office for lunch.

Special equipment: A food processor.
Prepare ahead: You can prepare this dish up to 3 days in advance. Refrigerate. Serve as directed.

FOR THE LENTILS

8 ounces brown lentils (about 1¼ cups)
1 teaspoon and ¾ teaspoon salt, divided
¼ cup basmati rice
⅓ cup and 1 tablespoon extra-virgin olive oil, divided
3 cups diced yellow onion (¼ inch)

To prepare the lentils

Check the lentils and discard any stones or debris. Place them in a fine-mesh sieve and rinse under cold running water for about 30 seconds.

Place the lentils, 4½ cups water, and 1 teaspoon salt in a medium pot over high heat, uncovered. Bring to a rolling boil, then reduce the heat to medium and simmer covered for 25 minutes. Test a couple of lentils to make sure they are tender. If they seem crunchy, continue to cook them until tender.

Place the rice and ¾ cup water in a small saucepan over high heat, uncovered. Once it comes to a boil, reduce the heat to medium-low and simmer covered for 10 minutes or until the water is absorbed. Remove from the heat and set aside, covered.

Drain the beans through a fine-mesh sieve and reserve ½ cup of the liquid. Set the pot aside for later use.

Place the cooked lentils and the reserved liquid in a food processor fitted with a metal blade. Pulse several times (do not overprocess) until the lentils are evenly ground. Return them to the pot, and set aside.

Double-line a dish with paper towels and set it aside. Preheat ⅓ cup olive oil in a medium skillet over

medium-high heat. Add the onions and ¾ teaspoon salt, and sauté until the onions are evenly reddish brown and caramelized. Remove the skillet from the heat, tilt it to one side, and use a slotted spoon to slide half of the onions to the top of the pan. Use the back of the spoon to press out as much oil as you can from the onions (pressing the oil out makes them crispier). Transfer the caramelized onions to the paper towel–lined dish and spread them out evenly; set aside.

Set the skillet over medium-high heat and gradually add ½ cup water (**caution**: it will splatter) followed by the cooked basmati rice. Cook, uncovered, stirring occasionally, until the water is absorbed. Stir this mixture into the pureed lentils.

Place the mixture of lentils and onions over medium-low heat and cook uncovered for 3 to 5 minutes, then stir in 1 tablespoon olive oil. Remove from the heat.

Spread the pureed lentils evenly over a shallow platter. Set aside to cool for several hours loosely covered with waxed paper. Once cooled, sprinkle most of the caramelized onions around the perimeter, and a few in the center. Garnish with a radish star and green onions.

To serve

This dish is best at room temperature. Offer with Pickled Turnips (page 17), small pickles and warmed pita bread, or Cabbage and Beet Salad (page 50).

{VARIATION}

Cumin: Add ½ teaspoon ground cumin to the cooked lentils before they are pureed.

Fordhook Lima Beans with Cilantro

SERVES 4

Fassolia bi Zeyt (fa-saul-lia bee zeyt)

These are the king of lima beans. Fordhook lima beans are plump with a buttery texture and are absolutely delicious. The lima beans are sautéed with onions, cilantro, and garlic in a rich tomato stew. This is one of my favorite dishes. It's ideal to take to a barbecue, picnic, or potluck. Since it is served at room temperature, you can platter it in advance.

Special equipment: A mortar and pestle (a garlic press will do).

Prepare ahead: You can prepare it up to 2 days in advance. The flavors develop as it marinates in the refrigerator. Serve as directed.

FOR THE BEANS

2 tablespoons and 1 tablespoon extra-virgin olive oil, divided

2 cups diced yellow onion (¼ inch)

1 teaspoon and ¾ teaspoon salt, divided

1 package (16 ounces, frozen) Fordhook lima
  beans
½ teaspoon coarsely ground black pepper
⅛ teaspoon sugar
2 large cloves garlic
2 cups boiling water
⅓ cup tomato paste
1 cup peeled and diced tomato (½ inch)
½ cup finely chopped cilantro; use green leafy
  parts and tender stems
3 tablespoons freshly squeezed lemon juice

To prepare the beans

Preheat 2 tablespoons olive oil in a large pot over medium-high heat. Add the onions and 1 teaspoon salt, and sauté for a minute or two. Add the frozen lima beans, pepper, and sugar.

Using a mortar and pestle, mash the garlic with ¾ teaspoon salt to a pulp. Add to the lima bean mixture and stir to combine. Add the boiling water, tomato paste, tomato, cilantro, and lemon juice, increase the heat to high, and stir well to dissolve the tomato paste. Bring the mixture to a rolling boil, then reduce the heat to medium-low and simmer covered, stirring periodically, for 25 minutes. Test a few beans to make sure they are tender, then remove from the heat. Stir in 1 tablespoon olive oil and set aside covered to cool.

To serve

Offer at room temperature with warm pita bread.

Lamb (or Beef) and Fordhook Lima Beans with Cilantro

SERVES 4

Fassolia bi Lahm (fa-saul-lia bee lah-him)

Special equipment: A mortar and pestle (a garlic press will do).

Prepare ahead: You can prepare it up to 2 days in advance. The flavors develop as it marinates in the refrigerator. Serve as directed.

FOR THE LAMB (OR BEEF)

1 recipe Fordhook Lima Beans with Cilantro (see previous recipe)

2 tablespoons extra-virgin olive oil

1 pound lean lamb from the leg, cut into 1-inch pieces

or: 1 pound lean beef (top round/London broil)

1 large clove garlic

1½ teaspoons salt

1 tablespoon freshly squeezed lemon juice

1 cup diced yellow onion (¼ inch)

¼ teaspoon coarsely ground black pepper

½ teaspoon allspice

½ teaspoon cinnamon

4 cups boiling water

½ cup tomato paste

⅓ cup finely chopped cilantro; use green leafy parts and tender stems

To prepare the lamb (or beef)

Prepare the Fordhook Lima Beans with Cilantro as described in the previous recipe; set aside.

Preheat the olive oil in a medium-sized pot over medium-high heat. Add the meat and fry until all of the moisture has evaporated and it is evenly browned (caramelized) on all sides.

Using a mortar and pestle, mash the garlic with the salt to a pulp and add to the pot with the meat, along with the lemon juice, onion, pepper, allspice, and cinnamon. Stir in the boiling water, tomato paste, and cilantro.

Increase the heat to high, stirring well to dissolve the tomato paste, and bring the mixture to a rolling boil. Reduce the heat to medium-low and simmer covered, stirring periodically, for 1 hour and 15 minutes. Test the meat with a fork; if it breaks apart easily, then it is done, if not, continue to cook until tender.

Use a slotted spoon to transfer the meat to the cooked beans. Mix well. Serve the leftover sauce from the meat on the side.

To serve

Offer warm with plain Basmati Rice (page 132) and a salad.

Chicken and Fordhook Lima Beans with Cilantro

Fassolia bi Djeaj (fa-saul-lia bee djeaj)

Special equipment: A mortar and pestle (a garlic press will do).

Prepare ahead: You can prepare it up to 2 days in advance. The flavors develop as it marinates in the refrigerator. Serve as directed.

FOR THE CHICKEN

1 recipe Fordhook Lima Beans with Cilantro (see recipe on page 146)

1 pound trimmed boneless skinless chicken breast, cut into 1-inch pieces

1 tablespoon apple cider vinegar

2 tablespoons extra-virgin olive oil

1 large clove garlic

1½ teaspoons salt

1 tablespoon freshly squeezed lemon juice

1 cup diced yellow onion (¼ inch)

¼ teaspoon coarsely ground black pepper

½ teaspoon allspice

¼ teaspoon cinnamon

2 cups boiling water

½ cup tomato paste

⅓ cup finely chopped cilantro (use the green leafy parts and tender stems)

To prepare the chicken

Prepare the Fordhook Lima Beans with Cilantro as described on page 146; set aside.

Rinse the chicken in 1 cup cold water with the vinegar to refresh the flavor of the chicken. Drain and cut into 1-inch pieces.

Preheat the olive oil in a medium pot over medium-high heat. Add the chicken and sauté until it is no longer pink. Using a mortar and pestle, mash the garlic with the salt to a pulp, and add to the pot with the chicken along with the lemon juice, onion, pepper, allspice, and cinnamon. Stir in the boiling water, tomato paste, and cilantro.

Increase the heat to high, stirring well to dissolve the tomato paste, and bring the mixture to a rolling boil. Reduce the heat to medium-low and simmer covered, stirring periodically, for 15 minutes. Remove from the heat.

Use a slotted spoon to transfer the chicken to the cooked beans, and mix well. Serve the sauce from the chicken on the side. Serve as directed above for Lamb (or Beef) with Fordhook Lima Beans and Cilantro.

Roasted Onion-Cumin Potato Spears

Batata bil Furren (ba-ta-ta bill fur-rin)

SERVES 6

Crisp spears of oven-roasted potatoes coated with olive oil, onion, paprika, and cumin are hard to resist. The crunchy texture of the seasonings on the outside of the potato is absolutely delicious. Serve with Roasted Lemon-Garlic Chicken (page 121) and a salad.

Prepare ahead: The potato spears can be cut and coated an hour in advance. Drape plastic wrap over the tray until ready to bake.

FOR THE POTATOES

4 russet potatoes, about ½ pound each, rinsed
   well, cut lengthwise (8 spears each)
3 tablespoons extra-virgin olive oil
3 tablespoons granulated onion (not powdered)
1½ teaspoons ground paprika
2 teaspoons ground cumin
1 teaspoon salt

To prepare the potatoes

Preheat the oven to 450°F. Combine the potato spears in a large bowl with the rest of the ingredients. Mix well to coat the individual spears.

Arrange the spears side-by-side, skin-side down, on a foil-lined baking sheet. Roast in the top of the oven for 15 minutes, then move the sheet to the middle rack for an additional 8 to 10 minutes or until browned and crisp on the outside and knife-tender. Remove from the oven, platter, and serve.

{VARIATION}

Substitute other herbs and spices such as rosemary, Italian seasoning, basil, oregano, or granulated garlic. You can also prepare these using sweet potatoes.

Scrambled Eggs with Beef Confit and Potatoes

Bied ma Qawarma (byied ma ka-war-ma)

I loved this tasty dish growing up and still enjoy it to this day. I remember waking up on Sunday mornings to the enticing aroma as it made its way up to my room. I couldn't wait to run downstairs and have a bite. It is a delicious combination of potatoes with onions, a touch of garlic, beef confit, and eggs. Serve with warm pita bread, and you are good to go! I often serve this at brunch with a platter of fresh fruits and cheeses.

Specialty ingredients: Beef confit, *qawarma* (page 136).

FOR THE SCRAMBLED EGGS WITH BEEF CONFIT AND POTATOES

1 tablespoon extra-virgin olive oil
1 tablespoon butter
1 cup peeled and diced russet potato (¼ inch)
½ cup diced yellow onion (¼ inch)
1 clove garlic (dice into small pieces)
¾ cup beef confit, without the rendered fat and broken into smaller pieces
6 large eggs, beaten

To prepare the scrambled eggs with beef confit and potatoes

Preheat the olive oil and butter in a large skillet over medium-high heat. Add the potatoes and fry them, turning occasionally until they begin to brown. Reduce the heat to medium. Add the onions and sauté until they are translucent and tender.

Stir in the garlic and beef confit and cook for about 1 minute more. Increase the heat to medium-high; then add the beaten eggs and scramble with the potatoes and beef until the eggs are no longer runny. Serve right away.

To serve

Offer with warm pita bread.

Spinach with Caramelized Onions

SERVES 4

Sabanekh bi Zeyt (sa-ban-nickh bee zeyt)

Caramelized onions sautéed with spinach and lemon draw out a sweet and tangy flavor. A topping of caramelized onions completes this dish. It is best served at room temperature.

Prepare ahead: You can prepare this up to 2 days in advance and refrigerate. Store the onions for the topping separately. Serve as directed.

FOR THE SPINACH WITH ONIONS

¼ cup and 1 tablespoon extra-virgin olive oil, divided

2 cups (well-packed) sliced yellow onions (⅛ inch)

½ teaspoon and ½ teaspoon salt, divided

1 pound frozen cut leaf spinach, thawed with half the moisture removed

¼ cup and 1 tablespoon freshly squeezed lemon juice, divided

1 tablespoon lemon zest

¼ teaspoon coarsely ground pepper

(You can substitute 2 pounds fresh spinach for the frozen: Rinse, dry, and cut into ½-inch strips, and steam until it begins to wilt; then squeeze out half the liquid.)

To prepare the caramelized onions

Preheat ¼ cup olive oil in a medium skillet over medium-high heat. Add the onions and ½ teaspoon salt, and sauté the onions until they are evenly reddish brown and caramelized. Remove the skillet from the heat and tilt it to one side, and use a slotted spoon to slide half of the onions to the top of the pan. Use the back of the spoon to press out as much of the oil as you can from the onions (pressing the oil out makes them crispier). Transfer the onions to a dish lined with paper towels, spreading them out evenly, and set aside.

To prepare the sautéed spinach

Return the skillet to the stove, and over low heat add the spinach, ¼ cup lemon juice, lemon zest, ½ teaspoon salt, and the pepper. Combine the onions with the spinach, cover, and continue to cook, stirring occasionally, for 5 to 7 minutes. Remove from the heat, and drizzle with 1 tablespoon each of olive oil and lemon juice. Mix well. Drape waxed paper over the sautéed spinach and set aside to cool.

To serve

Offer at room temperature. Arrange the spinach over a flat platter. Top with the toasted caramelized onions and surround with lemon wedges.

{VARIATION}

Dandelion with Caramelized Onions (Hindbi bi Zeyt): Follow the recipe above for Spinach with Caramelized Onions, replacing the spinach with 2 pounds fresh dandelion greens. Rinse the dandelion greens well, removing deeply embedded debris; shake out excess water and air-dry before you begin. Cut the greens into 2-inch lengths (width-wise) and steam just until they begin to wilt. Squeeze out half the liquid, then use the wilted dandelion greens in place of the spinach, following the procedure above.

Opposite page: Spinach with Caramelized Onions

Spinach with Minced Lamb and Pine Nuts

SERVES 4

Sabanekh bi Lahm Mafroom (sa-ban-nickh bee lah-him ma-froom)

This is a great way to convert the Spinach with Caramelized Onions recipe (page 152) into a meal of its own. It is a simple combination of two recipes. Once you have prepared the spinach with caramelized onions you arrange warm kibbi meat filling over the spinach; then top the meat filling with the caramelized onions and toasted pine nuts. The combination of flavors is divine and all of it can be prepared in advance and assembled just before serving.

FOR THE SPINACH AND ONIONS

1 recipe Spinach with Caramelized Onions (see
  recipe on page 152)

FOR THE TOPPING

1 recipe Lamb Kibbi Tray filling (see recipe on
  page 99)

To prepare the sautéed spinach with lamb topping

Prepare the caramelized onions and sautéed spinach as described on page 152.

For the topping, toast the pine nuts and prepare the lamb filling as described on pages 99–100 (you can substitute ground beef or ground chicken for the lamb). Reserve the toasted pine nuts to sprinkle over the top of the dish.

To serve

Arrange the warm sautéed spinach over a flat platter. Arrange the warm meat filling over the spinach. Top with the caramelized onions and toasted pine nuts. Serve with plain Basmati Rice (page 132), warm pita bread, and a salad.

Stewed Okra and Cilantro in Olive Oil

Bammee bi Zeyt (bam-mee bee zeyt)

SERVES 4

If you like okra, I believe you will enjoy this dish; if not, perhaps this dish will make you reconsider. The flavors of the tender stewed okra with garlic, onions, tomato, and cilantro are incredible. Served with warm pita bread, it makes for a great meal or an afternoon snack.

Special equipment: A mortar and pestle (a garlic press will do).

Prepare ahead: You can prepare this up to 2 days in advance and refrigerate. As it remains in the refrigerator, the flavors continue to develop. Serve as directed.

FOR THE OKRA

1 pound fresh okra (pick small ones 2 to 3 inches long)

2 tablespoons and 2 tablespoons and 1 tablespoon extra virgin olive oil, divided

2 cups diced yellow onion (¼ inch)

1 cup frozen pearl onions

1 teaspoon and 1 teaspoon salt, divided

½ teaspoon coarsely ground black pepper

2 teaspoons ground coriander

2 large cloves garlic

3 tablespoons freshly squeezed lemon juice

2 cups boiling water

½ cup tomato paste

1 cup peeled and diced tomato (½ inch)

½ cup finely chopped cilantro; use green leafy parts and tender stems

(**You can substitute** 1 pound frozen whole okra.)

To prepare the okra

Preheat the oven to 450°F. Rinse the okra several times in cold water, then drain and pat dry with a

kitchen towel. Trim any long stems so the tops are even. (Skip rinsing the okra if you are using frozen.)

Arrange the okra on a foil-lined baking sheet, side-by-side but not touching one another, and bake in the center of the oven for 5 minutes. Remove the tray and half-turn each piece of okra, then return the tray to the oven for an additional 5 minutes.

Remove the okra from the oven and half-turn each piece once again, but this time brush the tops of the okra, using 2 tablespoons olive oil. Return the okra to the oven for a final 5 minutes, then remove and set aside. (Baking the okra at a high temperature helps eliminate the slimy texture.)

Preheat a large pot with 2 tablespoons olive oil over medium-high heat. Add the diced onions, pearl onions, 1 teaspoon salt, pepper, and coriander, and sauté for 1 minute. Using a mortar and pestle, mash the garlic with 1 teaspoon salt to a pulp. Add the garlic pulp to the onion mixture and cook for an additional minute, then stir in the lemon juice, 2 cups boiling water, and the tomato paste.

Increase the heat to high and stir well, dissolving the tomato paste. Add the tomato, cilantro, and baked okra and gently fold all the ingredients together, bringing the mixture to a rolling boil. Reduce the heat to medium-low and simmer covered, stirring occasionally, for 15 to 20 minutes (stir gently to avoid breaking the pieces of okra). Test a piece of okra to make sure it is tender; if not, continue to cook until tender. Remove from the heat and gently stir in 1 tablespoon of olive oil. Set aside to cool, covered.

To serve
Offer at room temperature with warm pita bread.

Stewed Okra and Lamb (or Beef) with Cilantro

SERVES 4

Bammee bi Lahm (bam-mee bee lah-him)

Special equipment: A mortar and pestle (a garlic press will do).

Prepare ahead: You can prepare this up to 2 days in advance and refrigerate. As it remains in the refrigerator, the flavors continue to develop. Serve as directed.

FOR THE LAMB (OR BEEF)
1 recipe Stewed Okra and Cilantro in Olive Oil
   (see previous recipe)
2 tablespoons extra-virgin olive oil
1 pound lean lamb (from the leg), cut into
   1-inch pieces
or: 1 pound lean beef (top round/London broil)
2 tablespoons freshly squeezed lemon juice

1 cup diced yellow onion (¼ inch)
1 teaspoon and ½ teaspoon salt, divided
¼ teaspoon coarsely ground pepper
½ teaspoon ground allspice
¼ teaspoon ground cinnamon
1 teaspoon ground coriander
1 large clove garlic
4 cups boiling water
½ cup tomato paste
¼ cup finely chopped cilantro; use green leafy
   parts and tender stems

To prepare the lamb (or beef)
Prepare the Stewed Okra and Cilantro in Olive Oil as described in the previous recipe; set aside.

Preheat the olive oil in a medium pot over medium-high heat. Add the meat and fry until all of the moisture has evaporated and it is evenly browned (caramelized) on all sides. Stir in the lemon juice, onions, 1 teaspoon salt and the pepper, allspice, cinnamon, and coriander Using a mortar and pestle, mash the garlic with ½ teaspoon salt to a pulp, and add to the mixture. Stir in the boiling water, tomato paste, and cilantro.

Increase the heat to high, stirring well to dissolve the tomato paste, and bring the mixture to a rolling boil. Reduce the heat to medium-low and simmer covered, stirring periodically, for 1 hour and 15 minutes. At this point test the meat with a fork. If it breaks apart easily, then it is done; if not, continue to cook until tender. Use a slotted spoon to transfer the meat to the cooked okra, and gently fold in the meat (being careful not to break up the okra).

To serve

Serve the leftover sauce from the meat on the side. Offer warm with Basmati Rice with Toasted Noodles (page 134) and Pita Crouton Salad with Sumak Dressing (page 60).

Stewed Okra and Chicken with Cilantro

SERVES 4

Bammee bi Djeaj (bam-mee bee djeaj)

Special equipment: A mortar and pestle (a garlic press will do).

Prepare ahead: You can prepare this up to 2 days in advance and refrigerate. As it remains in the refrigerator, the flavors continue to develop. Serve as directed.

FOR THE CHICKEN

1 recipe Stewed Okra and Cilantro in Olive Oil
   (see recipe page 155)
1 pound trimmed boneless skinless chicken
   breast, cut into 1-inch pieces
1 tablespoon apple cider vinegar
2 tablespoons extra-virgin olive oil
1 cup diced yellow onion (½ inch)
1 teaspoon and ½ teaspoon salt, divided
½ teaspoon coarsely ground pepper
½ teaspoon ground allspice
¼ teaspoon ground cinnamon
1 teaspoon ground coriander
1 large clove garlic
2 cups boiling water
⅓ cup tomato paste
¼ cup finely chopped cilantro; use green leafy
   parts and tender stems

To prepare the chicken

Prepare the Stewed Okra and Cilantro in Olive Oil as described on page 155; set aside.

Rinse the chicken in 1 cup cold water with the vinegar to refresh the flavor of the chicken. Drain and cut into 1-inch pieces.

Preheat the olive oil in a medium pot over medium-high heat. Add the chicken and sauté until it is no *longer pink; then stir in the onions, 1 teaspoon salt, the pepper, allspice cinnamon, and coriander. Using a mortar and pestle, mash the garlic with ½ teaspoon salt to a pulp. Add it to the chicken mixture, along with the boiling water, tomato paste, and cilantro.*

Increase the heat to high, stirring to dissolve the tomato paste, and bring the mixture to a rolling boil. Reduce the heat to medium-low and sim-mer covered, stirring periodically, for 15 minutes. Remove the pot from the heat. Use a slotted spoon to transfer the chicken to the cooked okra, and gently fold in the chicken (being careful not to break the okra).

To serve

Serve the leftover sauce from the chicken on the side. Serve as directed in the previous recipe for Stewed Okra with Lamb (or Beef).

Stuffed Vegetables
Dolma (dol-ma)

16 PIECES

If you are looking for that one vegetable dish that's delicious and can serve as a centerpiece on your table, look no further. The variety of the small vegetables and the colors, flavors, and presentation of this dish make it a winner, and it can be prepared in advance. Your friends and family will be impressed by both the look and the taste.

Special equipment: A zucchini corer and a bread loaf pan that is about 9 x 5 x 2½ inches, both found at kitchen supply stores or online.

Special ingredients: If you have trouble finding the vegetables in the produce section of the grocery store you may have to go to a gourmet grocery store that carries specialty produce in smaller sizes.

Prepare ahead: You can prepare this dish up to 2 days in advance. Store covered in the refrigerator. Serve as directed. **Note:** The filling must be prepared 1 day in advance.

FOR THE FILLING
¼ cup toasted pine nuts
½ cup converted (also called parboiled) rice
1 teaspoon and ¾ teaspoon salt, divided

⅛ teaspoon black pepper
⅓ cup and ½ cup and 1½ tablespoons freshly squeezed lemon juice, divided
3 tablespoons and 2 tablespoons extra-virgin olive oil, divided
¼ cup currants
1 tablespoon finely chopped fresh dill
1 cup finely chopped flat-leaf parsley; use green leafy parts and tender stems
¾ cup (peeled) finely chopped tomato
¼ cup finely chopped green onion; use light and dark green parts
¼ cup finely chopped yellow onion
2 tablespoons finely chopped fresh mint
or: 1 teaspoon dry mint flakes
½ cup boiling water

FOR THE VEGETABLES (ALL AT ROOM TEMPERATURE)

4 small green zucchini, about 1½ inches wide at the base and about 3 to 4 inches long

4 small yellow squash, about 1½ inches wide at the base and about 3 to 4 inches long

4 small baby eggplants, about 1½ inches wide at the base and about 3 inches long

4 small firm roma (plum) tomatoes, about 3 inches long

1 yellow onion, sliced into ¼-inch rounds (to line the bottom of the pan)

To prepare the filling (1 day in advance)

Preheat the oven to 350°F. Spread the pine nuts over a foil-lined baking sheet and toast in the center of the oven, shaking the tray occasionally, for 5 to 7 minutes or until golden. Cool before adding them to the filling.

Combine the rice, 1 teaspoon salt, the pepper, ⅓ cup lemon juice, and 3 tablespoons olive oil in a bowl. Mix well. Add the currants, dill, parsley, tomato, both kinds of onion, and mint. Mix well. Cover and

refrigerate overnight to allow the rice to expand.

To prepare the vegetables

Start with room-temperature vegetables; they are easier to hollow and less likely to crack. Rinse the zucchini and the squash, using a vegetable brush to remove finely embedded sand. Prepare the zucchini and squash by turning them upside down and shaving the light brown tip off the bottom. Cut each to a 3-inch length by removing the top portion. Prepare the eggplants by cutting enough off the tops so that they are also about 3 inches long.

*Use a zucchini corer to core the squash, zucchini, and eggplants. Holding the vegetable in one hand, carefully insert the corer lengthwise into the cut top of the vegetable. Go deep enough to reach ¼ to ½ inch away from the bottom, being careful not to pierce through the bottom or sides. Keep a ¼-inch-thick wall around each vegetable as you gently turn the corer, removing and discarding the insides. (**Alternatively,** you can squeeze the excess liquid from the insides of the zucchini and squash [not the eggplant], and incorporate the pulp into the Mini*

159

Dill Omelets on page 14, as traditionally done in my family.) Once hollowed, set the vegetables aside.

Prepare the tomato by making a 1-inch circular cut into the top (stem side) and removing it. Keep the tops matched to the appropriate tomato. Hollow the tomatoes by removing and discarding the center rib, the pulp, and seeds; do not remove the flesh and inner ribs from the walls of the tomatoes.

To fill and cook the stuffed vegetables

Preheat the oven to 400°F. Line the bottom of a 9 x 5 x 2½-inch bread loaf pan with the onion rounds.

Remove the filling from the refrigerator and mix it well. Use a demitasse spoon to fill the zucchini, squash, and eggplant. Each time you add a spoonful, use your finger to press the filling down into the base of the vegetable until each is full ¼ inch from the top. This will allow space for the rice to expand while it cooks.

Stand the vegetables up in the pan. Use wedges of onion to fill in around the vegetables to support them in an upright position. (The vegetables must remain standing while they steam so the filling doesn't spill.) Combine ½ cup lemon juice, ¾ teaspoon salt, 2 tablespoons olive oil and ½ cup boiling water in a bowl and mix well. Pour this mixture around the vegetables in the pan. Cover the pan with aluminum foil, sealing it around the edges, place on the lowest shelf in the oven, and bake for 40 minutes.

In the meantime, place ¾ cups of the remaining filling in a bowl with 1½ tablespoons lemon juice and 2½ tablespoons water. Cover with plastic wrap and microwave on high for 2 minutes. Remove the bowl and set it aside covered for 15 minutes, then remove the plastic wrap and mix the filling well. Use a demitasse spoon to fill the tomatoes with the precooked filling. Replace their tops and set them aside.

After the vegetables have baked for 40 minutes, remove the pan from the oven and wedge the 4 stuffed tomatoes around the other vegetables. Replace the foil cover and return the pan to the oven for a final 5 minutes. Remove from the oven and cool covered. (**Note:** The tomatoes are prepared separately and steamed for the final 5 minutes to prevent them from collapsing.)

To serve

Offer at room temperature. Garnish with sprigs of parsley and lemon wedges.

Selecting vegetables

Choose zucchini and squash that are straight, as curved ones are harder to core. Choose vegetables that are the recommended size. While this may not always be possible (depending on availability), the "smaller" size of the vegetables is the key feature of this dish. Larger vegetables will do; however, you may have to increase the amount of prepared filling and use a larger loaf pan to stand them up in, allowing increased space to compensate for the larger sized vegetables.

Vegetable-Stuffed Cabbage Rolls

ABOUT 2 DOZEN

Mihshi Malfoof bi Zeyt (mihh-she mel-foof bee zeyt)

These delicious cabbage rolls are steamed with garlic in a lemon and mint broth. This is a great way to enjoy cabbage, and pretty healthy too. You can make these days in advance. Serve as an appetizer, side dish, or just keep them in the fridge to snack on.

Special equipment: A 13 x 9 x 2-inch baking pan.

Prepare ahead: The cooked cabbage rolls can be prepared up to 3 days in advance. Refrigerate. Serve as directed. **Note:** The filling must be prepared 1 day in advance.

FOR THE FILLING

½ cup converted (also called parboiled) rice

1 teaspoon salt

⅛ teaspoon coarsely ground black pepper

½ cup freshly squeezed lemon juice

3 tablespoon extra-virgin olive oil

1¼ cups finely chopped flat-leaf parsley; use
   green leafy parts and tender stems
¾ cup peeled and finely chopped tomato
¼ cup finely chopped green onion; use light
   and dark green parts
¼ cup finely chopped yellow onion
2 tablespoons finely chopped fresh mint or
   1 teaspoon dry mint flakes

FOR THE CABBAGE LEAVES
1 (3½–4-pound) head green cabbage, room
   temperature
2 teaspoons salt

FOR COOKING THE CABBAGE ROLLS
¼ cup garlic cloves, cut in half lengthwise
1 tablespoon chopped fresh mint leaves
or: ½ teaspoon dried mint flakes
1¼ teaspoons salt
2 cups boiling water
¼ cup freshly squeezed lemon juice
1 tablespoon extra-virgin olive oil

To prepare the filling (1 day in advance)
Combine the rice, salt, pepper, lemon juice, and olive oil in a bowl. Mix well, then stir in the remaining ingredients. Cover and refrigerate overnight to allow the rice to expand.

To prepare the cabbage leaves
Place a large pot with 20 cups of water and 2 teaspoons salt over high heat. Place a colander on a baking tray within reach. Insert a large two-pronged fork into the base of the head of cabbage. Once the water boils, submerge the cabbage head beneath the water. Rotate the fork with the head of

cabbage beneath the water. The individual leaves will begin to soften and separate from the head. Once this happens, you can use a knife to cut the individual leaves off from the base where they are attached to the stem and push them away. Let them continue to boil for a minute or so before removing them from the water. (Allowing the cabbage leaves to boil in the water will ensure they are pliable and easy to roll later.)

Remove the cabbage leaves one at a time from the boiling water. Stack them in the colander to drain. Continue rotating the head of cabbage, removing as many leaves as you can, or at least enough to make 24 rolls. Reserve the cabbage heart for later use. Spread the leaves over the tray to cool uncovered until they can be handled.

Use a knife to cut and remove the thick rib from the center of the larger leaves. Then cut the leaf in half, following the rib line. (Try to keep them equal in size.) Prepare the smaller leaves by cutting the lower third off the leaf. Reserve the ribs and extra pieces of cabbage for later use.

To roll the cabbage leaves

Place one cabbage leaf in front of you, dull-side up, with the rib line closest to you. Place 1 level tablespoon of filling along the rib line of the cabbage leaf and spread it lengthwise about 3 inches. Fold both sides (the right and left) of the cabbage leaf over the filling. Then tuck and roll the leaf neatly up toward the top. Repeat until the filling is finished. Each cabbage roll should be about 3 inches long.

To cook the cabbage rolls

Preheat the oven to 425°F, with one rack set on the lowest shelf in the oven. Brush olive oil over the bottom of a 13 x 9 x 2-inch pan. Arrange enough pieces of the reserved cabbage to cover the bottom of the pan to prevent sticking while the cabbage rolls steam.

Load the cabbage rolls in the pan over the cabbage pieces in rows of 8, placing them across the width of the pan, from left to right, one roll at a time, seam-side down, side-by-side (3 rows of 8). Make certain you have nestled one roll next to the other, securing them in place. (Placing them close together will prevent them from unraveling while they steam.) Sprinkle the garlic and mint over the cabbage rolls.

Dissolve the salt in 2 cups boiling water and mix well. Add the lemon juice and olive oil. Pour this mixture over the cabbage rolls. Cover and seal the top of the pan with aluminum foil. Place the pan on a foil-lined baking sheet on the lower rack of the oven and bake for 1 hour, then remove the pan from the oven and set it aside to cool, covered.

To serve

Offer the room-temperature cabbage rolls arranged on a dish with the cabbage heart in the center. Garnish with parsley, lemon, and grated carrot.

Selecting Heads Of Cabbage

Choose cabbages with smooth outer leaves (these will be easier to roll) and firm heads that are heavy for their size. Avoid those that seem light, as that is a sign the cabbage has lost much of its moisture.

Cabbage Rolls with Lamb (or Beef)

ABOUT 2 DOZEN

Mihshi Malfoof bi Lahm (mihh-she mel-foof bee lah-him)

Special equipment: A 13 x 9 x 2-inch baking pan.

Prepare ahead: The cooked cabbage rolls can be prepared up to 3 days in advance. Refrigerate. Serve as directed.

FOR THE FILLING

½ pound coarsely ground lamb (or beef)

½ cup converted (also called parboiled) rice

¾ teaspoon salt

¼ teaspoon coarsely ground black pepper

½ teaspoon ground allspice

¼ teaspoon ground cinnamon

¼ cup melted butter

¼ cup and ¼ cup cold water, divided

FOR THE CABBAGE LEAVES

1 (3½–4-pound) head green cabbage, room temperature

2 teaspoons salt

FOR COOKING THE CABBAGE ROLLS

¼ cup garlic cloves cut in half

1 tablespoon chopped fresh mint

or: ½ teaspoon dried mint flakes

1¼ teaspoons salt

1½ cups boiling water

⅛ teaspoon coarsely ground black pepper

¼ teaspoon ground allspice

⅛ teaspoon ground cinnamon

¼ cup freshly squeezed lemon juice

1 tablespoon extra-virgin olive oil

To prepare the filling

Combine the ground lamb (or beef) rice, salt, pepper, allspice, cinnamon, melted butter, and ¼ cup cold water in a bowl. Mix well, cover, and refrigerate for ½ hour. Then remove from the refrigerator, add ¼ cup cold water, and mix well. Roll and cook meat-filled cabbage leaves the same day.

To prepare and roll the cabbage leaves

Follow the procedure as described in the previous recipe for Vegetable-Stuffed Cabbage Rolls.

To cook the cabbage rolls

Follow the procedure as described in the previous recipe for Vegetable-Stuffed Cabbage Rolls with one exception. Once the cabbage rolls have been loaded in the pan, dissolve the salt and spices in 1½ cups boiling water and mix well. Add the lemon juice and olive oil. Pour this mixture over the cabbage rolls. Cover and seal the top of the pan with aluminum foil. Place the pan on a foil-lined baking sheet on the lower rack of the oven and bake for 1 hour, then remove the pan from the oven and set aside to cool for about ½ hour prior to serving.

To serve

Offer the warm cabbage rolls arranged on a dish with the cabbage heart in the center. Garnish with parsley, lemon, and grated carrot. Serve with Yogurt-Cucumber Salad on the side (page 63).

Lentil Noodle Stew

ABOUT 6 CUPS

Rashti (rush-tee)

In this hearty and rustic stew, the delicious flavor of the lentils is enhanced by the browned onions, garlic, and cilantro. Packed with iron, protein, and cholesterol-lowering fiber, lentils are quick and easy to prepare. This is the perfect starter to a meal when you want to avoid last minute heating. Serve with your favorite rustic bread.

Prepare ahead: You can prepare the stew several days in advance. As it remains refrigerated, the flavors continue to develop. You can also freeze the stew for several weeks in a well-sealed container. Serve as directed.

FOR THE STEW

1 cup brown lentils

1 teaspoon and ½ teaspoon and ¼ teaspoon salt, divided

¼ cup extra-virgin olive oil

1 tablespoon butter

3 cups diced yellow onion (¼ inch)

¼ teaspoon coarsely ground black pepper

1½ teaspoons ground coriander

4 large garlic cloves

1½ cups coarsely chopped cilantro; use leafy green parts and tender stems

¾ cup wide egg noodles

(**You can substitute** any flat noodles in place of the egg noodles.)

To prepare the stew

In a large pot, place the lentils, 1 teaspoon salt, and 7 cups water over high heat and cover. Once it comes to a boil, reduce the heat to medium-low, and simmer covered for 20 minutes.

In the meantime, preheat the olive oil and butter in a skillet over medium-high heat. Add the onions, ½ teaspoon salt, the pepper, and the coriander, and sauté until the onions are translucent, browned, and tender. Using a mortar and pestle, mash the garlic with ¼ teaspoon salt to a pulp and set it aside.

Once the onions are caramelized, stir in the garlic pulp, the cilantro, and the noodles and sauté for about a minute, then remove from the heat and set aside.

When the lentils are tender, add the onion and noodle mixture to the pot and increase the heat to high. Once the mixture comes to a boil, reduce the heat to medium-low, cover, and simmer for 10 minutes. Then remove from the heat and set aside to cool for half an hour.

To serve

For best results, serve slightly warm. If the soup seems too thick, you can thin it down with some boiling water.

Lentil Soup with Ruby Swiss Chard and Lemon

ABOUT 4 CUPS

Adas bi Hamood (aud-dus bee haum-mood)

Swiss chard is in the same family as beets and spinach, and contains an impressive list of health-promoting nutrients. This delicious combination of lentils, browned onions, cilantro, lemon, and Swiss chard provides a soup that is both healthy and flavorful.

Prepare ahead: You can prepare the soup several days in advance. As it remains refrigerated, the flavors continue to develop. You can also freeze the soup for several weeks in a well-sealed container. Serve as directed.

FOR THE SOUP

4 cups (lightly packed) sliced ruby Swiss chard (1-inch slices)

½ cup brown lentils

½ teaspoon and ¼ teaspoon and ¼ teaspoon salt, divided

¼ cup extra-virgin olive oil

2 cups diced yellow onion (¼ inch)

⅛ teaspoon coarsely ground black pepper

¾ teaspoon ground coriander

2 large garlic cloves

¾ cup coarsely chopped cilantro; use green leafy parts and tender stems

1½ teaspoons flour

2½ tablespoons freshly squeezed lemon juice

(**You can substitute** green Swiss chard.)

To prepare the soup

Rinse the Swiss chard well before slicing. Cut and discard the thick (celery-like) stalk from the leaf, then cut each leaf in half, lengthwise, following the rib-line to the top. Cut the leaves width-wise into 1-inch slices, and set aside until needed.

In a large pot, place the lentils, ½ teaspoon salt, and 4 cups water over high heat and cover. Once it comes to a boil, reduce the heat to medium-low and simmer covered for 20 minutes.

In the meantime, preheat the olive oil in a large skillet over medium-high heat. Add the onions, ¼ teaspoon salt, the pepper, and the coriander, and saute until the onions are translucent, browned, and tender. Using a mortar and pestle, mash the garlic with ¼ teaspoon salt to a pulp and set it aside.

Once the onions are caramelized, add the garlic pulp, the cilantro, the sliced Swiss chard, and the flour. Cook and stir until the Swiss chard has wilted. Remove from the heat and set the mixture aside.

When the lentils are tender, add the Swiss chard mixture and the lemon juice, and increase the heat to high. Once the mixture comes to a boil, reduce the heat to medium-low and simmer covered for 10 minutes. Remove the mixture from the heat and set aside to cool for 15 minutes.

To serve

For best results, serve slightly warm. If the soup seems too thick, you can thin it down with boiling water or additional lemon juice.

Opposite page: Lentil Soup with Ruby Swiss Chard and Lemon

166

Miniature Meatball Soup

ABOUT 6 CUPS

Shorba Keema (shore-ba kee ma)

As a child, my mother was so happy when she caught a cold because she knew her mother would always prepare this soup for her—a clear tomato broth with miniature meatballs and basmati rice, seasoned to perfection. I love to offer this soup on a cold day for lunch with a fresh loaf of bread right out of the oven. It is delicious as a meal, before a meal, or to cure the common cold! (See photo, page 130)

Prepare ahead: You can prepare the soup several days in advance. Refrigerate until needed. You can also freeze the soup for several weeks in a well-sealed container. Serve as directed.

FOR THE SOUP

⅓ cup minced and 1 cup diced (¼ inch) yellow onion, divided

½ pound ground beef (80%)

¼ cup and 2 tablespoons finely chopped flat-leaf parsley, divided

1½ teaspoons balsamic vinegar

½ teaspoon and ½ teaspoon salt, divided

¼ teaspoon coarsely ground black pepper

¼ teaspoon ground allspice

⅛ teaspoon ground cinnamon

1/16 teaspoon ground cloves

1/16 teaspoon ground nutmeg

3 tablespoons extra-virgin olive oil

6 cups chicken broth

2 tablespoons tomato paste

½ cup basmati rice (or long-grain rice)

1 cup peeled and diced tomato (½ inch)

2 tablespoons freshly squeezed lemon juice

To prepare the soup

Press the ⅓ cup minced onion between double-thick layers of paper towels. Once the excess moisture has been removed, combine the onion with the ground beef, ¼ cup parsley, the vinegar, ½ teaspoon salt, the pepper, allspice, cinnamon, cloves, and nutmeg. Mix well with your hand, using massage-like strokes to work the onions and parsley into the beef.

Divide the mixture into 1-tablespoon portions, then cut each tablespoon in half. Roll each half into a ball and set the meatballs aside (about 30 meatballs).

Preheat the olive oil in a large pot over medium-high heat. Add the meatballs and gently sauté them until evenly browned. Remove the pot off the heat and transfer the meatballs to a dish and set them aside. Reserve the pot.

Place the large pot over medium heat and add the 1 cup diced onion and ½ teaspoon salt. Sauté the onions until tender (if they begin to brown, slightly reduce the heat). Add the broth, tomato paste, and rice, and increase the heat to high. Once the mixture comes to a boil, add the meatballs, reduce the heat to medium-low, and simmer covered for 15 minutes. When the rice is cooked, add the tomato, lemon juice, and 2 tablespoons parsley. Bring the mixture to a boil and cook for 1 minute, then remove the soup from the heat.

To serve

Serve hot with a loaf of rustic bread.

Mixed Bean Stew

Makhlouta (makh-loot-ta)

A delightful and delicious combination of flavors and textures are brought together in this soup. So simple to prepare, it is slow-cooked with browned onions and cumin for a unique and distinct flavor. The beans provide a good source of nutrients, including iron and protein.

Special ingredients: Bean soup mix is sold in the dry bean section of grocery stores. It can contain an assortment of 16, 15, 14, and even 13 beans. I choose the 16 or 15 assorted mixes because of the variety of the beans and the overall flavor they give. Often these bean soup mixes come with a seasoning packet. You can discard the seasoning packet or save it for another use.

Prepare ahead: You can prepare the stew several days in advance. As it remains refrigerated, the flavors continue to develop. You can also freeze the stew for several weeks in a well-sealed container. Serve as directed.

FOR THE STEW

1 cup dry bean soup mix (15- or 16-bean soup mix)
¾ teaspoon and ½ teaspoon salt, divided
2 tablespoons extra-virgin olive oil
2 tablespoons butter
2 cups diced yellow onion (¼ inch)
⅛ teaspoon coarsely ground black pepper
1½ teaspoons cumin
⅓ cup brown lentils
2½ cups boiling water

To prepare the stew

Rinse the bean soup mix in a bowl, changing the water 3 times, and drain. Place the soup mix, ¾ teaspoon salt, and 4 cups water over high heat and cover. Once it comes to a boil, skim any foam off the top. Reduce the heat to medium-low and simmer covered for 30 to 40 minutes.

In the meantime, preheat the oil and butter in a skillet over medium-high heat. Add the onions, ½ teaspoon salt, and the pepper, and sauté the onions until they are tender and slightly browned, then add the cumin and mix well. Remove from the heat and set aside.

When the beans are slightly tender, add the lentils and continue to cook covered for about 20 minutes.

Add the boiling water to the browned onions and mix well. Pour this mixture over the beans and continue to cook, covered, for 10 to 15 minutes. Check to make certain the beans are tender, then remove the stew from the heat. Set aside to cool for 10 to 15 minutes prior to serving.

To serve

Serve with your favorite rustic bread. If the stew seems too thick, you can thin it down with some boiling water.

Baklava

Desserts

(HILLOU)

Whether you are the timid novice or the ultimate dessert pro, these recipes are fun to make and easy to devour. From the well-known and sweet, melt-in-your mouth Baklava to Turmeric Tea Cakes, Almond and Anise Fingers, Semolina Date Cookies, or Rice Pudding with Apricots, all are described with simple step-by-step instructions to guide you through the recipe. Enjoy Melt-Away Sugar Cookies and Sweet Semolina Yogurt Cakes at your next tea party, or Cashew Crescents at the next bake sale. Indulge your friends and family with desserts that are deliciously different. If you are looking for an impressive dessert to offer at your next gathering, then you should try Baked Kataifi with Cream, topped with pistachio and candied flower petals. For afternoon snacks, try Crunchy Anise Milk Cookies or Walnut Biscuits with Marshmallow Dip.

Almond Fingers 172
Baked Kataifi with Cream 173
Baklava 176
Syrup 179
Caramelized Bread Pudding with Cream . . 180
Cashew Crescents 182
Crunchy Anise Milk Cookies 185
Fresh Fruit 186
Glazed Anise Fingers 187
Honey Balls 189
Kataifi and Cream Nut Pie 191
Melt-Away Sugar Cookies 194
Clarified Butter 196
Mini Lebanese Pancakes with Cream 197

Mini Lebanese Half-Moon Pancakes
    with Walnuts 199
Rice Pudding with Apricots 200
Semolina Date Cookies 202
Semolina Walnut (or Almond)
    Cookies 204
Semolina Pistachio Cookies 205
Spicy Rice Pudding with Nuts 206
Sweet Semolina-Yogurt Cakes 208
Turkish Coffee 210
White Coffee 211
Turmeric Tea Cakes 212
Walnut Biscuits with Marshmallow Dip . . . 214

Almond Fingers

Asaibi Zainab (assaabee-zay-nub)

Layers of fillo dough wrapped around ground almonds scented with orange blossom water, this crunchy treat will quickly become a favorite around your home. These sweet crispy fingers are easy to make and are absolutely delicious.

Specialty ingredients: Fillo dough, found in most grocery stores or specialty markets (my favorite brand is Apollo); and *mazaher* (orange blossom water), found in specialty markets or online.

Special equipment: A food processor and a pastry brush.

Prepare ahead: You can bake these days in advance. Store them in an airtight container at room temperature for several days or refrigerate for several weeks. Serve at room temperature. Unbaked fingers can be frozen for several months. Freeze on a plastic-lined tray, then transfer to an airtight container. Thaw in the refrigerator, then bring to room temperature. Bake as directed.

FOR THE FINGERS

16 (12 x 17-inch) sheets of fillo dough (room temperature)

¾ cup syrup (see recipe on page 179)

2 cups finely ground almonds (about ½ pound)

3 tablespoons sugar

1 tablespoon mazaher

1 cup melted clarified butter (unsalted butter will do)

2 tablespoons finely ground unsalted pistachios

To prepare the fingers

Bring the fillo to room temperature (see "Handling Fillo Dough," page xiv). Prepare the syrup as described on page 179 and set it aside.

Combine the almonds and sugar in a bowl. Mix in the mazaher, using the back of a spoon to press the mazaher into the almonds and sugar until evenly blended and the nuts seem damp. Set aside.

Preheat the oven to 325°F. On a flat surface (I use a large, plastic cutting board because it's easier to clean), butter and layer 2 sheets of fillo, placing them lengthwise, one at a time, one on top of the other. (The long 17-inch side of the fillo should be facing you from left to right.) Brush each sheet with butter by starting at the corners and edges and working your way to the center.

Lift the bottom left and right corners up, folding the layered fillo in half lengthwise, making the dimen-

sion of the fillo 17 inches long and about 6 inches wide. The seam side should be towards you.

Place 3 tablespoons (lightly packed) almond filling in a line lengthwise (along the 17 inch length) from left to right, ½ inch above the seam. Use your fingers to distribute the filling evenly. Then fold the seam over the walnuts, securing them inside. Tightly and evenly roll the fillo toward the top.

Brush the entire outside of the 17-inch roll with butter (to prevent drying and cracking), then transfer it to a foil-lined baking sheet and place it seam-side down (this will prevent the roll from unraveling as it bakes). Repeat with the remaining fillo, placing each roll right up against the other, seam-side down. Cut each 17-inch roll into 5 fingers, equal in length (40 fingers total).

Place the tray on the middle rack of the oven and bake 35 to 45 minutes, or until the rolls are golden brown (check the bottoms to make sure they have browned). Remove from the oven and drizzle the cool syrup over them. Garnish the tops with ground pistachios. Cool completely. Serve at room temperature.

{VARIATION}

Substitute cashews, walnuts, or pistachios in the filling in place of the almonds. When using pistachios, add *maward* (rose water) instead of mazaher.

Baked Kataifi with Cream
Kneifi bi Kushta (knef-fee bee kush-ta)

SERVES 6

Two layers of crispy, shredded dough surround a warm cream center, then topped with candied flower petals and pistachios with a flavorful syrup drizzled over the individual servings. The traditional way of making the filling (kushta) is a process of skimming the thick skin that forms over cream after it has been simmering for a long period. No one really does this at home, though it is perhaps done at large markets in the Middle East that sell sweets. The cream used in this recipe is a tasty alternative. This dessert is the perfect ending to a great meal or even as an afternoon sweet with tea. Offer it with a plate of seasonal fresh fruit and Turkish coffee.

Specialty ingredients: Clarified butter (see page 196); kataifi shredded fillo dough (my favorite brand is Apollo); and *zaher lamoon* (sold as zaher jam or orange blossom jam, in specialty markets, or orange blossom jam online); you want the variety that actually has small candied petals.

Special equipment: A food processor and an 8-inch round cake pan.

Prepare ahead: You can prepare this up to 4 days in advance. Refrigerate covered. You can freeze it unbaked up to 2 months in an airtight wrapper. Bake directly from the freezer as directed. Serve as described.

FOR THE BAKED KATAIFI

1 cup syrup, see page 179

1 teaspoon and ½ cup melted clarified butter (unsalted butter will do), divided

½ pound kataifi shredded fillo dough (room temperature)

1 tablespoon zaher lamoon (garnish)

1 teaspoon freshly squeezed lemon juice

1 tablespoon ground pistachios (garnish)

FOR THE FILLING

1½ cups half-and-half

¼ cup farina (cream of wheat)

1½ tablespoons sugar

(**You can substitute** whole, reduced-fat, or fat-free milk in place of the half-and-half.)

To prepare the kataifi

Prepare the syrup as described on page 179 and set it aside. Brush the sides and bottom of an 8-inch round cake pan with 1 teaspoon melted butter, and set aside.

Cut the kataifi into 1-inch lengths. Place it in a food processor fitted with a sharp metal blade and process to fine pieces, about ¼ inch. Transfer the chopped kataifi to a bowl with ½ cup melted butter. Mix well with your hand until evenly blended.

Divide the kataifi mixture into two-thirds and one-third portions. Place the two-thirds portion into the greased cake pan. Evenly distribute and level the mixture, then use a flat-edged spatula to firmly press the kataifi mixture down evenly into the bottom of the pan. Set aside. Keep the one-third portion covered for later use.

Preheat the oven to 400°F. Lower one rack to the bottom shelf of the oven.

To prepare the filling

Rinse a medium saucepan with water (this will help prevent the half-and-half mixture from sticking). Combine the half-and-half and farina in the pan and mix well. Place the mixture over high heat, uncov-

ered, and stir constantly, using a flat-edged, heat-proof spatula, until it begins to boil. Reduce the heat to medium-low and continue to stir until the mixture thickens. If any lumps appear, use a whisk to blend them out. (**A word of caution**: When preparing the cream filling, do not use a wooden cooking utensil that you have used to sauté onions, garlic, or other foods. The filling will absorb that flavor.)

Test the desired thickness by dropping ½ teaspoon of the filling on a dish. Let it cool for 30 seconds. Turn the dish sideways; if it remains in one place, the filling is ready for the sugar. Add the sugar and cook for an additional minute.

To prepare the baked kataifi
Slowly pour the hot filling into the center of the cake pan over the layer of kataifi. Use the tines of a fork to evenly spread the cream mixture up to, but not touching, the sides of the pan, leaving a ¼-inch border free of filling.

Sprinkle the remaining one-third kataifi mixture over the top and sides of the cream filling. With your hand, evenly level and distribute the kataifi over the filling and down the sides; then, using a flat-edged spatula, gently press down on the kataifi to even it out.

Place the cake pan on the bottom rack in the oven and bake for 30 to 35 minutes, or until the top is golden brown and the kataifi has slightly pulled away from the edges of the pan. Remove from the oven and set aside to cool.

After 30 minutes, rotate the pan to loosen the shredded kataifi, and make sure it rotates freely in the pan. Place a serving platter flush against the cake pan and flip the shredded kataifi onto the platter, just as you would flip an upside-down cake.

In a small skillet, place the zaher lamoon and the lemon juice over low heat to dissolve the jam the orange blossom petals are stored in. Garnish the top with ground pistachios in a crisscross pattern, then place 2 orange blossom petals within each grid of pistachios.

To serve
Warm with the syrup on the side. Cut the kataifi into 6 pieces as follows: Begin cutting 2 inches from the outer edge. Cut an inner circle all the way around that is 2 inches in from the edge. Then cut the outer ring into 4 equal pieces and the inner circle in half. Let your guests pour the desired amount of syrup over their pieces.

{VARIATION}
Crispy Angel Hair with Cream (*Ismaliyeh*): This dessert is the same two layers of crispy angel hair with a warm cream center, except you do not grind the kataifi into fine pieces and you do not need to flip it upside down onto a platter. Cut the kataifi into 3-inch lengths and mix it with the melted butter. The rest of the recipe and procedure remain the same. Once baked and slightly cooled, transfer it to a platter and garnish and serve as described above. (To transfer it to a platter, gently flip it upside-down on to a dish, then carefully flip it right-side up on to your serving patter before garnishing it.)

Baklava

Baklawa bi Jouz (buck-la-wa bee jowz)

You can find baklava in many grocery stores and bakeries. These pastries come in many shapes and sizes and are traditionally diamond shaped, available with a variety of nut fillings, walnuts being most commonly used. What separates this baklava from store-bought is the clarified butter, the homemade syrup, and the fact that it is freshly baked from your oven. This sweet, crisp walnut strudel is so easy to prepare and is a delicious addition at any gathering (see photo, page 170).

Specialty ingredients: Fillo dough, found in most grocery stores or specialty markets (my favorite brand is Apollo), clarified butter (see page 196), and mazaher (orange blossom water), found in specialty markets or online.

Special equipment: A food processor, pastry brush, and a 9 x 13 x 2-inch baking pan.

Prepare ahead: You can bake baklava up to 3 days in advance. Cool completely and store in an airtight container. It can be refrigerated prior to baking for several days or frozen unbaked for several months. When refrigerating or freezing unbaked baklava, do not cut it into pieces until ready to bake. Press plastic wrap up against the top of the baklava and seal it around the edges to keep the moisture in; then place the pan in an airtight bag. When frozen, thaw overnight in the refrigerator. Always bring it to room temperature prior to baking.

FOR THE BAKLAVA

1 (16-ounce) package 12 x 17-inch fillo dough (room temperature)

1 cup cooled syrup (see the following recipe)

3 cups finely ground walnuts (about ¾ pound)

⅓ cup granulated sugar

4 teaspoons mazaher

1¼ cups melted clarified butter (unsalted butter will do)

2 tablespoons finely ground unsalted pistachios (garnish)

To prepare the baklava

Bring the fillo to room temperature (see "Handling Fillo Dough," page xiv). Prepare the syrup as described below and set it aside.

Combine the walnuts and sugar in a bowl. Mix in the mazaher, using the back of a spoon to press the mazaher into the walnuts and sugar until evenly blended and the nuts seem damp. Set aside.

Count the sheets of fillo dough (the number of sheets in a pound of fillo varies from box to box). Divide them, using one-third of the sheets for the bottom, 4 sheets for the center to hold the nuts, and the rest to be used on top. Keep the fillo dough covered with plastic to prevent drying.

Preheat the oven to 350°F. Brush the bottom of a 9 x 13 x 2-inch baking pan with melted butter. Place 1 sheet of fillo dough on the bottom of the tray. It will be slightly crumpled, which is no problem. Brush it with butter by starting at the corners and edges, working your way to the center. Continue layering one-third of the sheets on the bottom of the pan, making certain that you are brushing each

sheet with butter before placing the next. (Some of the sheets may tear while transferring them into the tray; it's okay, just adjust them as best you can.)

The next 4 sheets will line the edges of the pan to prevent the nuts from touching the sides of the pan and burning while baking. Place 1 sheet of fillo so that half of it is in the pan and the other half drapes over the edge. Brush the section in the pan with butter. Repeat this on the other 3 edges.

Transfer the walnut mixture to the pan. Use the tines of a fork to evenly distribute the mixture up to the corners and sides, right up to the fillo. Fold the pieces of fillo that are draped over the sides in and over the walnut mixture and brush them with butter.

Continue layering the sheets of fillo, brushing each sheet with butter before placing the next. (Always brush them from the corners and edges, working your way toward the center.) Carefully arrange the final 2 sheets so they are as flat as possible, brushing each layer with butter. Work your way around the border, using a small spatula, and tuck in any loose pieces. Brush the top and edges one final time with butter.

Place a piece of plastic wrap over the top of the baklava pan, and use a flat pancake turner to press down evenly over the entire top. (Doing this before cutting the baklava into individual pieces will ensure that the layers are even and will bake together.) Remove the plastic wrap and make 5 cuts lengthwise (from one

side to the other), about 1½ inches apart. Make 9 diagonal cuts widthwise (from one side to the other) that are also about 1½ inches apart.

Bake the baklava in the center of the oven for 50 to 60 minutes or until the top is golden brown. Evenly drizzle cooled syrup over the top of the hot baklava (oven-hot baklava absorbs syrup better), to coat each piece. (Do not pour warm or hot syrup over the baked baklava; it will decrease the crispy texture.) Set aside to cool for at least 4 hours before removing pieces.

To serve

Prior to serving the baklava, go over the cuts to loosen the individual pieces from the tray. Garnish the top of each piece with a pinch of ground pistachios. Serve at room temperature.

{VARIATION}

You can substitute 1 teaspoon cinnamon for the mazaher. Substitute almonds, cashews, or pistachios in place of the walnuts. When using pistachios, use maward (rose water) instead of mazaher (orange blossom water). The rest of the recipe and procedure remain the same.

Syrup
Atr (utt-terr)

Referred to by some as simple syrup, I think of it as essential syrup. While it's very easy to make, it is important not to over-boil the syrup. The longer you boil the sugar and water mixture, the thicker the syrup will become. When it gets too thick, it will not be absorbed as well by the sweets you are preparing it for.

Prepare ahead: You can prepare this days to weeks in advance. Cool completely prior to storing it in an airtight container at room temperature.

FOR THE SYRUP

2 cups granulated sugar

1 cup water

2 tablespoons freshly squeezed lemon juice, strained

To prepare the syrup

Dissolve the sugar and water together in a saucepan and mix well. (**A word of caution**: *Do not use a wooden cooking utensil that you have used to sauté onions, garlic, or other foods, as the syrup will absorb that flavor.*) *The syrup will appear cloudy at this stage.*

Place over high heat, uncovered. Once the mixture has come to a rolling boil and the surface seems engulfed by bubbles, set the timer and boil for 2 minutes. Then stir in the lemon juice and return to a boil for an additional 10 to 15 seconds. (Do not skip adding the lemon juice, otherwise the syrup will recrystallize when stored for longer periods.) Remove from the heat and set aside, uncovered. Cool completely before using. **Note**: *When preparing larger batches of syrup, you may need to allow the mixture to boil a bit longer accordingly.*

{VARIATION}

You can substitute lime juice for the lemon juice. You can add ½ tablespoon mazaher (orange blossom water) or maward (rose water) at the same time you add the lemon juice for scented syrups.

Caramelized Bread Pudding with Cream

SERVES 8 TO 10

Aysh el Sariya (Iiesh-ill sa-rye-ya)

This dessert of caramelized bread with a creamy filling topped with finely ground pistachios is a unique version of bread pudding very popular in Lebanon and countries throughout the Middle East. It makes for a great centerpiece dessert when entertaining larger groups. Offer it with a platter of fresh fruit and Turkish coffee.

Specialty ingredients: Mazaher (orange blossom water), maward (rose water), both found in specialty markets or online, and zaher lamoon (sold as zaher jam or orange blossom jam, in specialty markets, or orange blossom jam online); you want the variety that actually has small candied petals.

Special equipment: A 9 x 13 x 2-inch baking dish.

Prepare ahead: It can be prepared early in the day. Serve the same day as described.

FOR THE CARAMELIZED BREAD

1 pound loaf plain Italian bread, 8 large slices 1 inch thick
2 cups sugar
1 tablespoon and 2 teaspoons freshly squeezed lemon juice, divided
3 cups boiling water
1 tablespoon mazaher
1 tablespoon maward
1 teaspoon instant coffee
2 tablespoons ground pistachios (garnish)
2 tablespoons zaher lamoon (garnish)

FOR THE CREAM

5 slices white sandwich bread
2¼ cups milk
1½ tablespoons cornstarch
1½ teaspoons sugar

To prepare the caramelized bread

Preheat the oven to 175°F. Cut 8 1-inch-thick slices (widthwise) from the center of the loaf of bread. Cut off the crusts and discard them.

Place the pieces of bread, 1 inch apart, on a foil-lined baking sheet and bake in the center of the oven for 30 minutes, then turn each piece and return the tray to the oven for an additional 30 minutes.

*While waiting for the bread to bake, prepare the caramelized sugar. Place the sugar in a medium saucepan over medium-high heat and stir constantly until it has melted and is an amber color. Reduce the heat to medium-low and keep stirring the sugar, breaking down any lumps. Once all the lumps have melted and the sugar is caramel colored, carefully add 1 tablespoon lemon juice (**caution:** it will splatter), the boiling water, the mazaher, maward, and coffee. Reduce the heat to low and stir the mixture until all the sugar has dissolved.*

Remove the bread from the oven and increase the temperature to 350°F. Transfer the pieces of bread to a 9 x 13 x 2-inch baking dish. Pour the dissolved caramelized mixture over the bread. Allow the pieces of bread to absorb the liquid for a couple of minutes, then turn them once.

Place the baking dish in the center of the oven and bake the caramelized bread for 30 minutes, then remove from the oven and set aside to cool, uncovered, for 30 minutes. Turn the pieces of bread once, then set the bread aside to cool for an additional hour, uncovered. Store loosely covered at room temperature until ready to assemble.

To prepare the cream

Rinse a medium saucepan with water (this will help prevent the milk mixture from sticking). Remove and discard the crust from the 5 slices of white sandwich bread. Pull the bread apart into 1-inch pieces.

Combine the milk, the pieces of bread, cornstarch, and sugar in the saucepan. Place over medium-high heat and cook, stirring with a heat-proof, flat-edged spatula, until the mixture begins to bubble around the edges. Reduce the heat to medium and continue to cook, stirring constantly, for about 2 minutes. (**A word of caution**: When preparing the cream fill-ing, do not use a wooden cooking utensil that you have used to sauté onions, garlic, or other foods. The filling will absorb that flavor.)

Remove the cream from the heat and cover with a paper towel. Cool completely at room temperature before using. Once cooled, refrigerate until ready to assemble.

To assemble and serve

The bread pudding can be assembled 2 to 3 hours prior to serving. Arrange 5 pieces of the caramelized bread on a flat platter in the shape of a circle about 8 inches in diameter. Evenly spread the cream over the bread, distributing it up to (but not over) the edge. Arrange the last 3 pieces of caramelized bread in a "doughnut" shape on top of the cream.

Generously sprinkle ground pistachios around the perimeter of the pudding and over the center. In a small skillet, place the orange blossom petals and 2 *teaspoons lemon juice over low heat to dissolve the jam they are stored in. Garnish the exposed cream filling in the center and around the edges of the pudding with candied flower petals.*

Cover loosely with waxed paper and store in a cool, dry area. Serve at room temperature. Refrigerate leftover pudding.

Selecting bread

Italian bread is typically "spongier" than French bread. It is also a wider loaf, which is what you want for this recipe. It soaks up and retains the caramelized mixture better. If you can't find it, a large/wide 1-pound loaf of plain French bread will do. However, you will get superior results using good-quality Italian bread. (The loaf I use is about 12 inches long and about 4 inches wide.)

Cashew Crescents
Koul Weshkor (kool-wa-shkoorr)

ABOUT 3 DOZEN

The literal translation of the Arabic name for this type of baklava is "Eat and give thanks." These crescent-shaped pastries are filled with ground cashews, and as they bake, the crispy, crunchy layers fan apart. The cashew filling is like creamy butter, and the taste is sensational. Offer them as a dessert or snack.

Specialty ingredients: Fillo dough, found in most grocery stores or specialty markets (my favorite brand is Apollo), and mazaher (orange blossom water), found at specialty markets or online.

Special equipment: A food processor, pastry brush, and a 1½-inch round cookie cutter.

Prepare ahead: These can be made days in advance and stored in an airtight container at room temperature. Refrigerate for longer periods. Serve at room temperature.

FOR THE CRESCENTS
24 (12 × 17-inch) sheets fillo dough (room temperature)
1 cup cooled syrup (see page 179)
2 cups finely ground raw cashews (about ½ pound)

3 tablespoons granulated sugar
4 teaspoons mazaher
1 cup melted clarified butter (see page 196) (unsalted butter will do)
2 tablespoons finely ground unsalted pistachios

To prepare the crescents
Bring the fillo to room temperature (see "Handling Fillo Dough," page xiv). Prepare the syrup as described on page 179 and set it aside.

Combine the ground cashews and sugar in a bowl and mix well. Mix in the mazaher, using the back of a spoon to press the mazaher into the mixture until evenly blended and the nuts seem damp. Preheat the oven to 325°F.

On a flat surface (I use a large plastic cutting board; it's easier to clean), butter and layer 6 sheets of fillo dough and place them lengthwise one at a time, one on top of the other. (The long 17 inch side of the fillo should be facing you from left to right.) Brush each sheet with butter by starting at the corners and edges and working your way to the center.

Lift up the bottom left and right corners of the stack of fillo, folding it in half lengthwise, making the dimension of the fillo 17 inches long and about 6 inches wide. The seam side should be towards you. Brush the top with butter.

Fold the stack of fillo in half a second time lengthwise, making the dimension of the fillo 17 inches long and about 3 inches wide. The seam side should be towards you. Brush the top with butter.

Place 6 tablespoons (lightly packed) cashew filling along the center of the 17-inch folded fillo in a line from left to right. Use your fingers to distribute the filling evenly from left to right.

Carefully fold the fillo in half, tucking the filling inside and securing it in place. Brush the top with butter. The roll now is 17 inches long and about 1½ inches wide.

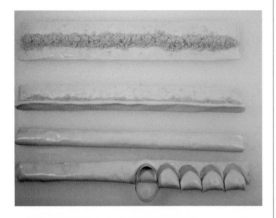

Use a 1½-inch round cookie cutter to cut the individual crescents. Start at one end of the 17-inch fillo roll. Cut through the fillo roll so that the cookie cutter is actually cutting just below the upper edge where the two flaps meet. By cutting just below these edges you will be cutting through the fillo creating layers that will fan apart as the crescents bake. (Do not cut through the seam side that is towards you, this is what holds the crescent together.)

Carefully transfer the crescent-shaped pastries to a baking sheet lined with foil and place one crescent next to the other, in rows. You should get about 9 crescents per 17-inch fillo roll. Repeat with the remaining fillo. (For a total of about 36 crescents.)

Place the tray on the middle rack of the oven and bake for 40 to 50 minutes, or until the crescents are golden brown (check the bottoms to see if they have browned to ensure they will be crispy), then remove them from the oven. Immediately drizzle cooled syrup over the individual crescents. Decorate the tops with ground pistachios. Cool completely before serving.

{VARIATION}

Substitute walnuts, almonds, or pistachios in place of the cashews in the filling. When using pistachios, use maward (rose water) instead of mazaher.

Crunchy Anise Milk Cookies

ABOUT 30 COOKIES

Ka'ak bi Haleeb (ka-ack bee ha-leeb)

These cookies are fun to prepare with the family and delicious any time of day. The crunchy texture will have everyone coming back for more. They are great for a snack in the afternoon with a glass of milk, or in the evening with a warm cup of tea. Pack them along on a hike or take them to the beach, they're delicious to munch on.

Special equipment: A coffee bean grinder (to grind the anise seeds).

Prepare ahead: You can prepare these several days in advance. Store them in an airtight container at room temperature.

FOR THE COOKIES

½ cup milk

½ cup and ½ cup granulated sugar, divided

¼ teaspoon yeast

3 cups unbleached flour

2½ teaspoons double acting baking soda

1 tablespoon ground anise seed

¼ teaspoon ground cloves

3 tablespoons melted unsalted butter

1½ tablespoons extra-virgin olive oil

Measuring flour: See page xiv.

To prepare the cookies

Warm the milk in a microwave for about 15 seconds or until it is lukewarm. Add ½ cup of the sugar and the yeast to the milk. Mix well, cover, and set aside.

In a bowl, combine the flour, baking soda, anise, and cloves. Add the rest of the sugar to the milk, followed by the butter and olive oil. Mix well, then pour over the dry ingredients and mix together with your hands to form the dough. Flatten the mixture into the bottom of the bowl (it may be a bit sticky,

that's okay). Do not add more flour, set it aside uncovered. Preheat the oven to 350°F. Foil-line a baking sheet and set it within reach.

After 5 minutes, divide the dough into ¼-cup portions. On a flat surface (I use a plastic cutting board—it has good traction and is easy to clean), evenly roll each portion into a rope 12 inches long. Cut each rope into 3 (4-inch) lengths. Working with one 4-inch length of dough at a time, wrap the ends around to form a circle. Pinch the ends together. Transfer the cookie to the foil-lined baking sheet. Repeat with the remaining dough, placing the cookies ½ inch apart.

*Use the tines of a fork to press an imprint on the top of each cookie 4 times. Place the tray of cookies in the center of the oven, and bake 25 to 30 minutes or until the tops are golden brown. (**Note**: For cookies that are less crunchy, remove them from the oven after 25 minutes.) Cool completely before serving.*

Fresh Fruit

SERVES 6

Fweicki (fweik-key)

Fresh fruit is a major part of most Lebanese gatherings. Offer a simple platter or an elaborate arrangement; the colors and flavors are always a welcome addition. Mix and match colors, textures, shapes, and flavors. Let your imagination go wild as you create colorful arrangements that entice your guests to taste the fruits of your labor.

Special equipment: A melon baller, skewers, and brochettes.
Prepare ahead: Prepare the fruit up to 1 day in advance. Refrigerate separately. Arrange the same day as serving.

FOR THE FRUIT (MIX AND MATCH ANY COMBINATION)

Cantaloupe, honeydew, watermelon

Mangoes, kiwis, papayas, star fruit (carambola), prickly pears

Cherries, peaches, nectarines

Strawberries, blueberries, raspberries, boysenberries

Oranges, clementines, tangerines, grapefruits

Grapes, pineapples

Medjool dates, figs

To prepare the fruit

Consider the type of event you are having. Will you provide a plate and fork, or is it easier to offer fruit on skewers or brochettes? Cut the fruit in different shapes and sizes. Use a melon baller for watermelon, cantaloupe, and honeydew balls. Peel and cut fresh peaches, oranges, grapefruits, or nectarines before adding them. Always peel and cut all of the fruit into individual servings prior to arranging them on a platter.

Arrange the fruit on flat or shallow platters. You can use the rind of some of the melons as serving bowls. The peel of some fruits, such as mangoes or oranges, can be rolled into roses. Select platters that contrast with the colors of the fruit. Use mirrors, glass platters, or black or cobalt platters so the vibrant colors will pop against the background.

{VARIATION}

Serve the fruit with various chocolate dipping sauces (dark, milk chocolate, or white chocolate). Or prepare dipping sauces of pureed raspberries, mangoes, blueberries, or strawberries. Incorporate fresh flowers such as orchids, roses, or lilies with your presentation.

Glazed Anise Fingers

Macaroon (mac-ca-roon)

These cookies are a combination of three kinds of flour, ground anise seeds, and olive oil shaped into fingers. Deep-fried and glazed, they are absolutely delicious. The crispy outer layer is enhanced by the soft and moist, sweetened center. Serve them with fresh fruit or as an afternoon snack.

Specialty ingredients: Ground mahlab (the pits of black cherries, when dried the beige colored drop-shaped kernels are ground producing a rose-scented powder that is slightly bitter with a faint almond-like taste), ground anise seeds, and semolina, found in specialty markets or online.

Special equipment: A grid cooling rack and a candy/fry thermometer, both found at kitchen supply stores or online.

Prepare ahead: The syrup (glaze) can be prepared several days in advance. The fingers can be prepared several days in advance and stored in an airtight container. The raw fingers can be frozen for several weeks. Freeze on a plastic-lined baking sheet, then store in an airtight container. Fry them directly from the freezer, as described.

Measuring flour: See page xiv.

FOR THE GLAZED ANISE FINGERS

1 recipe syrup, for the glaze (see recipe on page 179)

$1/16$ teaspoon active dry yeast

$1/16$ teaspoon sugar

7 tablespoons lukewarm water

1 cup and 2 tablespoons unbleached flour

½ cup and 2 tablespoons Wondra flour

¼ cup fine semolina

1 tablespoon ground anise seed

½ teaspoon ground mahlab

7 tablespoons extra-virgin olive oil

2 cups canola oil (for frying)

To prepare the glazed anise fingers

Prepare the syrup and set it aside.

In a small bowl, dissolve the yeast and sugar in the water. Cover and set it aside.

Combine the dry ingredients in a bowl. Add the olive oil and use your fingers to evenly blend the oil into the dry ingredients. Add the yeast mixture, mixing it in with your hands to quickly form the dough.

Measure the dough into ¼-cup portions. On a flat surface (I use a plastic cutting board—it has good

traction and is easy to clean), using your hands, roll each portion into an 8-inch rope, then cut each rope into 4 (2-inch) pieces. Take each 2-inch piece and roll it into a 3-inch finger with tapered ends.

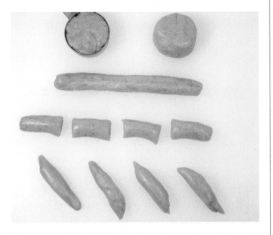

Place one 3-inch finger at a diagonal on the grid cooling rack, and gently flatten it onto the grid into the shape of a narrow leaf. Press gently to get the imprint of the grid on the backside of the dough. Carefully lift from one side and fold over toward the other side, forming a finger-shaped cookie tapered at each end. Repeat with remaining pieces of dough.

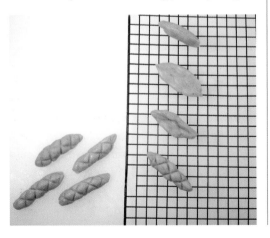

To fry the anise fingers

Place the canola oil in a small saucepan over medium-high heat. The oil should be about 1 inch deep. Heat the oil to 350°F, using a candy/fry thermometer to ensure proper temperature, and fry 6 anise fingers at a time.

Once golden brown, remove the fingers with a slotted spoon to a paper towel-lined dish. Then transfer them while still hot to a bowl with the cooled syrup. Continue soaking them in the syrup while the next batch is being fried. (Remove the anise fingers from the syrup just before the next batch goes into the syrup.) Repeat with the remaining fingers.

Recycle the oil: *See page xiv.*

*(**Alternatively**, the anise fingers can be baked. Preheat the oven to 350°F. Place the fingers on a foil-lined baking tray, decorative side facing up. After 30 minutes, remove them from the oven and place them hot into the syrup. Serve at room temperature. They are good baked, but they taste best fried.)*

To serve and store

Serve at room temperature. Store the cooled fingers in an airtight container with the leftover syrup poured over them. Always drain excess syrup from the fingers before serving.

Honey Balls
Awwamat (a-wham-mat)

ABOUT 100

Growing up, we called these Honey Balls, even though they are not prepared with honey. They were sweet, crunchy and yummy, and that was an easy name for them. These crispy balls of fried dough are soaked in syrup and are amazingly good. I like offering them when we have a group of eight or more with a colorful fruit platter next to them. I am always asked how I get them so crisp on the outside and light and airy on the inside. The answer is potato.

Special equipment: A food mill (a potato ricer will do), a stand mixer with a flat beater, a 14-inch wok that is about 4 inches deep and a candy/fry thermometer; all can be found at kitchen supply stores or online.

Prepare ahead: The honey balls can be prepared early in the day. They are best the day they are prepared, while they are crunchy. Store uncovered in a cool, dry area (so they retain their crunch). Here is the best-kept secret: Partially fried honey balls can be frozen for 2 months. Once they have cooled, freeze them on a plastic-lined tray and store in an airtight container. When ready to use, thaw to room temperature evenly spread over a tray. Fry and serve as described.

FOR THE HONEY BALLS

2 recipes cooled syrup (see page 179)
½ pound peeled russet potato (room
   temperature)
1 tablespoon dry active yeast
¼ teaspoon sugar
2 cups unbleached flour
1 (48-ounce) container of canola oil for frying

Measuring flour: See page xiv.

To prepare the honey balls
Prepare the syrup and set it aside.

Weigh the potatoes after they are peeled to ensure you have ½ pound potatoes. Dice them into 1-inch cubes. Place them in a medium saucepan with 4 cups of water over high heat and bring to a boil, then reduce the heat to medium-low, cover, and simmer for 15 minutes until tender.

Pour the cooked potatoes into a food mill. Once all the water has drained, pass the potatoes through the mill into a bowl. Set the bowl aside uncovered, allowing the potatoes to cool slightly.

189

While they are cooling, dissolve the yeast in ½ cup lukewarm water in a small bowl with the sugar. Mix well, then cover the bowl with a dish and set it aside for several minutes to proof the yeast (until it foams).

Place ¾ cup lukewarm water in the mixing bowl of a stand mixer fitted with a flat beater. On medium-low speed, add 1 cup of flour, ½ cup at a time. Mix until the batter is smooth. Add all the yeast mixture to the batter, followed by the second cup of flour, ½ cup at a time. Increase the speed to medium. Once the mixture is smooth, add the warm (not hot) potatoes and mix for a couple of minutes until well combined.

(**Alternatively**, if you do not have a stand mixer with a flat beater, you can mix the batter using a large hand whisk. The key is, once all the ingredients are in the bowl, to thoroughly beat enough air into the batter so the balls will be light, fluffy, and crisp when fried. I have not had good results using a handheld electric mixer, as the batter gets stuck and travels up the beaters before it is mixed thoroughly.)

Transfer the batter to a bowl that is large enough to allow it to double in volume. Cover the bowl with a dish and set it aside for 1½ hours to rise.

In the meantime, set up your "cook station" where you will be frying the honey balls. Pour enough oil into the wok so that is about 1½ inches away from the top rim. Place a flat tray within reach to transfer the partially fried honey balls on to. Prepare a bowl filled with the cooled syrup within reach. Place a colander with a bowl underneath it next to the tray.

To fry the honey balls

After the batter has risen, preheat the oil to 350°F, using a candy/fry thermometer to measure the temperature for accuracy. Once the oil has reached 350°F, adjust the heat to maintain the temperature. Do not to let the oil exceed 350°F; otherwise the balls will fry too quickly and the insides will not cook through properly.

Place a small bowl of ice water and a regular kitchen teaspoon (not a measuring spoon) within reach. (You will be using the tip of the teaspoon to drop portions of the batter into the hot oil.)

Using one hand, gently pat the batter down into the bowl. Using the same hand, gently clench some of the batter in the palm of your hand as you make a fist. As the batter squeezes up from the top of your fist, have the teaspoon ready in the other hand. Dip the rounded tip of the teaspoon in the bowl of cold water and shake off the excess water. (Dipping the tip of the spoon into the cold water helps prevent the batter from sticking to the spoon.) Then, using the rounded tip of the spoon, scoop a slightly larger than marble-sized portion of batter off the top of your fist. Carefully drop it into the hot oil. Drop it close to the surface of the oil to avoid splashing.

Repeat, gently clenching your hand into a fist and scooping portions off the top. Continue dipping the tip of the spoon in the cold water before scooping the batter as you keep a count of how many balls you are dropping into the oil.

Once you have about 33 balls in the oil, stir them around until they are evenly light golden in color. (If any of the portions stick to the bottom of the wok, use a metal slotted spoon to release them.) Once they are a light golden color, use the slotted spoon to remove them from the oil and transfer them to the tray. Repeat this procedure 2 more times.

Once all the partially fried balls are on the tray, transfer all of them back into the wok in one batch and fry them until they are a deep golden brown. Keep stirring them so they brown evenly on all sides.

Using the slotted spoon, transfer the balls (let as much oil as possible drain from the balls first) to the bowl of syrup. Mix well for several minutes, allowing the syrup to soak into the balls. Transfer them to the colander with the bowl underneath it (excess syrup will drain into the bowl). Transfer them to a container to cool, uncovered. Discard the drained syrup.

Recycle the oil: *See page xiv.*

To serve and store
Serve honey balls at room temperature the same day. Store them in a cool, dry area, lightly covered. Humidity will make the balls lose their crunch faster.

Kataifi and Cream Nut Pie
ONE 8-INCH PIE
Mafrouki (maa-frou-key)

This unique pie is easy to prepare and makes quite an impression. The crisp texture of the oven-baked kataifi sweetened with syrup complements the cream topping and buttery toasted pine nuts, almonds, and pistachios. Serve this dessert with fruit after a meal, or offer it at your next tea party for something deliciously different.

Specialty ingredients: Clarified butter (see page 196); kataifi shredded fillo (my favorite brand is Apollo), found at specialty markets or online.
Special equipment: A food processor and a 9-inch round cake pan.
Prepare ahead: The piecrust and topping can be prepared early in the day. Serve as described.

FOR THE PIECRUST
½ cup and ½ cup syrup (see page 179), divided
½ pound kataifi shredded fillo dough (room temperature)
½ cup melted clarified butter (unsalted butter will do)

FOR THE TOPPING
¼ cup toasted pine nuts
¼ cup toasted (unsalted) pistachios
¼ cup toasted slivered almonds
2 tablespoons melted butter
3 slices white sandwich bread
1½ cups milk
1 tablespoon cornstarch
1 teaspoon sugar

To prepare the piecrust
Prepare the syrup and set it aside until needed.

Select a flat serving dish about 12 inches in diameter. Lightly butter an 8-inch circle in the center of the dish, then set aside until needed.

Preheat the oven to 450°F and lower one rack to the bottom shelf of the oven. Cut the kataifi into 1-inch lengths. Place it in a food processor fitted with a sharp metal blade, and process to fine pieces about ¼ inch.

Combine the chopped kataifi in a 9-inch round cake pan with the ½ cup melted butter. Mix well with your hand until evenly blended. Spread it evenly in the cake pan and bake on the bottom rack of the oven for 12 to 15 minutes.

Remove the cake pan and stir the kataifi, using the tines of a fork to pull it away from the sides, separating the pieces. Once again, spread the kataifi evenly in the cake pan and place it back in the oven. After 5 minutes remove the cake pan and stir to ensure all the pieces are browning evenly. Return the pan to the oven for a final 2 to 5 minutes, or until the pieces are evenly reddish brown.

Remove from the oven and pour ½ cup syrup over the toasted kataifi. Use the tines of a fork to combine the syrup evenly until it has been absorbed. Transfer the toasted mixture to the center of the buttered dish. Using the backs of two spoons, press and shape the mixture into a flat crust about 8 inches in diameter, with a slightly raised lip around the border. Set the crust aside to cool, uncovered. After an hour and a half, cover it loosely with waxed paper and place it in a cool, dry area until ready to serve.

To prepare the topping

Preheat the oven to 350°F. Spread the 3 kinds of nuts separately over a foil-lined baking sheet, and toast in the center of the oven, shaking the pan occasionally, for 7 to 9 minutes or until golden. Drizzle 2 tablespoons melted butter over the nuts, mix well, and transfer to a dish double-lined with paper towels to cool.

Rinse a medium saucepan with water (this will help prevent the milk mixture from sticking). Remove and discard the crust from each slice of white sandwich bread. Pull the bread apart into 1-inch pieces. Combine the milk, bread, cornstarch, and sugar in the saucepan and place over medium-high heat. Using a heat-proof, flat-edged spatula to stir the mixture, cook until it begins to bubble around the edges, then reduce the heat to medium and cook, stirring constantly, for about 2 minutes. (**A word of caution:** When preparing the cream filling, do not use a wooden cooking utensil that you have used to sauté onions, garlic, or other foods; otherwise the filling will absorb that flavor.)

Remove the cream filling from the heat and cover with a paper towel. Cool completely at room temperature before placing it in the refrigerator.

To serve

About 2 or 3 hours prior to serving, remove the cream filling from the refrigerator. Stir the filling until smooth, using the tines of a fork, then spread it evenly over the toasted kataifi crust up to (but not over) the raised lip. Sprinkle the toasted nuts over the cream filling.

Garnish the edges of the platter with sliced strawberries. Cover loosely with waxed paper and store in a cool, dry area until ready to use. Serve ½ cup syrup on the side, allowing your guests to pour it over individual servings if they desire. Refrigerate leftover pie.

Opposite page: Kataifi and Cream Nut Pie

Melt-Away Sugar Cookies
Ghreibi (ghrey-bee)

ABOUT 2 DOZEN

These cookies literally melt in your mouth. A simple combination of clarified butter with sugar blended with flour, these pistachio-topped cookies are light and crisp. Enjoy them as an afternoon snack or a uniquely different cookie at a bake sale or tea party. These will quickly become a favorite around your home.

Specialty ingredients: Clarified butter, see page 196. (**Caution**: Unsalted butter, butter, or margarine will not work in this recipe.)

Special equipment: A hand mixer and a stir rod (one you would use to mix drinks).

Prepare ahead: You can prepare these cookies several days in advance and store them in an airtight container on the counter with plastic wrap in between the layers, or store them in the refrigerator for several weeks. Serve at room temperature.

FOR THE COOKIES
⅔ cup clarified butter (see recipe on page 196)
⅔ cup granulated sugar
2 cups unbleached flour
48 unsalted pistachio halves

Measuring flour: See page xiv.

To prepare the cookies
Combine the clarified butter and sugar in a bowl, using a hand mixer to blend them until light, smooth, and creamy.

Use a metal spoon to add the flour, half a cup at a time. Use the back of the spoon to press the flour into the butter until evenly blended. Press the mixture evenly into the bottom of the bowl. Cover and set aside.

After 30 minutes, mix the dough with your hands, using massage-like strokes, until the dough is pliable. (The warmth of your hands will soften the dough.) Measure the dough into ¼-cup portions. On a flat surface, roll each portion with your hands into a cylinder 3 inches long. Cut each cylinder into 3 (1-inch) pieces. Each piece will be a cookie.

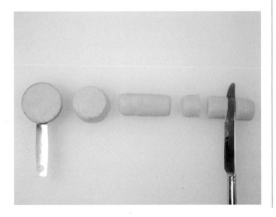

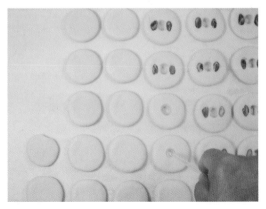

Cup a piece of dough in the palm of one hand, then cover it with your other palm. Gently rotate your hands in a circular motion to form a ball. Then, between your palms, gently flatten the ball into a cookie 2 inches in diameter. Place the cookie on a foil-lined baking sheet. Repeat with the remaining pieces of dough, placing the cookies ½ inch apart.

Preheat the oven to 350°F. Use a stir rod with a rounded tip (as you would use to mix drinks) to make a hole in the center of each cookie. Begin by gently rotating the rod clockwise in the center of the cookie, forming an opening. Gently press down while rotating the rod until you reach the bottom of the tray and the hole is about ½ inch in diameter. Repeat with the remaining cookies.

Place a half pistachio on either side of each cookie and gently press it into the dough. Place the tray on the middle rack in the oven and bake for 15 minutes, then remove and set aside. Cool completely (about 4 hours) before serving.

{VARIATION}

Add 1 tablespoon lemon zest, 1 tablespoon orange zest, or 1 tablespoon lime zest to the creamed butter and sugar mixture for a light lemon, orange, or lime flavor. To differentiate between the cookies, use slivered almonds for the lemon cookies, walnut pieces for the orange, and pecan pieces for the lime, in place of the pistachios.

Clarified Butter

ABOUT 3 CUPS

Samnee (sem-nee)

Clarified butter, also called drawn butter, enhances the flavor of several recipes in this book, especially sweets. You can store it for months in an airtight container in the refrigerator. When you clarify butter, you are separating the dairy solids and moisture from the butter fat, yielding a lighter flavor and butter that has a higher smoke point.

Prepare ahead: You can prepare this up to 2 days, 2 weeks, or 2 months in advance. Store it in an airtight container in the refrigerator.

FOR THE CLARIFIED BUTTER
2 pounds unsalted butter, cut into 1-inch pieces

To prepare the clarified butter
Place the butter in a medium saucepan over medium-low heat, uncovered. Melt the butter slowly and bring it to a gentle boil. If it begins to foam over, reduce the heat. Once it comes to a gentle boil, stir once and simmer uncovered over medium-low heat for 10 to 15 minutes or until it is a golden yellow color and is transparent. Remove from the heat. Skim any solids off the top. Set aside to cool uncovered for 30 minutes.

Pour the clarified butter through a fine-mesh sieve into an airtight container. Avoid pouring the dairy solids at the bottom of the pot into the sieve; discard the solids. Set the clarified butter aside uncovered to cool, then place it in the refrigerator uncovered. Make sure it is completely cooled before covering the container, to avoid condensation.

A word of advice: *Keep a watchful eye when clarifying butter. It can go from golden yellow to dark brown in under a minute. It cannot be used at that point, because it will have a bitter taste. Also, do not use a wooden cooking utensil that you have used to sauté onions, garlic, or other foods; otherwise the butter will absorb that flavor.*

Note: *Some recipes refer to ghee as clarified butter. I have found that the taste varies so much between brands of ghee that I avoid it. If you find a brand that you like, stick to it.*

Mini Lebanese Pancakes with Cream
Katayef bi Kushta (ka-tie-if bee kush-ta)

ABOUT 30 PANCAKES

Similar to Russian blinis, these delicious yeast-leavened pancakes are easy to prepare. Filled with cream and topped with candied flower petals and pistachios, these tiny treats are delicious. They are the perfect choice for a dessert buffet because they are beautiful to look at and they are so easy to pick up.

Specialty ingredients: Zaher lamoon (sold as zaher jam or orange blossom jam, in specialty markets, or orange blossom jam online; you want the variety that actually has small candied petals).

Special equipment: A stand mixer with a whisk (an electric hand mixer will do).

Prepare ahead: The pancakes can be prepared and filled several hours prior to serving. Garnish and refrigerate covered until ready to serve.

FOR THE PANCAKES
4 teaspoons yeast
¼ teaspoon sugar
½ cup and ¾ cups lukewarm water, divided
½ cup lukewarm milk
1 cup unbleached flour
½ cup Wondra flour
1 tablespoon rice flour

Measuring flour: See page xiv.

FOR THE FILLING
5 slices white sandwich bread
2¼ cups half-and-half
1½ tablespoon cornstarch
1½ teaspoons sugar

FOR THE TOPPING
1 cup syrup (see recipe on page 179)

Mini Lebanese Pancakes with Cream (front), Mini Lebanese Half-Moon Pancakes with Walnuts (sides), and Fried Mini Lebanese Half-Moon Pancakes with Walnuts (back)

Zaher lamoon
Ground pistachios

To prepare the pancakes
In a small bowl, dissolve the yeast and sugar in the ½ cup water. Mix well. Cover the bowl with a dish and set it aside for several minutes to proof the yeast (until it foams).

197

In the bowl of the stand mixer, add the ¾ cup water and the milk. On medium speed using the whisk attachment, add the flours, about ¼ cup at a time. Scrape down the sides of the bowl using a spatula. Once the batter is mixed well, add the yeast mixture. Scrape down the sides again. Increase the speed to high and mix for 1 minute. Remove the bowl, cover it with a dish, and set the pancake batter aside in a warm place to rise for 1½ hours.

To prepare the filling
While the pancake mixture is rising, prepare the filling. Remove and discard the crust from each slice of white sandwich bread, then pull the bread apart into 1-inch pieces.

Rinse a medium saucepan with water (this will help prevent the half-and-half mixture from sticking). Combine the bread, half-and-half, cornstarch, and sugar in the saucepan and place over medium-high heat. Using a heat-proof, flat-edged spatula to stir the mixture, cook until it begins to bubble around the edges, then reduce the heat to medium and cook, stirring constantly, for about 2 minutes. (**A word of caution:** When preparing the cream filling, do not use a wooden cooking utensil that you have sautéed onions, garlic, or other foods with; otherwise the filling will absorb that flavor.)

Remove the cream filling from the heat and cover with a paper towel. Cool completely at room temperature before filling the pancakes.

To cook the pancakes
When the batter has risen, preheat a pancake griddle over medium-high heat. Double-line a tray with paper towels, and set it within reach.

Use a hand whisk to mix the pancake batter for about a minute. The consistency should be thin. If the mixture seems thick, whisk in 1 tablespoon warm water.

Pour as many 1-tablespoon portions as will fit on the griddle top. Once the centers begin to bubble and the tops are full of holes and no longer moist (the tops must no longer be moist before removing), flip them onto the paper towel–lined tray, browned side facing up. Allow them to cool for several minutes before stacking them, browned-side up, 6 to a stack. Cover them loosely with plastic wrap until you are ready to fill them. Fill them within 1 hour.

To fill the pancakes
Hold a pancake in your hand, browned side against your hand, and place 2 teaspoons cream filling in the center of the pancake. Gently close the pancake from one side, pressing the edges together to form a cornucopia shape with the cream exposed from the other side. Repeat with the remaining pancakes. Sprinkle some ground pistachio over the exposed cream followed by 2 or 3 candied flower petals. Transfer them to a serving platter, cover loosely with waxed paper (not plastic wrap, it will stick to the flower petals), and refrigerate until ready to serve.

To serve
Serve at room temperature with syrup on the side. These are best prepared and served the same day.

Mini Lebanese Half-Moon Pancakes with Walnuts

ABOUT 30 HALF-MOONS

Katayef bi Jouz (ka-tie-if bee jouz)

To prepare mini Lebanese pancakes with walnuts, see the previous recipe for Mini Lebanese Pancakes with Cream. Prepare only the pancakes then fold them around a delicately flavored filling of ground walnuts as described below.

FOR THE PANCAKES WITH WALNUTS

1 recipe syrup (page 179)

1 recipe pancakes (page 197)

3 cups finely ground walnuts (about ¾ pound)

4½ tablespoons sugar

1½ tablespoons mazaher (orange blossom water)

2 tablespoons finely ground (unsalted) pistachio

To prepare the pancakes with walnuts

Prepare the syrup and set it aside.

Combine the walnuts and sugar in a bowl. Stir in the mazaher; use the back of a spoon to mix and press the mazaher into the mixture until evenly blended and the nuts seem damp.

Holding a pancake in your hand, with the browned side against your hand, place 2 teaspoons walnut mixture in the center of the pancake. Gently fold the pancake over the filling and press the edges together, sealing the nut mixture inside the half-moon shape. Repeat with the remaining pancakes. Transfer to a serving platter and sprinkle ground pistachio over the top. Cover and store at room temperature until ready to serve.

To serve

Offer with syrup on the side. These are best prepared and served the same day.

{VARIATION}

Fried Mini Lebanese Half-Moon Pancakes with Walnuts (Katayef bi Jouz Mickli): Prepare the recipe above for Mini Lebanese Half-Moon Pancakes with Walnuts. Preheat 2 cups canola oil in a small saucepan over medium-high heat to 350°F, using a candy/fry thermometer to ensure proper temperature. The oil should be about 1 inch deep. Fry 4 or 5 half-moons at a time. Once golden brown, remove them with a slotted spoon to a paper towel–lined dish, then transfer them while they are hot to a bowl with the cooled syrup. Continue soaking them in the syrup while the next batch is being fried. Remove them from the syrup just before the next batch goes into the syrup. Repeat with the remaining half-moons. Transfer to a serving platter and garnish with 2 tablespoons finely ground (unsalted) pistachios. Serve at room temperature. These are best the same day they are fried. Store loosely covered in a cool dry place until ready to serve.

Recycle the oil: *See page xiv.*

Rice Pudding with Apricots

SERVES 6

Mouhallabiyeh (moo-hella-bee-yee)

This unique and delicious dessert is a wonderful combination of rose and orange blossom waters, infused into a smooth and creamy pudding. You can add cardamom for a subtle change in flavor, or substitute vanilla essence in place of the rose and orange blossom water. Apricots, almonds, and pistachios top this pudding, complementing the overall flavor.

Specialty ingredients: Rice flour, mazaher (orange blossom water), and maward (rose water), found at specialty markets or online.

Prepare ahead: You can prepare this 1 day in advance. Chill in the refrigerator prior to covering it with plastic wrap. Serve as described.

FOR THE GARNISH

2 tablespoons toasted slivered almonds

½ tablespoon melted butter

6 dried apricots

1½ cups water

¼ cup sugar

1 tablespoon finely ground pistachios (unsalted)

FOR THE PUDDING

4 cups milk

7 tablespoons rice flour dissolved in ⅓ cup plus
  1 tablespoon cold water

½ cup sugar

1½ teaspoon mazaher

1½ teaspoon maward

To prepare the garnish

Preheat the oven to 350°F. Spread the almonds over a foil-lined baking sheet and toast in the center of the oven, shaking the pan occasionally, for 5 to 7 minutes or until golden brown. Mix the melted butter with the nuts. Transfer to a paper towel–lined dish and set aside to cool.

Place the apricots, 1½ cups water, and sugar in a small saucepan over high heat and bring to a rolling boil. Reduce the heat to medium-low, cover, and simmer for 20 minutes. Remove from the heat and set aside to cool completely before using.

To prepare the pudding

*Rinse a medium pot with cold water (this will help prevent the milk from sticking). Add the milk to the pot, place it over high heat, and bring to a boil uncovered. Use a flat-edged, heat-proof spatula to constantly stir and scrape the bottom and sides of the pot to prevent the milk from sticking and burning. (**A word of caution:** When preparing the pudding, do not use a wooden cooking utensil that you have used to sauté onions, garlic, or other foods; otherwise the pudding will absorb that flavor.)*

Once the milk comes to a boil, remove it from the heat. Add the dissolved rice flour, constantly stirring the mixture to prevent lumps. Return the pot to medium heat uncovered, and continue cooking, stirring constantly, using a whisk to break down any lumps that may appear. After 4 to 6 minutes the pudding will thicken. Once it coats the spatula,

drop 1 teaspoon of pudding on a saucer and set it aside to cool for 1 minute (meanwhile stirring the pudding). Turn the saucer sideways; if the pudding remains in place, add the sugar to the pot, stirring to dissolve the sugar.

After 2 to 4 minutes, place another teaspoon of pudding on the saucer and repeat the test. When the pudding remains in one spot, add the mazaher and maward. Cook the pudding for 2 more minutes, then pour it into a shallow, heat-proof serving dish. Cool completely, uncovered, before garnishing and serving. Refrigerate until needed.

To garnish and serve

Carefully separate the apricots into round halves and pat dry with a paper towel. Arrange 5 apricot halves to form a flower in the center of the pudding, and place 7 halves equally distanced around the edge of the pudding. Decoratively place 3 toasted slivered almonds over each apricot. Sprinkle ground pistachios around the perimeter of the pudding. Place small pinches of pistachios at the base of each of the apricots around the edge, with one final pinch in the center.

{VARIATIONS}

For a richer pudding, you can substitute half-and-half for the milk. For reduced calories, use reduced-fat or fat-free milk. Or, vary the flavoring of this versatile pudding.

Cardamom: For cardamom-flavored rice pudding, stir in 1 teaspoon ground cardamom with the mazaher and the maward; the rest of the procedure remains the same.

Vanilla: For vanilla-flavored rice pudding, substitute 1 teaspoon vanilla extract in place of the mazaher and maward; the rest of the procedure remains the same.

Semolina Date Cookies

ABOUT 2 DOZEN

Mamoul bi Tamer (maa-mool bee tum-mer)

Traditionally these cookies are offered around the holidays and on special occasions, although we never needed a special occasion to enjoy these treats. They are made of buttery semolina dough stuffed with a variety of fillings, then pressed into decoratively carved wooden molds of varying shapes and sizes. The different shapes include shallow, circular cookies filled with dates, as shown on the next page; circular dome-shaped ones filled with walnuts and dusted with powdered sugar; and long, tapered ones filled with pistachios also dusted with powdered sugar. The cookies remain a golden-blond color once baked.

Specialty ingredients: Clarified butter (see page 196). Semolina can found at specialty markets or online. *Deglet Noor* are dates that are chewy and a bit drier, used in baked goods.

Special equipment: Mamoul cookie molds, round, shallow decorative molds carved out of wood, found at specialty markets or online. (The size of the cookie mold used in this recipe is about 2¼ inches in diameter and about ½ inch deep.)

Prepare ahead: You can prepare these in advance and store them in an airtight container. Store the cookies at room temperature for several days or refrigerate for several weeks. Serve at room temperature.

FOR THE FILLING

½ pound finely chopped pitted dates (Deglet Noor)

3 tablespoons boiling water

1 tablespoon melted clarified butter (unsalted butter will do)

FOR THE DOUGH

1¾ cups semolina

½ cup Wondra flour

1 tablespoon sugar

⅔ cup melted clarified butter, slightly warm (unsalted butter will do)

⅓ cup lukewarm water

⅛ teaspoon yeast with a pinch of sugar

Measuring flour: See page xiv.

To prepare the filling

Cut the dates in half widthwise to ensure that no pits remain. Finely chop them by hand (or in a food processor for larger quantities). In a medium saucepan, combine the dates, boiling water, and butter. Place the pan over medium-low heat, cover, and simmer 10 minutes, stirring a couple of times. Remove from the heat and transfer the cooked dates to a buttered dish. Flatten them in the dish and refrigerate uncovered for 1 hour.

Measure the cooled date filling into 1-tablespoon portions. Cut the portions in half. Between your palms, roll each half into a ball. If the dates seem sticky, lightly butter your palms. Set the date balls aside.

To prepare the dough

Combine the semolina, Wondra flour, and sugar in a bowl. Pour the melted butter (melted butter that is slightly warm, not hot) over the flour mixture. Use the back of a spoon to mix and press the butter into the flour mixture until it is evenly blended. Flatten the mixture into the bottom of the bowl, using the back of the spoon. Cover and set aside at room temperature for 1 hour.

After 1 hour, mix the warm water and yeast with a pinch of sugar; cover and set aside.

Use your hand to loosen and break apart the soaked semolina, which may have hardened. Work the mixture loose until you have broken down any lumps. Pour the yeast mixture over the semolina. Use massage-like strokes to combine the ingredients with your hand (for about 1 minute), forming a ball of dough. Sprinkle a little bit of water over the dough if it seems dry and granular.

Measure the dough into ¼-cup portions. Roll each portion with your hands into a 3-inch cylinder, then cut each cylinder into 3 equal pieces. Drape plastic wrap over the pieces to prevent drying while you work.

Semolina Date Cookies, Semolina Walnut (or Almond) Cookies, and Semolina Pistachio Cookies

*Place a piece of dough in the palm of one hand and with the forefinger of your other hand, pierce the dough with your fingertip and hollow a cavity that is about 1¼ inches deep and 1¼ inches wide. Place a date ball in and close the dough, securing the filling inside. Repeat with the remaining dough. (**Note:** The warmth of your hands helps makes the dough pliable.)*

Place the date-filled dough ball into the cookie mold, seam side facing you. Press it firmly into the mold with your palm. Flip the mold, then tap the tip on a hard surface. Be prepared to catch the cookie with the other hand as it pops out. Repeat with the rest of the cookies, placing them on the foil-lined baking sheet ¼ inch apart. (If the filled dough balls begin to stick in the mold, dip them in a bit of Wondra flour before pressing them into the mold.)

To form and bake the cookies

Preheat the oven to 375°F. Line a baking sheet with foil and set it within reach.

Place the tray in the center of the oven and bake 18 to 22 minutes or until they are golden and the bottom edges begin to brown. Remove them from the oven and cool completely before serving. Serve at room temperature.

Semolina Walnut (or Almond) Cookies

ABOUT 2 DOZEN

Mamoul bi Jouz (maa-mool bee jouz)

Special Ingredients and Equipment: Clarified butter (see page 196), semolina, mazaher (orange blossom water), and a circular, dome-shaped cookie mold, all found at specialty markets or online. (The size of the cookie mold used in this recipe differs from the one used for the date filled cookies; it is a dome-shaped mold, about 2¼ inches in diameter and about 1¼ inches deep.) You will also need a food processor.

Prepare ahead: You can prepare these in advance and store them in an airtight container. Store the cookies at room temperature for several days or refrigerate for several weeks. Serve at room temperature.

FOR THE DOUGH

Follow the previous recipe for Semolina Date Cookies.

FOR THE FILLING

2 cups finely ground walnuts (about ½ pound)
or: 2 cups finely ground unsalted almonds (about ½ pound)
⅓ cup granulated sugar
4 teaspoons mazaher
¼ cup powdered sugar

To prepare the dough

Follow the procedure for preparing the dough as described in the previous recipe for Semolina Date Cookies.

To prepare the filling

Just before you are ready to fill the cookies, combine the nuts and granulated sugar in a bowl. Stir in the mazaher; use the back of a spoon to mix and press the mazaher into the mixture until evenly blended and the nuts seem damp. Set aside.

To form and bake the cookies

Follow the procedure in the previous recipe for forming the Semolina Date Cookies, except fill each cookie with 2 packed teaspoons of the nut mixture, gently pressing it into the cavity. Bake the cookies as described in the previous recipe for the date filled cookies.

Unlike the date filled cookies, generously dust the tops of these cookies with powdered sugar just as they come out of the oven. Serve at room temperature.

Semolina Pistachio Cookies

ABOUT 2 DOZEN

Mamoul bi Fistouk (maa-mool bee fis-touk)

Special ingredients and equipment: Clarified butter (see page 196), semolina, maward (rose water), and a long, tapered cookie mold, all found at specialty markets or online. (The size of the cookie mold used in this recipe differs from the one used for the date filled cookies; it is about 3½ inches long, about 1½ inches wide, and about ¾ inch deep.) You will also need a food processor.

Prepare ahead: You can prepare these in advance and store them in an airtight container. Store the cookies at room temperature for several days or refrigerate for several weeks. Serve at room temperature.

FOR THE DOUGH
Follow the recipe for Semolina Date Cookies (see page 202).

FOR THE FILLING
2 cups finely ground unsalted pistachios (about ½ pound)
6 tablespoons granulated sugar
5 teaspoons maward
¼ cup powdered sugar

To prepare the dough
Follow the procedure for preparing the dough as described for Semolina Date Cookies (pages 202–3).

To prepare the filling
Just before you are ready to fill the cookies, combine the pistachios and granulated sugar in a bowl. Stir in the maward; use the back of a spoon to mix and press the maward into the nuts until evenly blended and the nuts seem damp. Set aside.

To form and bake the cookies
Follow the procedure on page 203 for forming the Semolina Date Cookies, except fill each cookie with 2 packed teaspoons of the nut mixture, gently pressing it into the cavity. Bake the cookies as described on page 203.

Unlike the date filled cookies, generously dust the tops of these cookies with powdered sugar as they come out of the oven. Serve at room temperature.

Spicy Rice Pudding with Nuts
Mighli (mighh-lee)

This pudding is traditionally prepared to celebrate the birth of a new child or at Christmas. I have never needed a reason to prepare this delicious pudding. It is a unique combination of spices, including fresh ginger, cinnamon, anise, and cloves, boiled in water for the broth. Cream of rice is added to the broth with sugar, and the result is a spicy and unique rice pudding topped with nuts.

Specialty ingredients: *Kholengen,* found in some specialty markets or imported from the Middle East (also known as galangal root and found in Asian markets).

Special equipment: A coffee grinder to prepare the caraway and anise seeds.

Prepare ahead: You can prepare this several days in advance. Cover and refrigerate until needed. Refrigerate the nuts separately. Serve as directed.

FOR THE TOPPING

¼ cup pine nuts
¼ cup slivered almonds
¼ cup unsalted pistachios
¼ cup walnuts

FOR THE PUDDING

5 cups water
2½ teaspoons ground caraway seeds
1 tablespoon ground anise seeds
1 tablespoon ground cinnamon
1 (3–4-inch) cinnamon stick
¼ teaspoon ground cloves
⅛ teaspoon ground nutmeg
2 packed tablespoons freshly peeled and
  grated ginger
2 (2-inch) pieces kholengen (break into pieces)
5 tablespoons cream of rice dissolved in
  ⅓ cup water

½ cup granulated sugar
(**You may substitute** powdered rice flour in place of the cream of rice, for a smooth-textured pudding.)

To prepare the topping

Traditionally, the nuts are softened by soaking them in boiling water. Place the nuts separately in four dishes. Pour boiling water over each to cover with 2 inches of water, and soak for 30 minutes. Drain the water, once again pour boiling water over the nuts, and soak for 2 hours. Then drain the water, cover, and store the nuts separately until needed in the refrigerator.

(**Alternatively,** *for an extra crunch and texture, you can toast the nuts. Place them separately in rows on a foil-lined baking sheet and toast them in a preheated 350°F oven, shaking the pan occasionally, for 7 to 9 minutes or until golden. Cool completely before using.*)

To prepare the pudding

Combine the water and the next 8 ingredients in a medium-sized pot; mix well. Place over high heat uncovered and bring to a rolling boil, then reduce the heat to medium-low and simmer covered for 1 hour, scraping down the sides a few times. Strain the mixture through a fine-mesh sieve, using the back of

a spoon to gently stir the mixture to allow fine sediment to pass through with the broth. (You need the sediment because it carries the deep flavors.) Discard the leftover mixture in the sieve.

Measure the broth; if there is not quite 2 cups, add enough water to bring the measure to 2 cups. Separately, dissolve the cream of rice in ⅓ cup cold water and set it aside. Measure the sugar and set it aside.

Rinse out the pot. Return the 2 cups of broth containing the fine sediment to the pot. Add the dissolved cream of rice to the broth and mix well. Place the pot over high heat uncovered and bring to a boil, using a flat-edged, heat-proof spatula to continually stir and scrape the sides and bottom of the pot to prevent sticking as the mixture thickens. (**A word of caution:** When preparing the pudding, do not use a wooden cooking utensil that you have used to sauté onions, garlic, or other foods; otherwise the pudding will absorb that flavor.)

Then reduce the heat to medium, continuing to stir and scrape the sides and bottom of the pot (use a whisk to smooth out any lumps that appear). After 2 minutes, add the sugar and cook for 1 final minute as you continue to stir the mixture.

Transfer the pudding to a shallow heat-proof dish. Loosely drape waxed paper over the pudding and let it cool for a couple of hours. You can also portion the pudding in individual serving dishes and garnish them with the assorted nuts. (It is usually portioned into individual servings when it is being offered after the birth of a new baby. This way you can offer individual servings to guests who may come to visit at different times.)

To serve

Arrange the nuts in a decorative pattern. Place the walnuts along the edge of the pudding, followed by the almonds and pistachios in concentric circles, with the pine nuts in the center. Serve lightly chilled or at room temperature.

Sweet Semolina-Yogurt Cakes

ABOUT 3 DOZEN

Namoura (na-moo-r'ra)

These deliciously rich little cakes of semolina and yogurt are baked to perfection, then drenched in buttery syrup. They are easy to pick up and easy to eat. Offer as a pass-around dessert or on a dessert buffet, or take them to a potluck or bake sale—they'll go fast.

Specialty ingredients: Semolina, found at specialty markets or online.

Special equipment: A 9-inch round cake pan.

Prepare ahead: You can prepare these several days in advance. Store them in an airtight container at room temperature. Refrigerate for longer periods. Serve as described.

FOR THE SEMOLINA CAKES

1 recipe syrup (page 179)

1 tablespoon and 2 tablespoons unsalted butter, divided

1¾ cups fine semolina

¾ cup granulated sugar

½ teaspoon baking soda

⅔ cup plain yogurt (regular, reduced-fat, or fat-free)

1½ tablespoons slivered almonds (topping)

To prepare the semolina cakes

Prepare the syrup and set it aside.

Preheat the oven to 350°F. Melt 1 tablespoon butter, and use some of it to grease the sides and bottom of a 9-inch round cake pan; keep the rest aside for later use.

Combine the dry ingredients in a bowl. Add the yogurt and use your fingers to work it into the flour, forming the batter.

Transfer the batter to the cake pan and use a spatula (one you would ice a cake with) to distribute the batter evenly. Dip your fingers into the leftover tablespoon of melted butter, and gently pat the surface of the batter to smooth out the top. Score the top of the batter into 1 x 1-inch diamond shapes. Gently press a slivered almond into the center of each diamond shape. (**Note:** *Baking soda begins to react as soon as moisture is added, releasing air bubbles into the batter; therefore, work quickly to get the batter in the oven.*)

Bake the cake in the center of the oven for 30 minutes, or until the top is golden; then remove from the oven and set it aside.

Place the syrup and 2 tablespoons unsalted butter in a small saucepan over medium heat. Warm the syrup just until the butter melts. While waiting for the butter to melt, cut through the scored diamond shapes to the bottom of the pan, but do not remove any of the pieces. Once the butter has melted, pour the syrup over the top of the semolina cakes. Set them aside to cool for about 1 hour to allow the cakes to absorb the syrup. Serve at room temperature.

Sweet Semolina-Yogurt Cakes

Turkish Coffee

Qahwa (kah-wa)

4 DEMITASSE CUPS

Years ago, my cousin taught me the fine art of preparing the perfect cup of Turkish coffee. "One crucial note," she said: "Never take your eye off the pot; it can foam over in a flash!" Once the coffee has been poured into the individual cups, the grounds settle to the bottom, and you only drink the thinner liquid on top. Turkish coffee is delicious after meals and traditionally offered to all visiting guests. You will find many ways to enjoy this deeply rich and aromatic beverage.

Specialty ingredients: Fine-powder (finely ground) Turkish coffee, found at specialty markets or online.

Special equipment: An *ibrik* (a special metal brewing pot for the coffee) and demitasse cups (I use small ones that hold about ¼ cup liquid), both found at specialty markets or online.

FOR THE COFFEE

1¼ cups water

2½ teaspoons sugar

5 heaping teaspoons of fine-powder
   Turkish coffee

To prepare the coffee

Make certain the ibrik is large enough to allow the coffee to foam up. Combine the water and sugar in the ibrik and mix well. Add the coffee (it will be floating on the top), and do not stir it at this point.

Place the coffee pot over medium-high heat. The coffee will appear to "melt" into the water. After a few minutes, small bubbles will form around the edges. Keep a close eye; the coffee will suddenly begin to foam up. Let the coffee foam up to the top, but not over the edge of the ibrik.

*Remove the pot from the heat and gently swirl it around several times. Use a demitasse spoon to scoop a bit of the light brown surface foam off the top, and drop a bit into each cup. Return the ibrik to the heat to foam up again (**beware**: it will foam*

up faster each time). Remove it from the heat, then return it to the heat for a third and final foaming. Take from the heat and let the coffee pot stand for about half a minute to allow the grinds to settle before pouring.

Line the coffee cups in a row. Fill the cups by pouring a small amount into each cup, then go back and add a bit more, and then pour again until each cup is full. The very bottom of the wide base of the ibrik will contain the coffee-ground sediment. You can discard this.

My recommendation is not to prepare more than 6 cups at a time. Each time you prepare Turkish coffee, you will perfect the coffee–sugar–water ratio to suit your individual taste.

Reading your cup

When your cup is empty and all that remains is a bit of coffee and the grounds at the bottom, cover the cup with the saucer and rotate the entire cup. Then,

while still holding the saucer to the cup, quickly flip the cup upside down onto the saucer. After a couple of minutes, remove the cup, and the sediment will have formed letters and symbols on the inner walls of the cup. Try interpreting the letters and symbols. For a true and accurate prediction, it must be the cup you drank from. My aunt used to read our fortunes from the remaining coffee grounds, and it was always lots of fun.

Selecting and grinding turkish coffee

There are many brands of coffee available. Try several until you find the one you like best. I use Café Najjar Classic with cardamom. For die-hard Turkish coffee lovers, you can purchase a special coffee mill to grind the beans for fresh-ground powdered coffee. The mills can be found at specialty markets or online. The coffee beans can also be found at specialty markets or online.

White Coffee

4 DEMITASSE CUPS

Qahwa Bida (kah-wa bye-da)

This white coffee is traditionally offered after meals to aid in digestion. This fragrant, mellow combination of hot water mixed with orange blossom water will soothe your soul.

FOR THE WHITE COFFEE
1¼ cups boiling water
5 teaspoons mazaher (orange blossom water)

To prepare and serve the white coffee
Bring the water to a boil, then remove from the heat. Add the mazaher. Fill the demitasse cups and serve. **Alternatively,** you can offer the white coffee with sugar and a slice of lemon.

Turmeric Tea Cakes

Sfoof (sfoof)

ABOUT 1½ DOZEN

Turmeric is commonly found in curries and in some prepared mustards and is thought to have many beneficial medicinal properties. This deep yellow spice may not be what you would expect to find in a sweet tea cake. These small cakes are a tasty snack, delicious with a warm cup of tea or a glass of milk. You will find many ways to enjoy these brilliant yellow cakes.

Specialty ingredients: Tahini, found at specialty markets or online.

Special equipment: A 9-inch round cake pan.

Prepare ahead: You can prepare these several days in advance. Store them in an airtight container at room temperature.

FOR THE CAKES

1 tablespoon tahini, mixed well (butter will do)

1½ cups Wondra flour

½ cup unbleached flour

¼ cup nonfat dry milk

1 tablespoon turmeric

1 cup and 2 tablespoons granulated sugar

1½ teaspoons double-acting baking powder

¾ cup extra-virgin olive oil

⅔ cup water

2 tablespoons pine nuts

Measuring flour: See page xiv.

To prepare the cakes

Preheat the oven to 350°F. Spread the tahini over the bottom and sides of a 9-inch round cake pan.

In a bowl, combine the dry ingredients. Make a well in the center, then add the olive oil and water. Mix the batter thoroughly, using a flexible spatula.

Pour the batter into the cake pan. Rotate the pan, evenly distributing the batter around the sides of the pan. Lightly score the top of the batter (it's pretty loose, so be gentle) into 1½ x 1½-inch squares. Carefully place 3 pine nuts in the center of each square and 2 pine nuts on the smaller pieces around the sides. Gently press the nuts into place; do not submerge them. Work quickly because of the double-acting baking powder, which begins to react as soon as moisture is added (the second reaction occurs in the oven, releasing air bubbles into the batter).

Bake in the center of the oven for 30 to 35 minutes, or until the top is golden brown; then remove from the oven and set aside to cool for 60 minutes. Cut through the scored square shapes to the bottom of the pan and remove the pieces to a serving dish. Serve at room temperature.

Caution: *Do not substitute fresh milk in place of the dry milk—the result will not be the same.* **Avoid** *getting turmeric on counter tops or clothing as it stains easily.*

Tumeric Tea Cakes

Walnut Biscuits with Marshmallow Dip

2 DOZEN

Karrabeej ma Natef (karra-beej ma not-tif)

These light semolina biscuits filled with ground walnuts are baked till crisp and golden and are the perfect size to offer at a tea party or on a dessert buffet, or as an afternoon snack. The traditional way to make natef (a fluffy nougaty confection dipping sauce) involves a main ingredient that is very difficult to find in the United States and a procedure that you would not want to attempt, so I have substituted delicious marshmallow crème.

Specialty ingredients: Clarified butter (see page 196), semolina, and mazaher (orange blossom water), found at specialty markets or online.

Special equipment: A food processor.

Prepare ahead: You can prepare these several days in advance. Store them in an airtight container at room temperature, or for several weeks in the refrigerator. Serve at room temperature. The dip can be prepared up to 1 week in advance, stir before serving.

FOR THE BISCUITS

1¼ cups semolina

⅓ cup Wondra flour

2¼ teaspoons sugar

½ cup melted clarified butter (unsalted butter will do)

4½ tablespoons lukewarm water

⅛ teaspoon dry active yeast with a pinch sugar

1¼ cups finely ground walnuts (about ¼ pound)

3½ tablespoons granulated sugar

1¾ teaspoons mazaher

Measuring flour: See page xiv.

FOR THE DIP

1 (7-ounce jar) marshmallow crème

1 tablespoon water

2 tablespoons finely ground pistachios, unsalted

To prepare the biscuits

Combine the semolina, Wondra flour, and sugar in a bowl. Pour the melted butter over the flour mixture (the melted butter should be slightly warm, not hot). Use the back of a spoon to mix and press the butter evenly into the flour mixture, flattening the mixture into the bottom of the bowl. Cover with plastic wrap and set aside at room temperature for 1 hour.

After 1 hour, mix the warm water, yeast, and a pinch of sugar together in a small bowl. Cover and set it aside to proof the yeast for about 3 to 4 minutes. Meanwhile use your hand to loosen and break apart the soaked semolina, which may have hardened. Work the mixture loose until you have broken down any lumps.

Pour the yeast mixture over the semolina. Use massage-like strokes to combine the ingredients with your hand (for about 1 minute), forming a ball of dough. Sprinkle a little bit of water over the dough if it seems dry or granular.

Measure the dough into ¼-cup portions. Roll each portion into a 4-inch cylinder using your hands,

then cut each cylinder into 4 equal pieces. Drape plastic wrap over the pieces of dough to prevent drying while you work.

Combine the walnuts and sugar in a bowl. Stir in the mazaher; use the back of a spoon to mix and press the mazaher into the mixture until evenly blended and the nuts seem damp.

Preheat the oven to 350°F. Line a baking sheet with foil and set it within reach.

Holding a piece of dough in the palm of one hand, use the forefinger of your other hand to pierce the dough with your fingertip and hollow a cavity about 1 inch deep and 1 inch wide. (**Note:** It is the warmth of your hands that makes the dough pliable.) Place 1½ packed teaspoons of the walnut filling in the cavity. Gently press the filling down before closing the biscuit and securing the filling inside. Shape it into a 2½-inch finger that is tapered at both ends, and

place it on the baking sheet. Repeat with the remaining dough, placing the biscuits ¼ inch apart. Using the tines of a fork, gently pass over the top of each biscuit to score the top lengthwise, but do not pierce through it.

Bake in the center of the oven for 20 to 25 minutes or until the biscuits are golden and the bottom edges begin to brown. Serve at room temperature with the marshmallow dip on the side.

To prepare the marshmallow dip

Add the water to the jar of marshmallow crème. Use the tines of a fork to whip them together, then mix in the pistachios. Offer the dip in a separate dish next to the biscuits.

{VARIATION}

Substitute ground almonds, cashews, pine nuts, or pistachios for the walnuts. When using pistachios, substitute maward for the mazaher.

Suggested Menus

Tray-Passed Hors d'Oeuvres (Mezza)

Pumpkin Kibbi Balls 21
Vegetable-Stuffed Grape Leaves 42
Spinach Triangles 31
Lamb Turbans 11
Crispy Bean & Herb Patties 2
Hummus 8
Sumak Toasted Pita 40
Feta Cheese Fillo Rolls 36
Tangy Beef Fillo Rolls 35
Glazed Anise Fingers 187
Mini Lebanese Pancakes with Cream 197

Cocktail Buffet

Lamb Kibbi Balls 24
Spicy Red Pepper and Walnut Dip 30
Fried Cauliflower with Tahini Sauce 7
Pomegranate Beef Cheese Pies 18
Lamb-Stuffed Grape Leaves 45
Feta Cheese Fillo Rolls 36
Smoked Eggplant Dip 28
Paprika and Onion Toasted Pita 40
Olives, Cheese, Pickles, and Crudités 15
Baklava 176
Fresh Fruit Kabobs 186

Brunch

Mini Dill Omelets 14
Eggplant Salad 52

Feta Cheese Fillo Rolls 36
Green Beans in Tomato and Olive Oil 142
Spinach Triangles 31
Fava Beans with Garlic and Lemon 139
Thyme Pizzettas 37
Hummus 8
Olives, Cheese, Pickles, and Crudités 15
Labni 47
Pita Bread (store bought)
Rice Pudding with Apricots 200
Sweet Semolina-Yogurt Cakes 208
Fresh Fruit 186

Lavish Lebanese Mixed Grill

Grilled Chicken Kebabs 86
Grilled Lamb Rib Chops or
  Grilled Lamb Kebabs . . . . 88 and 90
Grilled Shrimp Kebabs 91
Grilled Beef Fingers 84
Grilled Vegetable Kebabs 92
Basmati Rice with Cumin, Lentils,
  and Onions 135
Parsley and Bulgur Wheat Salad 58
Robust Garlic Puree 26
Hummus with Horseradish 10
Smoked Eggplant Dip 28
Pita Bread (store bought)
Baked Kataifi with Cream 173
Honey Balls 189
Fresh Fruit 186
Turkish Coffee 210

Menus

Cardamom Chicken with Rice. 72
Jalapeño-Cilantro Salsa. 144
Pita Crouton Salad with Sumak Dressing. 60
Eggplant Moussaka. 138
Pita Bread (store bought)

Roast Leg of Lamb. 119
Grilled Vegetable Kebabs 92
Basmati Rice with Green Onions 134
Farmer's Salad with Tahini Dressing. 55
Pita Bread (store bought)

Grilled Chicken Kebabs. 86
Robust Garlic Puree 26
Roasted Onion-Cumin Potato Spears 150
Garbanzo Bean Salad 56
Pita Bread (store bought)

Grilled Shrimp Kebabs 91
Grilled Vegetable Kebabs 92
Lemon-Garlic Potato Salad. 57
Lentils with Caramelized Onions 145
Pita Bread (store bought)

Lamb Kibbi Trays 99
Smoked Eggplant Dip 28
Cabbage and Beet Salad or
   Yogurt-Cucumber Salad. . . . . 50 or 63
Pita Bread (store bought)

Miniature Meatball Soup 168
Chicken Kibbi Tray 99
Farmer's Salad. 55
Pita Bread (store bought)

Layered London Broil with Garlic Yogurt
   and Pita 105
Spinach with Caramelized Onions 152
Farmer's Salad. 55
Pita Bread (store bought)

Stewed Okra and Cilantro with Lamb. 156
Basmati Rice with Toasted Noodles 134
Pita Crouton Salad with Sumak Dressing. 60
Pita Bread (store bought)

Jute Mallow and Garlic-Cilantro Stew
   with Lamb. 94
Lamb Kibbi Trays 99
Smoked Eggplant Dip 28
Farmer's Salad. 55
Pita Bread (store bought)

Tilapia with Jalapeño–Pine Nut Sauce 128
Lima Beans with Cilantro 146
Pita Crouton Salad with Sumak Dressing. 60
Pita Bread (store bought)

Chicken and Spiced Rice with
   Toasted Nuts 75
Green Beans in Tomato and
   Olive Oil. 142
Yogurt-Cucumber Salad 63
Pita Bread (store bought)

Scrambled Eggs with Beef Confit
   and Potatoes. 151
Fava Beans with Garlic and Lemon 139
Romaine Salad 62
Pita Bread (store bought)

Lentil Soup with Ruby Swiss Chard
   and Lemon 166
Pumpkin Kibbi Trays. 102
Pita Crouton Salad with Sumak Dressing. 60
Pita Bread (store bought)

Cardamom Lamb with Rice. 74
Jalapeño-Cilantro Salsa. 144
Pita Crouton Salad with Sumak Dressing. 60
Lima Beans with Cilantro 146
Pita Bread (store bought)

The Pantry

(GLOSSARY)

Some of these items may already be in your pantry, while others may be a new addition.

A few of the items listed below will need to be refrigerated or frozen as directed on the package.

Items can be found at specialty markets or online. I suggest specialty Middle Eastern, Lebanese, Greek, Persian, Armenian, or Mediterranean markets. Google any of the above and include your zip code in the search to find stores near you.

Ackawi cheese Ackawi is a soft, smooth-textured white cheese prepared from cow's milk with a slight salty flavor. A delicious cheese for breakfast or served with fresh melons and fruit.

Allspice *(bahar hillou)* Allspice (whole or ground) is not a mixture of spices. The pea-sized fruits are picked from small evergreen trees when they are green, then dried. They resemble large peppercorns. The flavor is a combination of cinnamon, cloves, and nutmeg, and is slightly peppery.

Almonds *(louz)* Whole or ground nuts.

Anise *(yensoon)* Anise (whole seeds or ground) is a relative of dill, fennel, caraway, and cumin. Sweet and aromatic, it is the true taste of licorice. Anise flavoring is used in alcoholic beverages such as *araq* in Lebanon, Jordan, Iraq, and Syria; *ouzo* in Greece; or *sambuca* in Italy.

Basmati rice *(riz basmati)* A variety of long-grained rice, basmati is known for its fragrance and delicate flavor. The Hindi word *basmati* means fragrant. My preferred brands are imported from India or Pakistan.

Bulgur *(burghul)* Bulgur is wheat that is cooked (parboiled or steamed), removing the outer layers of bran, then ground into various-sized grains that are sun-dried. For tabbouli and kibbi, I recommend using bulgur (*burghul*) #1, fine. Larger grains can be steamed and prepared like rice.

Caraway *(crawya)* Caraway (whole seeds or ground) has an aromatic spicy, pungent anise-like flavor and aroma. It is used as a flavor in cooking, confectionery, and liqueurs.

Cardamom *(hale)* A member of the ginger family, cardamom produces green pods that can contain up to twenty aromatic seeds. The strong lemony flavor enhances both savory and sweet dishes, and is also found in varieties of Turkish coffee. Ground cardamom loses its flavor quickly, so it is best to keep the pods whole and grind the seeds as needed. Avoid purchasing brown cardamom pods; they are not true cardamom and differ in flavor.

Clarified butter This is butter that has had the milk solids and moisture removed (see recipe on page 196). It has a much higher smoke point, so it can tolerate higher temperatures without browning or burning. (**Note:** Ghee is a type of clarified butter that may be purchased; however, it may be infused with herbs or spices.)

Coriander *(kizbara)* Coriander (whole seeds or ground) has a slight hint of fresh cilantro leaves and an aromatic scent that is soothingly warm, nutty, and slightly fruity.

Cumin *(camoon)* Cumin (whole seeds or ground) has a strong, heavy, and warm aroma that is spicy-sweet. The flavor is pungent, powerful, and sharp, and when used in excess quantity can be bitter.

Curry powder Although there are many varieties of curry powder, this blend of spices usually includes coriander, turmeric, cumin, and fenugreek, along with additional ingredients. My favorite blend is CA RI NI AN DO–D&D GOLD MADRAS CURRY POWDER, found at specialty Asian markets or online.

Deglet Noor dates These are dates that are harvested from palm trees. They are the chewy bread-like date familiar to most, a bit drier than Medjool dates, and an excellent choice in baked goods, such as semolina date cookies (page 202).

Dibs ruman This concentrated pomegranate molasses adds a powerful sweet yet tart and savory flavor when added to recipes.

Farina This milled wheat cereal grain may already be familiar to you as cream of wheat.

Feta cheese This slightly grainy-textured curd cheese is commonly produced in blocks and stored in brine. Traditionally made from goat's or sheep's milk, it can also be made from cow's milk. Bulgarian feta cheese, made from sheep's milk, is my favorite variety—sharp, rich, and creamy.

Fillo dough (phyllo dough) These paper-thin sheets of raw, unleavened flour dough are used to prepare baklava (page 176), buraks (page 35), bastilla, and a large variety of other recipes. My favorite brand is Apollo.

Foul A variety of fava beans, foul are cooked and mixed with garlic and lemon juice to yield a dish known as *foul moudammas.*

Freekeh Freekeh is a highly nutritious grain made from fire-roasted green wheat. The grains are harvested while still young, therefore freekeh contains more protein, vitamins, and minerals than the same mature grains and has up to four times the fiber of brown rice. It is an excellent alternative to pasta, rice, or potatoes.

Garbanzo beans *(hoummos haab)* Also known as chickpeas, these delicious nutty-tasting, buttery-textured beans are the main ingredient when pureed in hummus (page 8). They are available canned or dried.

Grape leaves *(warac inab)* Whether fresh off the vine or from a jar, grape leaves may be stuffed with vegetables (page 42) or ground meat and rice (page 45), then steamed until tender.

Halloumi cheese This white sheep's milk cheese has a layered texture and a salty flavor.

Kashkaval cheese Also known as *achaouaine*, kashkaval ranges from mild to sharp varieties depending on the brand, it is a firm cheese made from sheep's milk and has a yellow hue.

Kataifi Consisting of very thin hair-like strands of shredded fillo dough, kataifi is traditionally used in a variety of desserts. It is very versatile and can be used to prepare appetizers and main dishes also. My favorite brand is Apollo.

Kholengen Dried galanga (a member of the ginger family), kholengen has a sharp sweet taste and is used to flavor both sweet and savory dishes. I use it to flavor spicy rice pudding (page 206), giving it an extra bite.

Kishk (or kashk powder) This is a mixture of fermented milk, salt, and bulgur, dried and ground into a cornmeal- to powder-like form with a tart flavor. It is used in preparing savory dishes and soups. Mixed with olive oil, sesame seeds, and spices, it is spread over dough and then baked into delicious red pepper pizzettas (page 39).

Mahlab powder Drop-shaped mahlab kernels are the pits of black cherries, beige in color. When ground, they produce a rose-scented powder that is slightly bitter with a faint almond-like taste.

Maward Rose flower water distilled from rose petals, maward is used to flavor sweets.

Mazaher Orange blossom water distilled from orange blossom flowers, mazaher is used to flavor sweets, and is added to hot water to prepare white coffee (page 211).

Mloukhiyeh (frozen) This green leafy vegetable, known as Jew's mallow or jute mallow, is "Lebanese spinach." Although it is seasonally available as fresh leaves or dried, I use the very convenient frozen chopped variety. Mloukhiyeh can be prepared as a stew and served with lamb, beef, and/or chicken, rice, toasted pita croutons, and an onion-vinegar sauce (page 94).

Moughrabiyeh Known as "Lebanese couscous," these are larger dried beads made from flour, salt, and water. When steamed in a rich broth with spices, they become deliciously tender "balls of pasta," served with lamb and/or beef and/or chicken with a pearl onion and chickpea onion broth on the side (page 108).

Olive oil *(zeyt zeytoon)* This is the prime component of the Lebanese/Mediterranean diet. Purchase a high-quality extra-virgin olive oil from the first pressing of the olives. Other grades include virgin, which comes from the second pressing; pure olive oil, which may be filtered and refined; and extra-light, which undergoes considerable processing and retains a very mild olive oil flavor. Keep olive oil stored in a cool, dark place in an airtight container.

Paprika *(filful hilou)* This spice is prepared by grinding dried sweet red peppers. The color can range from bright red to light pink. The flavor can also vary from spicy to sweet. Select brands that are sweet with a bright red color. Very versatile, it is used as a garnish as well as an ingredient in many recipes.

Pine nuts *(snobar)* Also called *pignoli* in Italian, these are the edible seeds extracted from some varieties of pine cones. These small, elongated ivory-colored seeds have a soft texture and a mild, nutty, buttery flavor. Lightly toasting them really brings out their flavor and adds a delicious crunch.

Pistachio *(fistouk)* Whole or ground nuts.

Plum sauce This delicious sauce is made from the pulp of plums with the distinctive flavors of vinegar, ginger, chili, and garlic. While it is not traditionally Lebanese, over the years it has become one of my favorite condiments to offer with curry. I buy Koon Chun, it is the brand I like best.

Purslane *(bakli)* This fresh, succulent seasonal summer vegetable has a mild sweet-and-sour flavor. I grew up picking it from the backyard in summertime and using it in *fattoush* salad. The succulent leaves and tender stems can be added to any green salad.

Rice flour This flour made from rice is used to thicken creamy puddings (such as rice pudding with apricots, page 200) and fillings.

Semolina flour *(smeed)* Semolina is coarsely ground durum wheat, used in pasta. It is used in these recipes to make light semolina butter cookies filled with dates, walnuts, almonds, or pistachios (see pages 202–205).

Sesame seeds *(simsoom)* Small seeds with a rich nutty flavor, sesame seeds are the main ingredient in tahini (sesame seed paste) and the heavenly confectionery halvah.

Shireeyee These are angel-hair pasta nests or cut fideo, *fideo cortado* in Italian. In this book the pasta is toasted to bring out a deep, rich flavor, then combined with basmati rice in a delicious pilaf (page 134).

Sumak These dried berries come from sumac bushes found throughout the Middle East. They are ground to produce sumak, fruity-tart and sour purplish red flakes, often mixed with salt. Sumak is used to flavor salad dressings, dips, and savory dishes. Select sumak that is deep purple-reddish in color. Avoid sumak that is light and pinkish in color; it is not as flavorful.

Tahini Produced from ground sesame seeds, tahini (sesame butter or paste) adds a rich, nutty flavor and creamy consistency to dips, sauces, and sweets. The thick paste separates from the oil, so for best results always mix well before using, reaching all the way to the bottom of the jar.

Turmeric Turmeric rhizomes are dried in hot ovens, then ground into a deep orange-yellow powder. Commonly used as a spice in curries, to add color to mustard, and is thought to have many beneficial medicinal properties. It is used in this book to flavor tumeric tea cakes (page 212).

Walnuts *(jouz)* Whole or ground nuts.

Wondra flour This instant flour is formulated to dissolve quickly, and is the perfect choice to have on hand for preparing lump-free sauces and gravies. I mix it with semolina when preparing semolina date cookies (page 202).

Zahtar An aromatic blend of thyme, sumak, and sesame seeds, zahtar is offered as a table condiment throughout the Middle East. Mixed with olive oil and onions, it is spread over flat dough and baked into delicious thyme pizzettas (page 37) or flat bread.

Zaher lamoon These delicate bright orange or red candied orange blossom petals are used to garnish sweets and are added to syrup, typically sold as zaher jam or orange blossom jam in specialty markets, or as orange blossom jam online. You want the variety that actually has small candied petals.

Metric Conversion Tables
APPROXIMATE U.S. METRIC EQUIVALENTS

Liquid Ingredients

U.S. MEASURES	METRIC	U.S. MEASURES	METRIC
¼ TSP.	1.23 ML	2 TBSP.	29.57 ML
½ TSP.	2.36 ML	3 TBSP.	44.36 ML
¾ TSP.	3.70 ML	¼ CUP	59.15 ML
1 TSP.	4.93 ML	½ CUP	118.30 ML
1¼ TSP.	6.16 ML	1 CUP	236.59 ML
1½ TSP.	7.39 ML	2 CUPS OR 1 PT.	473.18 ML
1¾ TSP.	8.63 ML	3 CUPS	709.77 ML
2 TSP.	9.86 ML	4 CUPS OR 1 QT.	946.36 ML
1 TBSP.	14.79 ML	4 QTS. OR 1 GAL.	3.79 L

Dry Ingredients

U.S. MEASURES		METRIC	U.S. MEASURES	METRIC
17⅗ OZ.	1 LIVRE	500 G	2 OZ.	60 (56.6) G
16 OZ.	1 LB.	454 G	1¾ OZ.	50 G
8⅞ OZ.		250 G	1 OZ.	30 (28.3) G
5¼ OZ.		150 G	⅞ OZ.	25 G
4½ OZ.		125 G	¾ OZ.	21 (21.3) G
4 OZ.		115 (113.2) G	½ OZ.	15 (14.2) G
3½ OZ.		100 G	¼ OZ.	7 (7.1) G
3 OZ.		85 (84.9) G	⅛ OZ.	3½ (3.5) G
2⅘ OZ.		80 G	¹⁄₁₆ OZ.	2 (1.8) G

Oven Temperatures

CELSIUS	FAHRENHEIT
110°C	225°F
120°C	250°F
140°C	275°F
150°C	300°F
160°C	325°F
170°C	350°F
180°C	350°F
190°C	375°F
200°C	400°F
220°C	425°F
230°C	450°F

Weight

METRIC	IMPERIAL
450 g	1 lb
600 g	1 lb 5 oz
900 g	2lb

Linear Measurements

METRIC	IMPERIAL
5 mm	¼ in
10 mm/1 cm	½ in
2.5 cm	1 in
4 cm	1 ½ in
5 cm	2 in
6 cm	2 ½ in
7.5 cm	3 in

Index

Italicized page references indicate photographs.

Achaouaine (kashkaval) cheese
    crudités platter with, 15–16, *16*
    definition, 221
Ackawi cheese
    crudités platter with, *15*, 15–16
    definition, 219
Adas bi hamood, 166–67, *167*
Ajeen, 20
Allspice, definition, 219
Almond(s)
    baklava with, *170*, 176–78, *177*, *178*
    biscuits with marshmallow dip, 214–15, *215*
    crescents, 182–84, *183*, *184*
    fingers, *172*, 172–73
    semolina cookies with, 202–3, *203*, *204*
Angel hair nests (shireeyee)
    basmati rice with toasted, 134
    definition, 222
Anise
    definition, 219
    fingers, glazed, *187*, 187–88, *188*
    milk cookies, crunchy, 185, *185*
Appetizers, 1–48
Apricots, rice pudding with, 200–201, *201*
Aradis bil curry, 80
Arnabeet mickli ma taratoor, *7*, 7–8
Arous jneini, 141, *141*
Asaibi zainab, *172*, 172–73
Atr, 179
Awwamat, *189*, 189–91
Aysh el sariya, 180–82, *181*

Baba ghannouj, 28–29, *29*
Baked kataifi with cream, 173–75, *174*
Baklava (Baklawa bi jouz), *170*, 176–78, *177*, *178*
Bammee bi djeaj, 157–58
Bammee bi lahm, 156–57
Bammee bi zeyt, *155*, 155–56

Basmati rice
    with cumin, lentils and onion, 135
    definition, 219
    green onions, 134
    plain, 132, *133*
    saffron, 132
    with toasted noodles, 134
Batata bil furren, 150, *150*
Bean(s), garbanzo
    bulgur pilaf with, 71
    definition, 220
    freezing cooked, 10
    and herb patties, 2–3, *3*
    hummus, 8–10, *9*
    and onion sauce, 109, 110
    salad, 56, *56*
    and tahini sauce, 98
    triangles with beef confit, 33
Beans, fava
    with garlic and lemon, 139–40, *140*
Beans, green
    in tomato and olive oil, 142, *142*
    in tomato and olive oil with lamb or beef, 143
Beans, lima
    chicken with cilantro and, 149
    with cilantro, 146–47, *147*
    lamb or beef with cilantro and, 148
Bean soup, mixed, 169
Beef. *See also* Beef, ground; Beef confit
    bulgur pilaf, 71
    cardamom, with rice, 74
    confit, 136–37, *137*
    curry, 80
    fire-roasted wheat with, *83*, 83–84
    green beans in tomato and olive oil, 143
    jute mallow garlic-cilantro stew, 94–96, *95*
    kabobs, grilled, 88–89, *89*
    kibbi balls with top round London broil, 24–26
    kibbi trays, 99–101, *100*, *101*
    layered with garlic yogurt and pita, *105*, 105–7
    Lebanese caraway couscous, 110

lima beans with cilantro, 148
raisin couscous and vegetable stew, 115–16
spiced rice and toasted nuts, 77
stewed okra and cilantro, 156–57
Beef, ground
fillo rolls, tangy, *35, 35–36, 36*
grilled fingers, 84–85, *85*
hummus with pine nuts and, 11
kibbi balls, 24–26
kibbi balls in cilantro yogurt, 96–97, *97*
kibbi balls in garbanzo bean tahini sauce, 98,
99–101, *100, 101*
Lebanese meatloaf, *111,* 111–12
meatball soup, miniature, *130,* 168
pomegranate and cheese pies, *18,* 18–20, *19*
pomegranate crescents, 6
stuffed cabbage rolls, 164
stuffed eggplant with pine nuts, 66–67, *67*
stuffed grape leaves, 45
stuffed squash and grape leaves, 122–24, *123*
stuffed zucchini in tomato sauce with,
125–27, *126*
tortellini in cilantro yogurt, 68–70, *69, 70*
turbans, 12
Beef confit
basic recipe for, 136–37, *137*
garbanzo bean triangles, 33
omelets, mini, 15
scrambled eggs and potatoes with, 151, *151*
Beet(s)
and cabbage salad, 50, *50*
turnips, pickled, 17, *17*
Bied ma qawarma, 151, *151*
Biscuits, almond, 214–15, *215*
Bread pudding, caramelized, 180–82, *181*
Bulgur
definition, 219
kibbi balls, 24–26
kibbi trays, 99–101, *100, 101*
and parsley salad, 58–59, *59*
pilaf with chicken, lamb, or beef, 71
tabbouli bites, 34, *34*
Burak bi djeaj, 36
Burak bi jibni, 36
Burak bi lahm, *35,* 35–36, *36*
Burghul bidfeen ma djeaj, 71
Burghul bidfeen ma lahm, 71

Butter, clarified. *See* Clarified butter

Cabbage
and beet salad, 50, *50*
rolls stuffed with meat, 164
rolls stuffed with vegetables, 161, 161–63,
162, 163
Cakes
semolina-yogurt, sweet, 208–9, *209*
turmeric tea cake, 212–13, *213*
Canapés, yogurt cheese, 46, *46*
Caramelized dishes
bread pudding, 180–82, *181*
cumin rice, for red snapper, 116–18, *117*
onions with dandelions, 152
onions with lentils, *145,* 145–46
onions with spinach, 152–53, *153*
Caraway
definition, 219
Lebanese, couscous with chicken, 108–10, *109*
Cardamom
chicken with rice, 72–73, *73*
definition, 219
lamb or beef with rice, 74
rice pudding with apricots, 201
Cashew(s)
baklava, *170,* 176–78, *177, 178*
biscuits with marshmallow dip, 214–15, *215*
crescents, 182–84, *183, 184*
fingers, *172,* 172–73
Castaleta mishwi, 90, *90*
Cauliflower, fried, with tahini sauce, 7, 7–8
Cheese. *See also* Feta cheese; Yogurt cheese
Ackawi, definition, 219
choosing, 16
crudités platter with, 15–16, *16*
Halloumi, definition, 220
kashkaval (achaouaine), definition, 221
Chicken. *See also* Chicken, ground
bulgur pilaf, 71
cardamom, with rice, 72–73, *73*
curry, 78–80, *79*
fire-roasted wheat with, 84
grilled lemon-garlic or ginger, *121,* 121–22
hummus with pine nuts and, 11
jute mallow garlic-cilantro stew, 96
kebabs, grilled, 86–87, *87*

layered with garlic yogurt and pita, 107–8
Lebanese caraway couscous, 108–10, *109*
lima beans with cilantro, 149
pita crouton salad with sumac dressing, 61
raisin couscous and vegetable stew, 115
roasted lemon-garlic or ginger, *64, 121*, 121–22
spiced rice with toasted nuts, 75–76, *76*
stewed okra with cilantro, 157–58
Chicken, ground
    fillo rolls, tangy, 36
    kibbi balls, 24–26
    kibbi balls in cilantro sauce, 96–97, *97*
    kibbi balls in garbanzo-tahini sauce, 98
    kibbi trays, 99–101, *100, 101*
    pomegranate and cheese pies, 20
    pomegranate crescents, 6
    stuffed eggplant with pine nuts, 66–67, *67*
    stuffed zucchini in tomato sauce, 125–27, *126*
    tortellini in cilantro yogurt, 68–70, *69, 70*
    turbans, 11–13, *13*
Chocolate dip for fresh fruit, 186
Cilantro
    chicken and lima beans with, 149
    and jalapeño salsa, 144, *144*
    jute mallow stew with garlic and chicken, 96
    jute mallow stew with garlic and meat, 94–96, *95*
    lamb or beef with lima beans and, 148
    lima beans with, 146–47, *147*
    stewed okra in olive oil with, *155*, 155–56
    stewed okra in olive oil with chicken and,
        157–58
    stewed okra in olive oil with lamb or beef and,
        156–57
    yogurt, beef tortellini in, 68–70, *69, 70*
    yogurt, kibbi balls in, 96–97, *97*
    yogurt, stuffed zucchini in, 127
Clarified butter
    almond fingers, *172*, 172–73
    baked kataifi with cream, 173–75, *174, 175*
    baklava, *170*, 176–78, *177, 178*
    cashew crescents, 182–84, *183, 184*
    definition, 220
    melt-away sugar cookies, 194–95, *195*
    recipe, 196
    semolina cookies, 202–3, *203*, 204, 205
    walnut biscuits with marshmallow dip,
        214–15, *215*

Cod baked in citrus tahini, *81*, 81–82
Coffee
    Turkish coffee, *210*, 210–11
    white, 211
Cookies
    anise fingers, glazed, *187*, 187–88, *188*
    anise milk, crunchy, 185, *185*
    semolina almond, 202–3, *203*, 204
    semolina date, 202–3, *203*
    semolina pistachio, 202–3, *203*, 205
    semolina walnut, 202–3, *203*, 204
    sugar, melt-away, *194*, 194–95, *195*
Coriander, definition, 220
Cousa mihshi warac inab, 122–24, *123*
Couscous
    Lebanese caraway, with chicken, 108–10, *109*
    raisin, with chicken and vegetable stew, 115
    raisin, with lamb or beef and vegetable stew,
        115–16
    raisin, with vegetable stew, 112–14, *113, 114*
Couscous ma djeaj, 115
Couscous ma khudra, 112–14, *113, 114*
Couscous ma lahm, 115–16
Cream
    angel hair with, crispy, 175
    for caramelized bread pudding, 180–82, *181*
    kataifi with, baked, *173*, 173–75, *174*
    mini Lebanese pancakes with, *197*, 197–98
Crispy angel hair with cream, 175
Crispy bean & herb patties, 2–3, *3*
Crudités, 15–16, *16*
Crunchy anise milk cookies, 185, *185*
Cucumber(s)
    crudités platter with, 15–16, *16*
    eggplant salad with, 48, 52–54, *53*
    farmer's salad with, 55
    garbanzo bean salad with, 56, *56*
    garden wraps with, 141, *141*
    pita crouton salad with sumak dressing,
        60–61, *61*
    yogurt cheese canapés with, 46, *46*
    and yogurt salad, 63, *63*
Cumin
    basmati rice with lentils, onion and, 135
    caramelized, rice for red snapper, 116–18, *117*
    definition, 220
    hummus with, 10

roasted onion and potato spears, 150, *150*
Curry
    beef or lamb, 80
    chicken, 78–80, *79*
    potato, 80
    shrimp, 80
Curry powder, definition, 220

Dandelion(s)
    with caramelized onions, 152
    salad, 51, *51*
    salad with yogurt, 52
Date(s)
    Deglet Noor, definition, 220
    semolina cookies, 202–3, *203*, 204, 205
Desserts, 171–215
Dibs ruman (pomegranate molasses)
    beef and pine nut-stuffed eggplant, 66–67, *67*
    definition, 220
    lamb turbans, 11–13, *13*
    pomegranate and cheese pies, *18*, 18–20, *19*
    pomegranate-beef crescents, 6
    pumpkin kibbi balls, *21*, 21–23, *22* , *23*
    red pepper and walnut spread, 30, *31*
    red pepper pizzettas, 39
    thyme pizzettas, *37*, 37–38, *38*
Dill, mini omelets with, *14*, 14–15
Dips and spreads
    eggplant, smoked, 28–29, *29*
    hummus with tahini, 8–10, *9*, 11
    marshmallow, 214–15, *215*
    red bell pepper and walnut, spicy, 30, *30*
Djeaj bil curry, 78–80, *79*
Djeaj bil furrin, *121*, 121–22
Djeaj ma riz boukhari, 72–73, *73*
Djeaj ma riz haswi, 75–76, *76*
Dolma, 158–60, *159*, *160*
Douggas, 144, *144*
Dough, basic, 20. *See also* Fillo dough
Drawn (clarified) butter, 196
Dressings, salad
    for eggplant salad, 53, 54
    sumak, for pita crouton salad, 60–61, *61*
    tahini, for romaine salad, 62

Egg(s)
    beef confit omelets, mini, 15

dill omelets, mini, *14*, 14–15
    potato omelets, mini, 15
    scrambled, with beef confit and potatoes,
        151, *151*
    zucchini omelet, mini, 15
Eggplant
    moussaka, *138*, 138–39
    salad, *48*, 52–54, *53*
    smoked dip, 28–29, *29*
    stuffed vegetables with, 158–60, *159*, *160*
    stuffed with beef and pine nuts, 66–67, *67*

Fakhed ghannem, *119*, 119–20
Falafel, 2–3, *3*
Falafel molds, 3
Farina
    baked kataifi with cream, 173–75, *174*, *175*
    definition, 220
Farmer's salad with tahini dressing, 55, *55*
Fassolia bi djeaj, 149
Fassolia bi lahm, 149
Fassolia bi zeyt, 146–47, *147*
Fatayer bi hoummous, 33
Fatayer bi sbanekh, *31*, 31–32, *32*
Fatteh ma djeaj, 107–8
Fatteh ma khundra, 107
Fatteh ma lahm, *105*, 105–7
Fattoush, 60–61, *61*
Fava beans with garlic and lemon, 139–40, *140*
Feta cheese
    crescents, *4*, 4–6, *5*
    definition, 220
    fillo rolls, 36
    spinach triangles with, 32
Fillo dough (phyllo dough)
    almond fingers, *172*, 172–73
    baklava, *170*, 176–78, *177*, *178*
    definition, 220
    rolls, beef, chicken or feta cheese, *35*, 35–36, *36*
    shredded, and baked with cream, 173–75, *174*,
        175
    shredded, and cream nut pie, 191–93, *193*
    shredded, angel hair with cream, 175
Fire-roasted wheat with lamb (or beef), *83*, 83–84
Fish
    cod baked in citrus tahini, *81*, 81–82
    kibbi trays, 102–3

red snapper with caramelized cumin rice,
116–18, *117*
tilapia with jalapeño pine nut sauce, 128–29, *129*
Fordhook lima beans
chicken with cilantro and, 149
with cilantro, 146–48, *147*
lamb or beef with cilantro and, 148
Foul, definition, 220
Foul moudammus, 139–40, *140*
Freekeh, definition, 220
Freekeh ma djeaj, 84
Freekeh ma lahm, *83*, 83–84
Fried cauliflower with tahini sauce, *7*, 7–8
Fried mini Lebanese half-moon pancakes with
walnuts, 199
Fruit, fresh (Fweicki), 186, *186*

Galangal root (kholengen)
definition, 221
rice pudding with nuts, 206–7, *207*
Garbanzo bean(s)
bulgur pilaf with, 71
definition, 220
freezing cooked, 10
& herb patties, 2–3, *3*
hummus, 8–10, *9*
and onion sauce, 109, 110
salad, *56*, *56*
and tahini sauce, 98
triangles with beef confit, 33
Garden wraps, 141, *141*
Garlic
cilantro and jute mallow stew, 94–96, *95*
fava beans with lemon and, 139–40, *140*
and lemon chicken, roasted, *64*, *121*, 121–22
and lemon potato salad, *57*, *57*
puree, robust, 26–27, *27*
and yogurt sauce, 106, 107
Ghreibi, *194*, 194–95, *195*
Glazed anise fingers, *187*, 187–88, *188*
Glossary, 219–23
Grape leaves
definition, 220
meat-stuffed, 45
with stuffed squash, 122–24, *123*
vegetable-stuffed, *42*, 42–44
working with, 43–44, *44*

Green beans
in tomato and olive oil, 142, *142*
in tomato and olive oil with lamb or beef, 143
Green bell peppers, with crudités platter, 15–16, *16*
Green onions, with basmati rice, 134
Grilled dishes
beef fingers, 84–85, *85*
chicken kebabs, 86–87, *87*
lamb kebabs, 88–89, *89*
lamb rib chops, 90, *90*
lemon-garlic (or ginger) chicken, *64*, 122
shrimp kebabs, *91*, 91–92
vegetable kebabs, 92–93, *93*

Halloumi cheese
crudités platter with, 15–16, *16*
definition, 220
Hillou, 171–215
Honey balls, *189*, 189–91
Horseradish hummus with tahini, 10
Hoummos bi tahini, 8–10, *9*
Hoummos bi tahini ma lahm mafroom, 11
Hummus
basic recipe with tahini, 8–10, *9*
with chicken, 11
with cumin, 10
with horseradish, 10
with meat and pine nuts, 11
with roasted red bell peppers, 10
with sun-dried tomatoes, 10

Ijjie batata, 15
Ijjie cousa, 15
Ijjie qawarma, 15
Ijjie shimra, *14*, 14–15
Ismaliyeh, 175

Jalapeño
and cilantro salsa, 144, *144*
and pine nut sauce, 128
Jute mallow (Lebanese spinach)
definition (mloukhiyeh), 221
and garlic-cilantro stew, 94–96, *95*

Ka'ak bi haleeb, 185, *185*
Kablama bi banadora, 125–27, *126*
Kablama bi laban, 127

Karabeej ma nateef, 214–15, *215*
Kashik powder. *See* Kishk
Kashkaval (achaouaine) cheese
    crudités platter with, 15–16, *16*
    definition, 221
Kashk powder. *See* Kishk
Kataifi
    angel hair with cream, 175
    baked, with cream, 173–75, *174, 175*
    and cream nut pie, 191–93, *193*
    definition, 221
Katayef bi jouz, 199
Katayef bi jouz mickli, 199
Katayef bi kushta, *197*, 197–98
Kebabs, grilled
    chicken, 86–87, *87*
    lamb, 88–89, *89*
    shrimp, *91*, 91–92
    vegetable, 92–93, *93*
Kefta bil saniyeh, *111*, 111–12
Kefta mishwi, 84–85, *85*
Khibz arabi imhammas, 40–41, *41*
Kholengen
    definition, 221
    rice pudding with nuts, spicy, 206–7, *207*
Kibbi arnabiyeh, 96–97, *97*
Kibbi balls
    chicken, lamb or beef, 24–26
    in cilantro yogurt, 96–97, *97*
    in garbanzo tahini sauce, 98
    potato, 23–24
    pumpkin, *21*, 21–23, *22, 23*
Kibbi bi saniyeh, 99–101, *100, 101*
Kibbi bi saniyeh luctine, 102–3
Kibbi bi saniyeh samak, 103–4
Kibbi kebab batata, 23–24
Kibbi kebab djeaj, 26
Kibbi kebab lahm, 24–26
Kibbi kebab luctine, *21*, 21–23, *22, 23*
Kibbi labaniyeh, 96–97, *97*
Kibbi tray
    fish, 103–4
    lamb, beef, or chicken, 99–101, *100, 101*
    pumpkin, 102–3
Kishk (kashk powder)
    dandelion salad with, 51, *51*
    definition, 221

red pepper pizzettas with, 39
Kneifi bi kushta, 173–75, *174, 175*
Koul weshkor, 182–84, *183, 184*

Laban bi khyar, 63, *63*
Labni, 47, *47*
Labni canapé, 46, *46*
Lahm bi ajeen, 11–13, *13*
Lahm bil curry, 80
Lahm ma riz boukari, 74
Lahm ma riz haswi, 77
Lamb. *See also* Lamb, ground
    bulgur pilaf, 71
    cardamom, with rice, 74
    curry, 80
    fire-roasted wheat with, *83*, 83–84
    green beans in tomato and olive oil, 143
    jute mallow garlic-cilantro stew, 94–96, *95*
    kebabs, grilled, 88–89, *89*
    kibbi balls, 24–26
    layered with garlic yogurt and pita, *105*, 105–7
    Lebanese caraway couscous, 110
    lima beans with cilantro, 148
    raisin couscous and vegetable stew, 115–16
    rib or loin chops, grilled, 90, *90*
    roast leg of, *119*, 119–20
    spiced rice with toasted nuts, 77
    stewed okra and cilantro, 156–57
Lamb, ground
    grilled fingers, 84–85, *85*
    hummus with pine nuts and, 11
    kibbi balls in cilantro yogurt, 96–97, *97*
    kibbi balls in garbanzo tahini sauce, 99–101, *100, 101*
    kibbi trays, 99–101, *100, 101*
    Lebanese meatloaf, *111*, 111–12
    pomegranate and cheese pies, *18*, 18–20, *19*
    pomegranate crescents, 6
    stuffed cabbage rolls, 164
    stuffed eggplant with pine nuts, 66–67, *67*
    stuffed grape leaves, 45
    stuffed squash and grape leaves, 122–24, *123*
    stuffed zucchini in tomato sauce, 125–27, *126*
    tortellini in cilantro yogurt, 68–70, *69, 70*
    turbans, 11–13, *13*
Layered chicken with garlic yogurt and pita, 107–8

Layered London broil with garlic yogurt and pita, *105*, 105–7
Lebanese caraway couscous with lamb (or beef), 110
Lebanese meatloaf, *111*, 111–12
Lemon(s)
    citrus tahini, for baked cod, *81*, 81–82
    fava beans with garlic and, 139–40, *140*
    and garlic chicken, roasted, *64*, *121*, 121–22
    and garlic potato salad, *57*, *57*
    and ginger chicken, grilled, 122
    lentil soup with Swiss chard and, 166–67, *167*
Lentil(s)
    basmati rice with cumin and onions, 135
    with caramelized onions, *145*, 145–46
    noodle stew, 165
    soup with Swiss chard, lemon and, 166–67, *167*
Lettuce, romaine
    pita crouton salad with, 60–61, *61*
    salad, *62*, *62*
Lift, *17*, *17*
Lima beans. *See* Fordhook lima beans
Loubi bi lahm, 143
Loubi bi zeyt, *142*, *142*

Macaroon, *187*, 187–88, *188*
Mafrouki, 191–93, *193*
Mahlab powder
    anise fingers, glazed, *187*, 187–88, *188*
    definition, 221
Main meals, 65–130
Makhlouta, 169
Mamoul bi fistouk, 205
Mamoul bi jouz, 202–3, *203*, 204
Mamoul bi tamer, 202–3, *203*
Manakeesh bi flaifli, 39
Manakeesh bi zahtar, *37*, 37–38, *38*
Marshmallow dip, 214–15, *215*
Maward
    baklava with pistachios, 178
    bread pudding, caramelized, 180–82, *181*
    definition, 221
    pistachio fingers, 173
    rice pudding with apricots, 200–201, *201*
    semolina cookies with walnuts or almonds, 202–3, *203*, 204
    syrup with, 179

white coffee, 211
Mazaher
    almond fingers, *172*, 172–73
    baklava, *170*, 176–78, *177*, *178*
    bread pudding, caramelized, 180–82, *181*
    cashew crescents, 182–84, *183*, *184*
    definition, 221
    Lebanese half-moon pancakes, 199
    rice pudding with apricots, 200–201, *201*
    syrup with, 179
    walnut biscuits with marshmallow dip, 214–15, *215*
Meatball soup, miniature, *130*, 168
Meatloaf, Lebanese, *111*, 111–12
Melt-away sugar cookies, 194–95, *195*
Menus, suggested, 217–18
Metric conversion tables, 224–25
Mighli, 206–7, *207*
Mihshi malfoof bi lahm, 164
Mihshi malfoof bi zeyt, *161*, 161–63, *162*, *163*
Miniature meatball soup, *130*, 168
Mini beef confit omelets, 15
Mini dill omelets, *14*, 14–15
Mini Lebanese half-moon pancakes with walnuts, 199
Mini Lebanese pancakes with cream, *197*, 197–98
Mini potato omelets, 15
Mini zucchini omelets, 15
Mint
    garden wraps, *141*, *141*
    parsley and bulgar wheat salad, 58–59, *59*
    pita crouton salad, 60–61, *61*
    vegetable-stuffed grape leaves, *42*, 42–44, *44*
    yogurt cheese canapés, *46*, *46*
    yogurt-cucumber salad, *63*, *63*
    and yogurt sauce, for beef tortellini, 70
Mixed bean soup, 169
Mloukhiyeh, definition, 221
Mloukhiyeh bi djeaj, 96
Mloukhiyeh bi lahm, 94–96, *95*
Moughrabiyeh, definition, 221
Moughrabiyeh ma djeaj, 108–10, *109*
Moughrabiyeh ma lahm, 110
Mouhallabiyeh, 200–201, *201*
Mouhamarra, *30*, *30*
Mousaka'a batinjan bi zeyt, *138*, 138–39
Mujaddara, *145*, 145–46

Namoura, 208–9, *209*
Nuts. *See also specific types of nuts*
    chicken, beef, or lamb and spiced rice with
      toasted, 75–76, *76, 77*
    kataifi and cream nut pie, 191–93, *193*
    melt-away sugar cookies with, 194–95, *195*
    rice pudding with, 206–7, *207*

Okra
    stewed, with cilantro, olive oil, beef or lamb,
      156–57
    stewed, with cilantro, olive oil and chicken,
      157–58
    stewed, with cilantro and olive oil, *155,* 155–56
Olive oil, definition, 221
Olives
    crudités platter with, 15–16, *16*
    garden wraps with, 141, *141*
    yogurt cheese canapés with, 46, *46*
Omelets, mini, *14,* 14–15
Onion(s)
    basmati rice with cumin, lentils and, 135
    caramelized, with dandelions, 152
    caramelized, with lentils, *145,* 145–46
    caramelized, with spinach, 152–53, *153*
    and cumin potato spears, roasted, 150, *151*
    and cumin sauce, 118
    pearl, bulgur pilaf with chicken, 71
    red, pita crouton salad with, 61
    stuffed vegetables with, 158–60, *159, 160*
Onions, green, with basmati rice, 134
Orange blossom jam. *See* Zaher lamoon
Orange blossom water. *See* Mazaher

Pancakes, mini
    with cream, *197,* 197–98
    half-moon, with walnuts, 199
    half-moon, with walnuts fried, 199
Paprika
    definition, 221
    and onion pita dippers, toasted, 40
    red pepper pizzettas, 39
Parsley and bulgur wheat salad, 58–59, *59*
Peppers
    green bell, crudités platter with, 15–16, *16*
    hot, pickled turnips and, 17
    red bell, and walnut spread, spicy, 30, *30*

red bell, hummus with roasted, 10
    roasting, 30
Phyllo dough. *See* Fillo dough
Pickled turnips, 17, *17*
Pickles, crudités platter with, *15,* 15–16
Pie(s)
    kataifi and cream nut, 191–93, *193*
    pomegranate and cheese with meat, *18,*
      18–20, *19*
Pilafs, basmati rice, 132
Pine nut(s)
    and beef-stuffed eggplants, 66–67, *67*
    biscuits with marshmallow dip, 214–15, *215*
    definition, 222
    hummus with minced lamb and, 11
    and jalapeño sauce, for tilapia, 128
    lamb turbans with, 11–13, *13*
    pomegranate-beef crescents, 6
    spinach triangles with, 32
    spinach with minced lamb and, 154
    vegetable-stuffed grape leaves with, *42,* 42–44
Pistachio(s)
    baklava with, *170,* 176–78, *177, 178*
    biscuits with marshmallow dip, 214–15, *215*
    crescents, 182–84, *183, 184*
    fingers, *172,* 172–73
    semolina cookies with, *203,* 204
    sugar cookies, melt-away, *194,* 194–95, *195*
Pita
    beef or lamb layered with garlic yogurt and,
      105, 105–7
    chicken layered with garlic yogurt and, 107–8
    croutons, eggplant salad with, *48,* 52–54, *53*
    croutons, salad with sumak dressing, 60–61, *61*
    dippers, toasted, 40–41, *41*
    garden wraps, 141, *141*
Pizzettas
    red pepper, 39
    thyme, *37,* 37–38, *38*
Plum sauce
    chicken curry, 78–80, *79*
    definition, 222
Pomegranate. *See also* Dibs ruman
    beef and cheese pies, *18,* 18–20, *19*
    and beef crescents, 6
    chicken and cheese pies, 20
    smoked eggplant dip, garnish for, 29

Pomegranate molasses. *See* Dibs ruman
Potato(es)
    honey balls, *189, 189*–91
    kibbi balls, 23–24
    lemon-garlic, salad, 57, *57*
    mini omelets with, 15
    roasted onion-cumin spears, 150, *150*
    vegetarian curry, 80
Pudding(s)
    caramelized bread, with cream, 180–82, *181*
    rice, with apricots, 200–201, *201*
    rice, with nuts, 206–7, *207*
Pumpkin
    kibbi balls, *21,* 21–23, *22, 23*
    kibbi trays, 102–3
Purslane
    definition, 222
    pita crouton salad with, 61

Qahwa, *210,* 210–11
Qahwa bida, 211
Qawarma, 136–37, *137*

Raisins, golden
    couscous with vegetable stew, 112–14, *113, 114*
    spinach triangles with, 32
Rashti, 165
Red bell peppers
    hummus with roasted, 10
    roasting, 30
    and walnut spread, spicy, 30, *30*
Red pepper pizzettas, 39
Red snapper with caramelized cumin rice, 116–18, *117*
Rice, basmati
    with cumin, lentils and onion, 135
    definition, 219
    green onions, 134
    plain, 132, *133*
    saffron, 132
    with toasted noodles, 134
Rice, converted/parboiled
    caramelized cumin, for red snapper, 116–18, *117*
    cardamom chicken with, *72,* 72–73
    cardamom lamb or beef with, 74
    and lamb-stuffed grape leaves, 45
    spiced, with chicken and toasted nuts, 75–76, *76*

    and vegetable-stuffed grape leaves, *42, 42*–44
Rice pudding
    with apricots, 200–201, *201*
    with nuts, 206–7, *207*
Riz basmati, 132
Riz basmati ma addas, 135
Riz basmati ma bussel ukhdar, *133,* 134
Riz basmati ma shireeyee, *133,* 134
Riz basmati ma zafaron, 132, *133*
Riz haswi, 75–76, *76*
Roasted lemon-garlic chicken, *121,* 121–22
Roasted lemon-ginger chicken, 122
Roasted onion and cumin potato spears, 150, *150*
Roast leg of lamb, *119,* 119–20
Robust garlic puree, 26–27, *27*
Romaine lettuce
    pita crouton salad with, 60–61, *61*
    salad, 62, *62*
Rosemary, toasted pita dippers with, 40
Rose water. *See* Maward

Sabanekh bi lahm mafroom, 154
Sabanekh bi zeyt, 152–53, *153*
Salads, 48–63
Salata batata, 57, *57*
Salata batinjan, *48,* 52–54, *53*
Salata felaheen, 55, *55*
Salata hindbi ma kishk, 51, *51*
Salata hindbi ma laban, 52
Salata hoummos haab, 56, *56*
Salata khus, 62, *62*
Salata malfoof ma shamandar, 50, *50*
Salsa, jalapeño-cilantro, 144, *144*
Samakeh harrah, 128–29, *129*
Sambousik bi jibni, *4,* 4–6, *5*
Sambousik bi lahmi, 6
Samnee, 196
Sauces
    cilantro yogurt, 68
    cumin-onion, 118
    curry, 78–79
    garbanzo bean-onion, 109, 110
    garbanzo-tahini, 98
    garlic-yogurt, 106, 107
    jalapeño-pine nut, 128
Sayadiyeh, 116–18, *117*

Scrambled eggs with beef confit and potato, 151, *151*
Semolina
  anise fingers, glazed, *187*, 187–88, *188*
  cookies with pistachios, 202–3, *203*, 205
  cookies with walnuts or almonds, 202–3, *203*, 204
  date cookies, 202–3, *203*
  definition, 222
  walnut biscuits with marshmallow dip, 214–15, *215*
  yogurt cakes, sweet, 208–9, *209*
Sfiha djeaj, 20
Sfiha lahm, *18*, 18–20, *19*
Sfoof, 212–13, *213*
Sheesh aradis mishwi, *91*, 91–92
Sheesh barak, 68–70, *69*, *70*
Sheesh kabob mishwi, 88–89, *89*
Sheesh khoudra mishwi, 92–93, *93*
Sheesh tawook mishwi, 86–87, *87*
Shiekh el mihshi, 66–67, *67*
Shireeyee, definition, 222
Shorba keema, *130*, 168
Shrimp
  curry, 80
  kebabs, grilled, *91*, 91–92
  pita crouton salad with sumac dressing, 61
Side dishes, 131–69
Smoked eggplant dip, 28–29, *29*
Soups
  lentil, with Swiss chard and lemon, 166–67, *167*
  miniature meatball, *130*, 168
Spanakopita, spinach filling for, 31
Spicy red pepper and walnut spread, 30, *30*
Spicy rice pudding with nuts, 206–7, *207*
Spinach
  with caramelized onions, 152–53, *153*
  with minced lamb and pine nuts, 154
  thawing, 32
  triangles, *31*, 31–32, *32*
Spinach, Lebanese. *See* Jute mallow
Squash
  stuffed, and grape leaves, 122–24, *123*
  stuffed, in tomato sauce, 125–27, *126*
  stuffed vegetables with, 158–59, *159*, *160*
Stews
  jute mallow and garlic-cilantro, 94–96, *95*

lentil noodle, 165
mixed bean, 169
okra and cilantro in olive oil, *155*, 155–56
okra and lamb or beef with cilantro in olive oil, 156–57
okra with chicken, cilantro in olive oil, 157–58
Stuffed
  cabbage rolls, *161*, 161–63, *162*, *163*
  eggplant, 66–67, *67*
  grape leaves, *42*, 42–44, *45*
  squash and grape leaves, 122–24, *123*
  vegetables, 158–60, *159*, *160*
  zucchini in cilantro yogurt, 127
  zucchini in tomato sauce with meat, 125–27, *126*
Sugar cookies, melt-away, *194*, 194–95, *195*
Sumak
  definition, 222
  dressing, 60
  eggplant salad with, *48*, 52–54, *53*
  lamb kibbi balls, 24–26
  pita dippers, toasted, with, 40
  pomegranate-beef crescents with, 6
  red pepper pizzettas with, 39
  thyme pizzettas with, *37*, 37–38, *38*
Sun-dried tomatoes, hummus with, 10
Sweet semolina-yogurt cakes, 208–9, *209*
Swiss chard and lentil soup, 166–67, *167*
Syrup, 179

Tabbouli, 58–59, *59*
Tabbouli bites, 34, *34*
Tahini
  citrus, cod baked in, *81*, 81–82
  definition, 222
  dressing, for farmer's salad, 55
  dressing, for romaine salad, 62
  eggplant dip, smoked, 28–29, *29*
  garbanzo sauce, 98
  hummus, 8–10, *9*
  pomegranate, beef and cheese pies with, *18*, 18–20
  sauce, *7*, 7–8
  turmeric tea cakes, 212–13, *213*
  yogurt-cucumber salad with, *63*, 63
Tajin, *81*, 81–82
Tangy beef fillo rolls, *35*, 35–36, *36*

Tangy chicken fillo rolls, 36
Thyme pizzettas, *37*, 37–38, *38*
Tilapia with jalapeño pine nut sauce, 128–29, *129*
Toasted pita dippers, 40–41, *41*
Tomato(es)
    cherry, tabbouli bites with, 34, *34*
    eggplant salad with, *48*, 52–54, *53*
    farmer's salad with, 55, *55*
    garbanzo bean salad with, 56, *56*
    green beans in olive oil and, 142, *142*
    jalapeño-cilantro salsa, 144, *144*
    lamb with green beans, olive oil and, 143
    parsley and bulgur wheat salad with, 58–59, *59*
    pita crouton salad with, 60–61, *61*
    stuffed vegetables with, 158–60, *159*, *160*
    sun-dried, hummus with, 10
Tomato sauce, stuffed zucchini in, 125–27, *126*
Toom, 26–27, *27*
Turkish coffee, *210*, 210–11
Turmeric
    definition, 222
    tea cakes, 212–13, *213*
Turnips, white
    crudités platter with, *15*, 15–16
    eggplant salad with, *48*, 52–54, *53*
    pickled, 17, *17*

Vegetable(s)
    crudités platter, 15–16, *16*
    kebabs, grilled, 92–93, *93*
    layered, with garlic yogurt and pita, *105*, 105–7
    stew with raisin couscous, 112–14, *113*, *114*
    stew with raisin couscous and chicken, 115
    stew with raisin couscous and lamb or beef,
        115–16
    stuffed, *158*, 158–60, *160*
    stuffed cabbage rolls, *161*, 161–63, *162*, *163*
    stuffed grape leaves, *42*, 42–44, *44*

Walnut(s)
    baklava, *170*, 176–78, *177*, *178*
    biscuits with marshmallow dip, 214
    crescents, 182–84, *183*, *184*
    definition, 222

fingers, *172*, 172–73
    Lebanese half-moon pancakes with, 199
    and red pepper spread, spicy, 30, *31*
    semolina cookies with, *203*, 204
Warac inab bi lahm, 45
Warac inab bi zeyt, *42*, 42–44, *44*
White coffee, 211
Wondra flour
    anise fingers, glazed, *187*, 187–88, *188*
    definition, 222
    Lebanese pancakes, mini, *197*, 197–98
    turmeric tea cakes, 212–13, *213*
Wraps, garden, 141, *141*

Yogurt. *See also* Yogurt cheese
    cilantro, sauce, 68
    and cucumber salad, 63, *63*
    dandelion salad with, 52
    and garlic sauce, 106, 107
    semolina cakes, sweet, 208–9, *209*
Yogurt cheese
    basic recipe for, *47*, 47
    canapés, 46, *46*
    garden wraps with, 141, *141*
    pomegranate beef pie with, *18*, 18–20, *19*

Zaher lamoon
    caramelized bread pudding with cream,
        180–82, *181*
    definition, 223
    kataifi with cream, baked, 173–75, *174*, *175*
    Lebanese pancakes, mini, *197*, 197–98
Zahtar
    definition, 223
    pita dippers with, 40
    pizzettas, *37*, 37–38, *38*
Zeytoun, jibni, kabese ma khudra, 15–16, *16*
Zucchini
    chicken kebabs with, grilled, 86–87, *87*
    mini omelets with, 15
    stuffed, 158–60, *159*, *160*
    stuffed, and grape leaves, 122–24, *123*
    stuffed, in cilantro yogurt, 127
    stuffed, in tomato sauce, 125–27, *126*

About the Author

Chef Kamal Al-Faqih, a Lebanese-American, began his career in 1986 as the owner and head chef of Med Catering, the first exclusively Mediterranean catering company in the Washington, D.C., area. During his twenty years there, his reputation became unmatched as his authentic dishes were offered at the White House and embassy events, and for notables from Jordan's King Abdullah to Placido Domingo. In 2005, Chef Kamal relocated to California, where he tested and wrote the recipes that comprise *Classic Lebanese Cuisine*. He lives in Ladera Ranch, California.